Other Books and Series by Jeff Bowen

Applications for Enrollment of Chickasaw Newborn Act of 1905
Volumes I thru VII

Cherokee Intermarried White 1906 Volume I thru X

Applications for Enrollment of Creek Newborn Act of 1905
Volumes I thru XIV

Applications for Enrollment of Choctaw Newborn Act of 1905
Volume I, II, III, IV, V, VI, VII, VIII & IX

Visit our website at **www.nativestudy.com** to learn more about these and other books and series by Jeff Bowen

APPLICATIONS FOR ENROLLMENT OF CHOCTAW NEWBORN ACT OF 1905

VOLUME X

TRANSCRIBED BY
JEFF BOWEN

NATIVE STUDY
Gallipolis, Ohio
USA

Other Books and Series by Jeff Bowen

1901-1907 Native American Census Seneca, Eastern Shawnee, Miami, Modoc, Ottawa, Peoria, Quapaw, and Wyandotte Indians (Under Seneca School, Indian Territory)

1932 Census of The Standing Rock Sioux Reservation with Births And Deaths 1924-1932

Census of The Blackfeet, Montana, 1897- 1901 Expanded Edition

Eastern Cherokee by Blood, 1906-1910, Volumes I thru XIII

Choctaw of Mississippi Indian Census 1929-1932 with Births and Deaths 1924-1931 Volume I
Choctaw of Mississippi Indian Census 1933, 1934 & 1937, Supplemental Rolls to 1934 & 1935 with Births and Deaths 1932-1938, and Marriages 1936-1938 Volume II

Eastern Cherokee Census Cherokee, North Carolina 1930-1939 Census 1930-1931 with Births And Deaths 1924-1931 Taken By Agent L. W. Page Volume I
Eastern Cherokee Census Cherokee, North Carolina 1930-1939 Census 1932-1933 with Births And Deaths 1930-1932 Taken By Agent R. L. Spalsbury Volume II
Eastern Cherokee Census Cherokee, North Carolina 1930-1939 Census 1934-1937 with Births and Deaths 1925-1938 and Marriages 1936 & 1938 Taken by Agents R. L. Spalsbury And Harold W. Foght Volume III

Seminole of Florida Indian Census, 1930-1940 with Birth and Death Records, 1930-1938

Texas Cherokees 1820-1839 A Document For Litigation 1921

Choctaw By Blood Enrollment Cards 1898-1914 Volumes I thru XVII

Starr Roll 1894 (Cherokee Payment Rolls) Districts: Canadian, Cooweescoowee, and Delaware Volume One
Starr Roll 1894 (Cherokee Payment Rolls) Districts: Flint, Going Snake, and Illinois Volume Two
Starr Roll 1894 (Cherokee Payment Rolls) Districts: Saline, Sequoyah, and Tahlequah; Including Orphan Roll Volume Three

Cherokee Intruder Cases Dockets of Hearings 1901-1909 Volumes I & II

Indian Wills, 1911-1921 Records of the Bureau of Indian Affairs Books One thru Seven;
Native American Wills & Probate Records 1911-1921

Other Books and Series by Jeff Bowen

Turtle Mountain Reservation Chippewa Indians 1932 Census with Births & Deaths, 1924-1932

Chickasaw By Blood Enrollment Cards 1898-1914 Volume I thru V

Cherokee Descendants East An Index to the Guion Miller Applications Volume I
Cherokee Descendants West An Index to the Guion Miller Applications Volume II (A-M)
Cherokee Descendants West An Index to the Guion Miller Applications Volume III (N-Z)

Applications for Enrollment of Seminole Newborn Freedmen, Act of 1905

Eastern Cherokee Census, Cherokee, North Carolina, 1915-1922, Taken by Agent James E. Henderson   Volume I (1915-1916)
Volume II (1917-1918)
Volume III (1919-1920)
Volume IV (1921-1922)

Complete Delaware Roll of 1898

Eastern Cherokee Census, Cherokee, North Carolina, 1923-1929, Taken by Agent James E. Henderson   Volume I (1923-1924)
Volume II (1925-1926)
Volume III (1927-1929)

Applications for Enrollment of Seminole Newborn Act of 1905 Volumes I & II

North Carolina Eastern Cherokee Indian Census 1898-1899, 1904, 1906, 1909-1912, 1914 Revised and Expanded Edition

1932 Hopi and Navajo Native American Census with Birth & Death Rolls (1925-1931) Volume 1 - Hopi
1932 Hopi and Navajo Native American Census with Birth & Death Rolls (1930-1932) Volume 2 - Navajo

Western Navajo Reservation Navajo, Hopi and Paiute 1933 Census with Birth & Death Rolls 1925-1933

Cherokee Citizenship Commission Dockets 1880-1884 and 1887-1889 Volumes I thru V

Copyright © 2013
by Jeff Bowen

ALL RIGHTS RESERVED
No part of this publication may be reproduced
or used in any form or manner whatsoever
without previous written permission from the
copyright holder or publisher.

Originally published:
Baltimore, Maryland
2013

Reprinted by:

Native Study LLC
Gallipolis, OH
www.nativestudy.com
2020

Library of Congress Control Number: 2020918113

ISBN: 978-1-64968-103-4

Made in the United States of America.

This series is dedicated to the descendants of the Choctaw newborn listed in these applications.

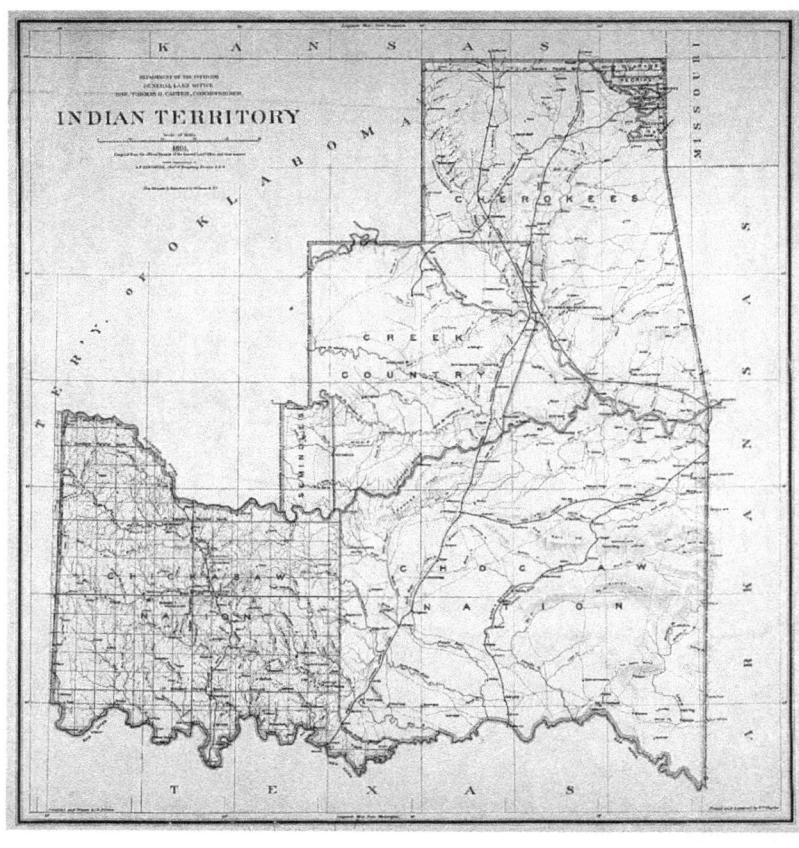

This map of Indian Territory shows how large the Choctaw and Chickasaw Nations' land base was that contained huge deposits of asphalt and coal. Just the size and territory involved was flooded with the "Grafters".

DEPARTMENT OF THE INTERIOR.
Commissioner to the Five Civilized Tribes.

NOTICE.

Opening of Land Office at Wewoka,
IN THE SEMINOLE NATION, INDIAN TERRITORY.

Notice is hereby given that on Monday, September 4, 1905, the Commissioner to the Five Civilized Tribes will establish a land office at Wewoka, in the Seminole Nation, Indian Territory, for the purpose of allowing citizens and freedmen of the Seminole Nation to select allotments of land for their minor children enrolled under the Act of Congress approved March 3, 1905 (33 Stat. L 1060), and for the further purpose of allowing citizens and freedmen of the Seminole Nation, whose allotments are incomplete, to select additional land in order to bring the value of their allotments up to the standard of $309.09, as nearly as may be practicable.

Each child whose enrollment in accordance with the Act of March 3, 1905, has been duly approved by the Secretary of the Interior, is entitled to receive an allotment of forty acres without regard to the character or value of the land selected.

Selection of allotments for minor children must be made by their citizen or freedmen parents or by a duly appointed guardian, or curator, or by a duly appointed administrator.

TAMS BIXBY,
Commissioner.

Muskogee, Indian Territory,
July 29, 1905.

This particular notice for the Seminole and Creek Newborn makes mention of the Act of 1905. It is likely that a similar notice was posted in the Choctaw and Chickasaw Nations for the registration of newborn children.

DEPARTMENT OF THE INTERIOR,
Commission to the Five Civilized Tribes.

Rules and Regulations Governing the Selection of Allotments and the Designation of Homesteads in the Choctaw and Chickasaw Nations.

1. Selections of allotments and designations of homesteads for adult citizens and selections of allotments for adult freedmen must be made in person except as herein otherwise provided.

2. Applications to have land set apart and homesteads designated for duly identified Mississippi Choctaws must be made personally before the Commission to the Five Civilized Tribes. Fathers may apply for their minor children and if the father be dead the mother may apply. Husbands may apply for wives. Applications for orphans, insane persons and persons of unsound mind may be made by duly appointed guardian or curator, and for aged and infirm persons and prisoners by agents duly authorized thereunto by power of attorney, in the discretion of said Commission.

3. At the time of the selection of allotment each citizen and duly identified Mississippi Choctaw shall designate as a homestead out of said selection land equal in value to one hundred and sixty acres of the average allottable land of the Choctaw and Chickasaw Nations, as nearly as may be.

4. Each Choctaw and Chickasaw freedman, at the time of allotment shall designate as his or her allotment of the lands of the Choctaw and Chickasaw Nations, land equal in value to forty acres of the average allottable land of the Choctaw and Chickasaw Nations.

5. Citizens, freedmen and identified Mississippi Choctaws who are married, whether they have attained their majority or not, will be regarded as of age for the purpose of making selections.

6. Selections may be made by citizen and freedman parents for unmarried male children under twenty-one years of age and for unmarried female children under eighteen years of age, and a male citizen or freedman may make selection for his wife, if she is entitled to make selection, unless she shall, at the time or previously thereto, protest in writing.

7. Where the father of an unmarried minor citizen, freedman or identified Mississippi Choctaw is a non-citizen, the citizen, freedman or identified Mississippi Choctaw mother of such children must make selection in person in behalf of said children.

8. Selections of allotments and designations of homesteads for minor citizens and selections of allotments for minor freedmen may be made by the citizen father or mother or freedman father or mother, as the case may be, or by a guardian, curator, or an administrator having charge of their estate, in the order named.

9. Selections of allotments and designations of homesteads for citizen, and selections of allotment for freedmen, prisoners, convicts, aged and infirm persons and soldiers and sailors of the United States on duty outside of Indian Territory, may be made by duly appointed agents under power of attorney, and for incompetents by guardians, curators, or other suitable person akin to them.

10. Selections may be made and homesteads designated by duly identified Mississippi Choctaws, who have, within one year after the date of their identification as such, made satisfactory proof of bona fide settlement within the Choctaw-Chickasaw country, at any time within six months after the date of their said identification.

11. Persons authorized to make selections by power of attorney, as provided in rules 2 and 9 hereof, must be the husband or wife, or a relative not further removed than a cousin of the first degree of the person for whom such selection is made.

12. It shall be the duty of the Commission to the Five Civilized Tribes to see that selections of allotments and designations of homesteads for the classes of persons mentioned in rules 2, 6, 7, 8 and 9 hereof, are made for the best interests of such persons.

13. Selections of allotments for citizens, freedmen and identified Mississippi Choctaws who have died subsequent to September 25, 1902, and before making a selection of allotment, shall be made by a duly appointed administrator or executor. If, however, such administrator or executor be not duly and expeditiously appointed, or fails to act promptly when appointed, or for any other cause such selections be not so made within a reasonable and practicable time, the Commission to the Five Civilized Tribes shall designate the lands thus to be allotted.

14. In determining the value of a selection the appraised value of the land selected shall be increased by the appraised value of such pine timber on such land as has heretofore been estimated by the Commission to the Five Civilized Tribes.

15. Selections of allotments may be made only by citizens and freedmen whose enrollment has been approved by the Secretary of the Interior, and by persons duly identified by the Commission to the Five Civilized Tribes as Mississippi Choctaws, and by none others.

16. When a selection of land has been made by a citizen, freedman or identified Mississippi Choctaw, and the land so selected is claimed by a person whose rights as a citizen or freedman have not been finally determined, contest for the land so selected may be instituted by the person claiming the land, formal application for the land being first made as is required by the Rules of Practice in Choctaw and Chickasaw allotment contest cases.

THE COMMISSION TO THE FIVE CIVILIZED TRIBES.
TAMS BIXBY, Chairman.

Muskogee, Indian Territory, March 24, 1903.

The above statement published prior to 1905, was established for what was supposed to be a set of guidelines when it came to allotments. But with supplemental agreements and Congressional legislation, time frames as well as rules and regulations often changed and were not the same for every tribe.

INTRODUCTION

The *Applications for Enrollment of Choctaw Newborn Act of 1905*, National Archive film M-1301, Rolls 50-57, are found under the heading of Applications for Enrollment of the Commission to the Five Civilized Tribes. For this series, I have transcribed the application forms filled out by individuals applying for enrollment in the Five Civilized Tribes under the Dawes Commission. These applications contain considerably more information than stated on the census cards found in series M-1186. M-1301 possesses its own numerical sequence, separate from M-1186. To find each party's roll number you would have to reference M-1186.

The Choctaw as well as the Chickasaw allotments were likely some of the most sought after properties in Indian Territory. There was supposed to be a 25-year restriction on the sale or lease of any Indian lands so as to insure that the owners wouldn't be swindled, but that isn't what happened. This fact is borne out in the Dawes Commission General Allotment Act, of February 8, 1887, Section 5, which "Provides that after an Indian person is allotted land, the United States will hold the land 'in trust [1] for the sole use and benefit of the Indian' (or his heirs if the Indian landowner dies) for a period of 25 years. (Land held in trust by the United States government cannot be sold or in anyway alienated by the Indian landowner, since the United States government considers the underlying ownership of the land held by itself and not the tribe. After the period of trust ends, the Indian landowner is free to sell the land and is free from any encumbrance from the United States.)"[1] Instead, Native Americans were exploited by the devious. The Choctaw and Chickasaw Districts both had huge asphalt and coal deposits, so there was pressure from outsiders to acquire them from the minute they were discovered. After repeated attacks throughout the years and many legislative changes, President "Roosevelt finally signed the Five Tribes Bill at noon on April 26, 1906, the forces seeking to end all restrictions were disappointed. Section 19 removed restrictions from the sale of all inherited land but directed that no full-bloods could sell their land for twenty-five years. The Act also prohibited leases for more than one year without the approval of the Secretary of the Interior."[2]

Angie Debo described the opportunists that wanted these Native American allotments as, "Grafters". The parents of the newborns enumerated within this series would no sooner receive the approval for their child's allotment than there would be someone there with cash in hand holding a new deed or lease for the parents to sign their child's birthright away. Angie Debo said it best, "As the business incapacity of the allottees became apparent, a horde of despoilers fastened themselves upon their property." According to Debo, "The term 'grafter' was applied as a matter of course to dealers in Indian land, and was frankly accepted by them. The speculative fever also affected Government employees so that it was almost impossible to prevent them from making personal investments."[3]

---

[1] General Allotment Act, Act of Feb. 8, 1887 (24 Stat. 388, ch. 119, 25 USCA 331)
[2] The Dawes Commission and the Allotment of the Five Civilized Tribes, 1893-1914 by Kent Carter, pg. 173
[3] And Still the Waters Run, Angie Debo, p. 92.

INTRODUCTION

According to the Department of Interior in 1905, "It is estimated that there will be added to the final rolls of the citizens and freedmen of the Choctaw and Chickasaw nations the names of 2,000 persons, including 1,500 new-born children to be enrolled under the provisions of the act of Congress approved March 3, 1905."[4]

The quote below explains, in detail, the requirements for qualifying as a newborn Choctaw, "By the act of Congress approved March 3, 1905 (H.R. 17474), entitled 'An act making appropriations for the current and contingent expenses of the Indian Department and for fulfilling treaty stipulations with various Indian tribes for the fiscal year ending June 30, 1906, and for other purposes,' it was provided as follows:

'That the Commission to the Five Civilized Tribes is hereby authorized for sixty days after the date of the approval of this act to receive and consider applications for enrollment of infant children born prior to September twenty-fifth, nineteen hundred and two, and who were living on said date, to citizens by blood of the Choctaw and Chickasaw tribes of Indians whose enrollment has been approved by the Secretary of the Interior prior to the date of the approval of this act; and to enroll and make allotments to such children.'

'That the Commission to the Five Civilized Tribes is authorized for sixty days after the date of the approval of this act to receive and consider applications for enrollment of children born subsequent to September twenty-fifth, nineteen hundred and two, and prior to March fourth, nineteen hundred and five, and who were living on said latter date, to citizens by blood of the Choctaw and Chickasaw tribes of Indians whose enrollment has been approved by the Secretary of the Interior prior to the date of the approval of this act; and to enroll and make allotments to such children.'

"Notice is hereby given that the Commission to the Five Civilized Tribes will, up to and inclusive of midnight, May 2, 1905, receive applications for the enrollment of infant children born prior to September 25, 1902, and who were living on said date, to citizens by blood of the Choctaw and Chickasaw tribes of Indians whose enrollment has been approved by the Secretary of the Interior prior to March 3, 1905."[5]

Following is the scope of these transcriptions: Besides the applications themselves, researchers will find the identities of other individuals within these applications -- doctors, lawyers, mid-wives, and other relatives -- that may help with you genealogical research.

Jeff Bowen
Gallipolis, Ohio
NativeStudy.com

---

[4] Annual Reports of the Department of the Interior For the Fiscal Year Ended June 30, 1905, p. 609.
[5] Annual Reports of the Department of the Interior For the Fiscal Year Ended June 30, 1905, p. 593.

Applications for Enrollment of Choctaw Newborn
Act of 1905 Volume X

<u>Choc New Born 600</u>
    Alton Olive Moran b. 2-5-04

BIRTH AFFIDAVIT.

IN RE-APPLICATION FOR ENROLLMENT, as a citizen of the   Choctaw   Nation, of Alton Olive Moran , born on the 5th day of Feby , 190 4

Name of Father: James E Moran   a citizen of the Choctaw Nation.
Name of Mother: Fannie Moran   a citizen of the Choctaw Nation.

                     Postoffice   Hinton I.T.

AFFIDAVIT OF MOTHER.

UNITED STATES OF AMERICA, INDIAN TERRITORY, }
     Southern   District.

I, Fannie Moran , on oath state that I am 29 years of age and a citizen by Marriage , of the Choctaw Nation; that I am the lawful wife of James E Moran , who is a citizen, by Birth of the Choctaw Nation; that a male child was born to me on 5th day of Feby , 1904 , that said child has been named Alton Olive Moran , and is now living.

                               Fannie Moran
Witnesses To Mark:

     Subscribed and sworn to before me this 27th day of March , 1905.

My commission expires   Price Statler
Jany 1st 1906   Notary Public.

AFFIDAVIT OF ATTENDING PHYSICIAN OR MID-WIFE.

UNITED STATES OF AMERICA, INDIAN TERRITORY, }
     Southern   District.

I, H.A. Ellis , a Physician , on oath state that I attended on Mrs. Fannie Moran , wife of James Moran on the 5th day of Feb. , 190 4; that there was born to her on said date a male child; that said child is now living and is said to have been named Alton

                         H.A. Ellis M.D.

Witnesses To Mark:

Applications for Enrollment of Choctaw Newborn
Act of 1905   Volume X

Subscribed and sworn to before me this   21   day of   March   , 1905.

Date of expiration of my   *(Name Illegible)*
commission June 1 1905   Notary Public.

Choc New Born 601
    Henry A. Whiteman   b. 7-27-03

7-NB-601.

Muskogee, Indian Territory, May 26, 1905.

W. J. Whiteman,
    Goodwater, Indian Territory.

Dear Sir:

    There is enclosed you herewith for execution application for the enrollment of your infant child, Henry A. Whiteman, born July 27, 1903.

    In the affidavits filed in this office on the 7th ultimo, the date of the applicant's birth is given as July 27, 1903, while in those filed on the 26th ultimo, it is given as July 26, 1905. In the enclosed application the former date, which is apparently correct, is inserted. Please have these affidavits executed and return them to this office.

    In having these affidavits executed care should be exercised to see that all names are written in full, as they appear in the body of the affidavit, and in the event that either of the persons signing the affidavit are unable to write, signatures by mark must be attested by two witnesses. Each affidavit must be executed before a Notary Public and the notarial seal and signature of the officer must be attached to each separate affidavit.

Respectfully,

VR 26-5.   Chairman.

Applications for Enrollment of Choctaw Newborn
Act of 1905   Volume X

7-N.B. 601.

Muskogee, Indian Territory, June 5, 1905.

W. J. Whiteman,
    Goodwater, Indian Territory.

Dear Sir:

    Receipt is hereby acknowledged of the affidavits of Mattie J. Whiteman and W. H. McBrayer to the birth of Henry A. Whiteman, July 26, 1903, son of W. J. and Mattie J. Whiteman, and the same have been filed with our records in the matter of the enrollment of said child.

                  Respectfully,

                  Commissioner in Charge.

Affidavit of Attending Physician or Midwife

UNITED STATES OF AMERICA, }
    INDIAN TERRITORY,
  Central   DISTRICT

    I, W H McBrayer a Physician on oath state that I attended on Mrs. Mattie J Whiteman wife of W.J. Whiteman on the 27th day of July, 190 5, that there was born to her on said date a male child, that said child is now living, and is said to have been named Henry A. Whiteman

                W. H. McBrayer   M. D.

Subscribed and sworn to before me this the 1 day of March 1905

                C.L. Evans
                    Notary Public.

WITNESSETH:
Must be two witnesses { *(Name Illegible)*
who are citizens and
know the child.   Joe Tompson[sic]

    We hereby certify that we are well acquainted with Dr WH McBrayer a **Physician**   and know him to be reputable and of good standing in the community.

          Must be two citizen { H.C. Dukes
              witnesses.   Nelson Wilson

Applications for Enrollment of Choctaw Newborn
Act of 1905   Volume X

NEW BORN AFFIDAVIT

No _____

CHOCTAW ENROLLING COMMISSION

IN THE MATTER OF THE APPLICATION FOR ENROLLMENT as a citizen of the Choctaw Nation, of   Henry A Whiteman   born on the 27th day of   July   190 3

Name of father   W.J. Whiteman   a citizen of   Choctaw   Nation, final enrollment No.   64
Name of mother   M.C. Whiteman   a citizen of   Choctaw   Nation, final enrollment No.   2883

Goodwater   Postoffice.

AFFIDAVIT OF MOTHER

UNITED STATES OF AMERICA
   INDIAN TERRITORY
DISTRICT   Central

I   Mattie J. Whiteman   , on oath state that I am   24   years of age and a citizen by   Blood   of the   Choctaw   Nation, and as such have been placed upon the final roll of the   Choctaw   Nation, by the Honorable Secretary of the Interior my final enrollment number being _____; that I am the lawful wife of   William J Whiteman   , who is a citizen of the   Choctaw   Nation, and as such has been placed upon the final roll of said Nation by the Honorable Secretary of the Interior, his final enrollment number being   64   and that a   Male   child was born to me on the   27th   day of July   190 5; that said child has been named   Henry A Whiteman   , and is now living.

WITNESSETH: Mattie J Whiteman

Must be two witnesses   { H.C. Dukes
who are citizens   { Nelson Wilson

Subscribed and sworn to before me this, the   1   day of   March   , 190 5

C.L. Evans
Notary Public.

My Commission Expires: 10 day of Mrch 1908

Applications for Enrollment of Choctaw Newborn
Act of 1905   Volume X

BIRTH AFFIDAVIT.

DEPARTMENT OF THE INTERIOR.
COMMISSION TO THE FIVE CIVILIZED TRIBES.

IN RE APPLICATION FOR ENROLLMENT, as a citizen of the   Choctaw   Nation, of   Henry A Whiteman   , born on the   27th day of July   , 1903

Name of Father: W.J. Whiteman   a citizen of the   Choctaw   Nation.
Name of Mother: Mattie J. Whiteman   a citizen of the   Choctaw   Nation.

Postoffice   Goodwater I.T.

AFFIDAVIT OF MOTHER.

UNITED STATES OF AMERICA, Indian Territory, }
   Central   DISTRICT.

I,   Mattie J. Whiteman   , on oath state that I am   25   years of age and a citizen by   Blood   , of the   Choctaw   Nation; that I am the lawful wife of   W. J. Whiteman   , who is a citizen, by Intermarriage   of the   Choctaw   Nation; that a   male   child was born to me on 27th day of July   , 1903; that said child has been named   Henry A Whiteman   , and was living March 4, 1905.

Mattie J Whiteman

Witnesses To Mark:
 { Lula McLaughlin
 { M. H. Maynor

Subscribed and sworn to before me this   31   day of   March   , 1905

C.L. Evans
Notary Public.

AFFIDAVIT OF ATTENDING PHYSICIAN OR MID-WIFE.

UNITED STATES OF AMERICA, Indian Territory, }
   Central   DISTRICT.

I,   W H McBrayer   , a   Physician   , on oath state that I attended on Mrs.   Mattie J Whiteman   , wife of   W. J. Whiteman   on the 27th day of July   , 1903; that there was born to her on said date a   male   child; that said child was living March 4, 1905, and is said to have been named   Henry A. Whiteman

W. H. McBrayer M.D.

Applications for Enrollment of Choctaw Newborn
Act of 1905   Volume X

Witnesses To Mark:
{

    Subscribed and sworn to before me this 31 day of March , 1905

                            C.L. Evans
                                  Notary Public.

BIRTH AFFIDAVIT.

DEPARTMENT OF THE INTERIOR.
COMMISSION TO THE FIVE CIVILIZED TRIBES.

IN RE APPLICATION FOR ENROLLMENT, as a citizen of the Choctaw Nation, of Henry A Whiteman , born on the 27 day of July , 1903

Name of Father: W.J. Whiteman   a citizen of the Choctaw Nation.
Name of Mother: Mattie J. Whiteman   a citizen of the Choctaw Nation.

                Postoffice   Goodwater Ind. Ter.

AFFIDAVIT OF MOTHER.

UNITED STATES OF AMERICA, Indian Territory,
....**DISTRICT.**

    I, Mattie J. Whiteman , on oath state that I am 25 years of age and a citizen by blood , of the Choctaw Nation; that I am the lawful wife of W. J. Whiteman , who is a citizen, by intermarriage of the Choctaw Nation; that a male child was born to me on 27 day of July , 1903; that said child has been named Henry A Whiteman , and was living March 4, 1905.

                              Mattie J Whiteman

Witnesses To Mark:
{

    Subscribed and sworn to before me this 31 day of May , 1905

                              C.L. Evans
                                  Notary Public.

Applications for Enrollment of Choctaw Newborn
Act of 1905 Volume X

AFFIDAVIT OF ATTENDING PHYSICIAN OR MID-WIFE.

UNITED STATES OF AMERICA, Indian Territory,
....DISTRICT.

I, W H McBrayer , a Physician , on oath state that I attended on Mrs. Mattie J Whiteman , wife of W. J. Whiteman on the 27 day of July , 1903; that there was born to her on said date a male child; that said child was living March 4, 1905, and is said to have been named Henry A. Whiteman

W. H. McBrayer M.D.

Witnesses To Mark:
{

Subscribed and sworn to before me this 31 day of May , 1905

C.L. Evans
Notary Public.

Choc New Born 602
    Sam Willis b. 1-11-05
    Edward Willis b. 2-23-03
    Died prior to March 4, 1905
    No. 2 Dismissed 6-28-05

DEPARTMENT OF THE INTERIOR,
COMMISSION TO THE FIVE CIVILIZED TRIBES.

Record in the matter of the application for enrollment as a citizen by blood of the Choctaw Nation of:

    EDWARD WILLIS   7-NB-602.

Applications for Enrollment of Choctaw Newborn
Act of 1905   Volume X

DEATH AFFIDAVIT

NO._____

Choctaw Enrolling Commission.

IN THE MATTER OF THE DEATH OF   Edward Willis a citizen of the   Choctaw   Nation, who formerly resided at or near   Rufe Ind. Ter., and died on the   21st day of   August   190 3

AFFIDAVIT OF RELATIVE.
UNITED STATES OF AMERICA
INDIAN TERRITORY
   Central   DISTRICT.

I,   Gracie Willis   on oath, state that I am   24   years of age, and a citizen of the   Choctaw   Nation, and as such have been finally enrolled by the Honorable Secretary of the Interior, my enrollment number being .... ; that my postoffice address is Rufe   , Ind. Ter.; that I am   the mother   of   Edward Willis   who was a citizen, by blood   , of the   Choctaw   Nation; and that said   Edward Willis   died on the   21st day of   August   , 190 3

WITNESSETH:

Must be two witnesses who are Citizens.
- James Woolery
- Willie Caldwell

her
Gracie x Willis
mark

Subscribed and sworn to before me this the   22   day of Feb   190 5

W. A. Shoney   Notary Public.

AFFIDAVIT OF ACQUAINTANCE.
UNITED STATES OF AMERICA
INDIAN TERRITORY
   Central   DISTRICT.

I,   Annie Woolery   on oath, state that I am   19   years of age, and a citizen by   blood   of the   Choctaw   Nation; that my post-office address is Valliant   Ind. Ter.; that I was personally acquainted with   Edward Willis   the deceased child above named, who was a citizen of   Choctaw   Nation by blood, and that said   Edward Willis   died on the   21st day of   August   , 190 3

Annie Woolery

Subscribed and sworn to before me this   22   day of   Feb   190 5

W.A. Shoney   Notary Public.

My Commission Expires: Jan 10, 1909

Applications for Enrollment of Choctaw Newborn
Act of 1905 Volume X

W.J.
7-NB-602.

DEPARTMENT OF THE INTERIOR,
COMMISSION TO THE FIVE CIVILIZED TRIBES.

In the matter of the application for the enrollment of Edward Willis as a citizen by blood of the Choctaw Nation.

---oOo---

It appears from the record herein that on April 25, 1905 there was filed with the Commission application for the enrollment of Edward Willis as a citizen by blood of the Choctaw Nation.

It further appears from the record herein and the records of the Commission that the applicant was born February 23, 1903; that he is a son of Willie Willis, a recognized and enrolled citizen by blood of the Choctaw Nation whose name appears opposite number 1588 upon the final roll of citizens by blood of the Choctaw Nation, approved by the Secretary of the Interior December 12, 1902, and Gracie Willis, a recognized and enrolled citizen by intermarriage of said nation; and that said applicant died August 21, 1903.

The Act of Congress approved March 3, 1905 (Public No. 212) among other things provides:

"That the Commission to the Five Civilized Tribes is authorized for sixty days after the date of the approval of this act to receive and consider applications for enrollment of children born subsequent to September twenty-fifth, nineteen hundred and two, and prior to March fourth, nineteen hundred and five, and who were living on said latter date, to citizens by blood of the Choctaw and Chickasaw tribes of Indians whose enrollment has been approved by the Secretary of the Interior prior to the date of the approval of this act; and to enroll and make allotments to such children."

It is, therefore, hereby ordered that the application for the enrollment of Edward Willis as a citizen by blood of the Choctaw Nation be dismissed in accordance with the order of the Commission of March 31, 1905.

COMMISSION TO THE FIVE CIVILIZED TRIBES,

Tams Bixby
Chairman.

Muskogee, Indian Territory.
JUN 28 1905

Applications for Enrollment of Choctaw Newborn
Act of 1905   Volume X

7-NB-602.

Muskogee, Indian Territory, June 28, 1905.

W. Willis, **COPY**
    Rufe, Indian Territory.

Dear Sir:

    Inclosed herewith you will find a copy of the order of this Commission, dated June 28, 1905, dismissing the application for the enrollment of Edward Willis as a citizen by blood of the Choctaw Nation.

                      Respectfully,
                          SIGNED

                        Tams Bixby

Registered.   Chairman.
Incl. 7-NB-602.

7-NB-602.

Muskogee, Indian Territory, June 28, 1905.

Mansfield, McMurray & Cornish, **COPY**
    Attorneys for Choctaw and Chickasaw Nations,
        South McAlester, Indian Territory.

Gentlemen:

    Inclosed herewith you will find a copy of the order of this Commission, dated June 28, 1905, dismissing the application for the enrollment of Edward Willis as a citizen by blood of the Choctaw Nation.

                      Respectfully,
                         SIGNED

                        Tams Bixby
                          Chairman.

Incl. 7-NB-602.

Applications for Enrollment of Choctaw Newborn
Act of 1905   Volume X

NEW-BORN AFFIDAVIT.

Number.............

...Choctaw Enrolling Commission...

IN THE MATTER OF THE APPLICATION FOR ENROLLMENT, as a citizen of the Choctaw Nation, of Edward Willis

born on the 23rd day of February 190 3

Name of father   W Willis   a citizen of   Choctaw
Nation final enrollment No. ....
Name of mother   Gracie Willis   a citizen of   Choctaw
Nation final enrollment No. ....

Postoffice   Rufe, I T

AFFIDAVIT OF MOTHER.

UNITED STATES OF AMERICA
INDIAN TERRITORY
Central   DISTRICT

I   Gracie Willis   , on oath state that I am 24 years of age and a citizen by Intermarriage of the Choctaw Nation, and as such have been placed upon the final roll of the Choctaw Nation, by the Honorable Secretary of the Interior my final enrollment number being ....; that I am the lawful wife of   W Willis   , who is a citizen of the Choctaw Nation, and as such has been placed upon the final roll of said Nation by the Honorable Secretary of the Interior, his final enrollment number being .... and that a   male   child was born to me on the 23rd day of February 190 3; that said child has been named Edward Willis , and is now living.

                                                    her
                                        Gracie x Willis

Witnesseth.   mark

Must be two Witnesses who are Citizens.   } James Woolery
Annie Woolery

Subscribed and sworn to before me this   22   day of   Feb   190 5

                                      W A Shoney
                                              Notary Public.

My commission expires: Jan 10, 1909

Applications for Enrollment of Choctaw Newborn
Act of 1905 Volume X

Choctaw 665.

Muskogee, Indian Territory, April 7, 1905.

Claud P. Spriggs,
    Ft. Towson, Indian Territory.

Dear Sir:

    Receipt is hereby acknowledged of your letter of April 1, enclosing the affidavits of Gracie Willis and J. G. Ball to the birth of Sam Willis, son of Willie and Gracie Willis, January 11, 1905, and the same have been filed with our records as an application for the enrollment of said child.

        Respectfully,

                Commissioner in Charge.

BIRTH AFFIDAVIT.

DEPARTMENT OF THE INTERIOR.
COMMISSION TO THE FIVE CIVILIZED TRIBES.

IN RE APPLICATION FOR ENROLLMENT, as a citizen of the Choctaw Nation, of Sam Willis, born on the 11th day of January, 1905

Name of Father: Willie Willis   a citizen of the Choctaw Nation.
Name of Mother: Gracie Willis   a citizen of the Choctaw Nation.

Postoffice   Fort Towson

AFFIDAVIT OF MOTHER.

UNITED STATES OF AMERICA, Indian Territory,
    Central   DISTRICT.

    I, Gracie Willis, on oath state that I am 23 years of age and a citizen by intermarriage, of the Choctaw Nation; that I am the lawful wife of Willie Willis, who is a citizen, by Blood of the Choctaw Nation; that a male child was born to me on 11th day of January, 1905; that said child has been named Sam Willis, and was living March 4, 1905.

                    her
              Gracie x Willis
                   mark

Applications for Enrollment of Choctaw Newborn
Act of 1905   Volume X

Witnesses To Mark:
{ Claud P Spriggs
  Mrs T Fennell

Subscribed and sworn to before me this ? day of   April   , 1905

Thomas Fennell
Notary Public.

AFFIDAVIT OF ATTENDING PHYSICIAN OR MID-WIFE.

UNITED STATES OF AMERICA, Indian Territory, }
Central   DISTRICT.

I,   Dr J G Ball   , a   Physician   , on oath state that I attended on Mrs.   Gracie Willis   , wife of   Willie Willis   on the 11 day of   January   , 1905; that there was born to her on said date a   male   child; that said child was living March 4, 1905, and is said to have been named Sam Willis

J G Ball M.D.

Witnesses To Mark:
{

Subscribed and sworn to before me this ? day of   April   , 1905

Thomas Fennell
Notary Public.

AFFIDAVIT OF ATTENDING PHYSICIAN OR MIDWIFE

UNITED STATES OF AMERICA
INDIAN TERRITORY
   Central   DISTRICT

I,   J G Ball   a   Physician
on oath state that I attended on Mrs.   Gracie Willis   wife of   W. Willis
on the 11th day of January , 190 5, that there was born to her on said date a   male   child, that said child is now living, and is said to have been named   Samuel Willis

J. G. Ball   M.D.

WITNESSETH:
Must be two witnesses { Rufus L Wilson
who are citizens and   {
know the child.   Timothy J Cephus

13

Applications for Enrollment of Choctaw Newborn
Act of 1905 Volume X

Feb   Subscribed and sworn to before me this, the   22nd   day of
           190 5

W A Shoney   Notary Public.

We hereby certify that we are well acquainted with   J G Ball
a   Physician   and know   him   to be reputable and of good standing in the community.

H. L. Fowler

L.N. Isham

NEW-BORN AFFIDAVIT.

Number...........

...Choctaw Enrolling Commission...

IN THE MATTER OF THE APPLICATION FOR ENROLLMENT, as a citizen of the Choctaw   Nation, of   Samuel Willis

born on the   11th   day of   January   190 5

Name of father   W Willis   a citizen of ....
Nation final enrollment No. ....
Name of mother   Gracie Willis   a citizen of   Choctaw
Nation final enrollment No. ....

Postoffice   Rufe, I.T.

AFFIDAVIT OF MOTHER.

UNITED STATES OF AMERICA
INDIAN TERRITORY
   Central   DISTRICT

I   Gracie Willis   , on oath state that I am   24   years of age and a citizen by   Intermarriage   of the   Choctaw   Nation, and as such have been placed upon the final roll of the   Choctaw   Nation, by the Honorable Secretary of the Interior my final enrollment number being .... ; that I am the lawful wife of   W Willis   , who is a citizen of the   Choctaw   Nation, and as such has been placed upon the final roll of said Nation by the Honorable Secretary of the Interior, his final enrollment number being .... and that a   Male   child was born to me on the   11th   day of   January   190 5; that said child has been named   Samuel Willis   , and is now living.

Applications for Enrollment of Choctaw Newborn
Act of 1905   Volume X

her
Gracie x Willis
mark

Must be two Witnesses who are Citizens. } H.L. Fowler

Annie Woolery

Subscribed and sworn to before me this   22   day of   Feb   190 5

W A Shoney
Notary Public.

My commission expires: Jan 10, 1909

Choc New Born 603
    James C. Runton   b. 6-30-04
    Dora M. Runton   b. 3-27-03
    Died Dec 26, 1903
    No. 2 Dismissed 1-22-05

Choctaw 2351.

Muskogee, Indian Territory, April 7, 1905.

Carnolie Runton,
    Heavener, Indian Territory.

Dear Sir:

    Receipt is hereby acknowledged of the affidavits of Tabitha A. Runton and J. D. Fowler to the birth of James C. Runton, son of Carnolie and Tabitha A. Runton, June 3, 1904, and the same have been filed with our records as an application for the enrollment of said child.

Respectfully,

Commissioner in Charge.

Applications for Enrollment of Choctaw Newborn
Act of 1905   Volume X

NEW-BORN AFFIDAVIT.

Number..................

...Choctaw Enrolling Commission...

IN THE MATTER OF THE APPLICATION FOR ENROLLMENT, as a citizen of the Choctaw Nation, of James C. Runton

born on the 30th day of __June__ 190 4

Name of father   Carnolie Runton   a citizen of   Choctaw
Nation final enrollment No.   6804
Name of mother   Tabitha A. Runton   a citizen of   United States
Nation final enrollment No.   40

Postoffice   Heavener I.T.

AFFIDAVIT OF MOTHER.

UNITED STATES OF AMERICA
INDIAN TERRITORY
Central   DISTRICT

I   Tabitha A Runton   , on oath state that I am 31 years of age and a citizen by marriage of the Choctaw Nation, and as such have been placed upon the final roll of the Choctaw Nation, by the Honorable Secretary of the Interior my final enrollment number being Forty ; that I am the lawful wife of   Carnolie Runton   , who is a citizen of the   Choctaw   Nation, and as such has been placed upon the final roll of said Nation by the Honorable Secretary of the Interior, his final enrollment number being   6804   and that a   Male   child was born to me on the 30th day of   June   190 4; that said child has been named   James C Runton   , and is now living.

Tabitha A Runton

Witnesseth.   his
Must be two ⎱ Loman x Jack
Witnesses who ⎰   her mark
are Citizens.   Hanna x Jack
                      mark

Witness Subscribed and sworn to before me this   13   day of   Jan   190 5
to mark
Joseph Jackson   J M Young
                                              Notary Public.
My commission expires: March-6-1905

Applications for Enrollment of Choctaw Newborn
Act of 1905 Volume X

AFFIDAVIT OF ATTENDING PHYSICIAN OR MIDWIFE

UNITED STATES OF AMERICA
INDIAN TERRITORY
   Central   DISTRICT

   I,   J D Fowler   a   Practicing Physician
on oath state that I attended on Mrs. Tabitha A Runton wife of   Carnolie Runton
on the   30th   day of   June , 190 4 , that there was born to her on said date a   male child, that said child is now living, and is said to have been named   James C Runton

                                        J D Fowler   *M.D.*

          Subscribed and sworn to before me this, the   14   day of
          January   190 5

WITNESSETH: his   J M Young   Notary Public.
Must be two witnesses { Loman x Jack   *Witness to mark*
who are citizens   her mark   *Joseph Jackson*
                  Hanna x Jack
                      mark
   We hereby certify that we are well acquainted with   J D Fowler
a   Practicing Physician   and know   him   to be reputable and of good standing in the community.

        Joseph Jackson   Heavener Ind Ter

        (Illegible) Collin   Heavener Ind Ter

7-NB-603.   **COPY**

                          Muskogee, Indian Territory, January 22, 1906.

Carnolie Runton,
       Heavener, Indian Territory.

Dear Sir:

       You are hereby advised that on January 22, 1906, the Commissioner to the Five Civilized Tribes dismissed the application for the enrollment of your child, Dora M. Runton, as a citizen by blood of the Choctaw Nation, for the reason that she died prior to March 4, 1905.
                            Respectfully,
                  SIGNED

                                      Tams Bixby
                                          Commissioner.

Applications for Enrollment of Choctaw Newborn
Act of 1905 Volume X

BIRTH AFFIDAVIT.

DEPARTMENT OF THE INTERIOR.
COMMISSION TO THE FIVE CIVILIZED TRIBES.

IN RE APPLICATION FOR ENROLLMENT, as a citizen of the Choctaw Nation, of Dora M Runton, born on the 27 day of Mch, 1903

Name of Father: Carnolie Runton   a citizen of the Choctaw Nation.
Name of Mother: Tabitha A Runton   a citizen of the U. S. Nation.

Postoffice   Heavener I.T.

AFFIDAVIT OF MOTHER.

UNITED STATES OF AMERICA, Indian Territory,
Central   DISTRICT.

I, Tabitha A Runton, on oath state that I am 31 years of age and a citizen by ~~blood~~ *intermarriage*, of the Choctaw Nation; that I am the lawful wife of Carnolie Runton, who is a citizen, by blood of the Choctaw Nation; that a female child was born to me on 27" day of March, 1903; that said child has been named Dora M Runton, and ~~was living March 4, 1905~~.

Died December 26, 1903

Tabitha A Runton

Witnesses To Mark:
{

Subscribed and sworn to before me this 1ˢᵗ day of April, 1905

J.M. Young
Notary Public.

AFFIDAVIT OF ATTENDING PHYSICIAN OR MID-WIFE.

UNITED STATES OF AMERICA, Indian Territory,
Central   DISTRICT.

I, J.D. Fowler, a Physician, on oath state that I attended on Mrs. Tabitha A Runton, wife of Carnolie Runton on the 27 day of March, 1903; that there was born to her on said date a female child; that said child was living March 4, 1905, and is said to have been named Dora M Runton

J D Fowler

Applications for Enrollment of Choctaw Newborn
Act of 1905 Volume X

Witnesses To Mark:
{

    Subscribed and sworn to before me this 1st day of April , 1905

                        J.M. Young
My Com Exp Mch 9 1909   Notary Public.

DEPARTMENT OF THE INTERIOR.
COMMISSION TO THE FIVE CIVILIZED TRIBES.

    In the matter of the death of   Dora M Runton   a citizen of the   Choctaw Nation, who formerly resided at or near   Howe   , Ind. Ter., and died on the   26 day of Dec , 1903

AFFIDAVIT OF RELATIVE.

UNITED STATES OF AMERICA, Indian Territory,
    Central   DISTRICT.

    I,   Carnolie Runton   , on oath state that I am   33   years of age and a citizen by blood , of the Choctaw Nation; that my postoffice address is   Heavener I.T. , Ind. Ter.; that I am   The Father   of   Dora M Runton   who was a citizen, by blood , of the Choctaw   Nation and that said   Dora M Runton   died on the   26   day of Dec , 1903

                        Carnolie Runton
Witnesses To Mark:
{

    Subscribed and sworn to before me this 1st   day of   April , 1905.

                        J.M. Young
my com exp Mch 9, 1909   Notary Public.

AFFIDAVIT OF ACQUAINTANCE.

UNITED STATES OF AMERICA, Indian Territory,
    Central   DISTRICT.

    I,   Loman Jack   , on oath state that I am about 62   years of age, and a citizen by blood   of the Choctaw   Nation; that my postoffice address is   Howe   , Ind. Ter.; that I was personally acquainted with   Dora M Runton   who was a citizen, by blood , of the   Choctaw Nation; and that said   Dora M Runton   died on the   26   day of Dec , 1903

Applications for Enrollment of Choctaw Newborn
Act of 1905 Volume X

            his
          Loman x Jack
Witnesses To Mark: mark
 { Joseph Jackson
  Eastman McNail

  Subscribed and sworn to before me this 1st day of April , 1905.

         J.M. Young
my com exp Mch 9, 1909   Notary Public.

BIRTH AFFIDAVIT.

DEPARTMENT OF THE INTERIOR.
COMMISSION TO THE FIVE CIVILIZED TRIBES.

 IN RE APPLICATION FOR ENROLLMENT, as a citizen of the   Choctaw   Nation, of James C Runton , born on the 30 day of June , 1904

Name of Father: Carnolie Runton   a citizen of the   Choctaw   Nation.
Name of Mother: Tabitha A Runton   a citizen of the   U.S.   Nation.

      Postoffice   Heavener I.T.

AFFIDAVIT OF MOTHER.

UNITED STATES OF AMERICA, Indian Territory, ⎫
  Central   DISTRICT. ⎭

 I,   Tabitha A Runton , on oath state that I am 31   years of age and a citizen by   Intermarriage , of the   Choctaw   Nation; that I am the lawful wife of   Carnolie Runton   , who is a citizen, by blood   of the   Choctaw Nation; that a   male   child was born to me on   30" day of June , 1904; that said child has been named   James C Runton , and was living March 4, 1905.

        Tabitha A Runton

Witnesses To Mark:
{

  Subscribed and sworn to before me this 1st day of April , 1905

       J. M. Young
         Notary Public.

Applications for Enrollment of Choctaw Newborn
Act of 1905   Volume X

AFFIDAVIT OF ATTENDING PHYSICIAN OR MID-WIFE.

UNITED STATES OF AMERICA, Indian Territory, }
Central   DISTRICT.

I,   J. D. Fowler   , a   Physician   , on oath state that I attended on Mrs.   Tabitha A Runton   , wife of   Carnolie Runton   on the   30" day of   June , 1904; that there was born to her on said date a   male   child; that said child was living March 4, 1905, and is said to have been named   James C Runton

J. D. Fowler

Witnesses To Mark:

{

Subscribed and sworn to before me this 1st day of   April   , 1905

J. M. Young

my com exp Mch 9-1909   Notary Public.

Choc New Born 604
   Nonie Esner Bacon   b. 9-14-03

Choctaw 1483.

Muskogee, Indian Territory, April 7, 1905.

L. D. Horton,
   Boswell, Indian Territory.

Dear Sir:

Receipt is hereby acknowledged of your letter of April 1, enclosing the affidavits of Mame Bacon and Nancy Chapman to the birth of Nonie Esner Bacon, daughter of Mame and Dave Bacon, September 14, 1903, and the same have been filed with our records as an application for the enrollment of said child.

Respectfully,

Commissioner in Charge.

Applications for Enrollment of Choctaw Newborn
Act of 1905 Volume X

BIRTH AFFIDAVIT.

DEPARTMENT OF THE INTERIOR.
COMMISSION TO THE FIVE CIVILIZED TRIBES.

    IN RE APPLICATION FOR ENROLLMENT, as a citizen of the Choctaw Nation, of Nonie Esner Bacon, born on the 14th day of September, 1903

Name of Father: Dave Bacon   a citizen of the Choctaw Nation.
Name of Mother: Mame Bacon   a citizen of the Choctaw Nation.

    Postoffice   Boswell Ind Ter

AFFIDAVIT OF MOTHER.

UNITED STATES OF AMERICA, Indian Territory, }
    Central   DISTRICT.

    I, Mame Bacon, on oath state that I am 33 years of age and a citizen by Blood, of the Choctaw Nation; that I am the lawful wife of Dave Bacon, who is a citizen, by blood of the Choctaw Nation; that a Female child was born to me on 14th day of September, 1903, that said child has been named Nonie Esner Bacon, and is now living.

                       her
                Mame x Bacon
Witnesses To Mark: mark
 { Sam Brimm
    JE McCleary

    Subscribed and sworn to before me this 30th day of March, 1905.

                     V. Branaugh
                        Notary Public.

AFFIDAVIT OF ATTENDING PHYSICIAN OR MID-WIFE.

UNITED STATES OF AMERICA, Indian Territory, }
    Central   DISTRICT.

    I, Nancy Chapman, a Mid Wife, on oath state that I attended on Mrs. Mame Bacon, wife of Dave Bacon on the 14th day of September, 1903; that there was born to her on said date a Female child; that said child is now living and is said to have been named Nonie Esner Bacon

                       her
                Nancy x Chapman
                   mark

Applications for Enrollment of Choctaw Newborn
Act of 1905   Volume X

Witnesses To Mark:
   { J E McCleary
     F. F. Willcutt

    Subscribed and sworn to before me this   30th   day of   March   , 1905.

                                  V. Branaugh
                                    Notary Public.

<u>Choc New Born 605</u>
      Allen Payton   b. 2-24-03
      Walter Payton   b. 1-10-05

                                               Choctaw 3793.

                     Muskogee, Indian Territory, April 7, 1905.

L. D. Horton,
    Boswell, Indian Territory.

Dear Sir:

    Receipt is hereby acknowledged of your letter of April 1, transmitting the affidavits of Josephine Payton and Minerva Dwight to the birth of Allen and Walter Payton, children of Ned and Josephine Payton, February 24, 1903, and January 10, 1905, respectively, and the same have been filed with our records as an application for the enrollment of said children.

                                Respectfully,

                                              Commissioner in Charge.

BIRTH AFFIDAVIT.
DEPARTMENT OF THE INTERIOR.
COMMISSION TO THE FIVE CIVILIZED TRIBES.

    IN RE APPLICATION FOR ENROLLMENT, as a citizen of the   Choctaw   Nation, of   Allen Payton   , born on the   24   day of   February   , 1903

Name of Father: Ned Payton   a citizen of the   Choctaw   Nation.
Name of Mother: Josephine Payton   a citizen of the   Choctaw   Nation.

Applications for Enrollment of Choctaw Newborn
Act of 1905   Volume X

Postoffice   Boswell, I.T.

AFFIDAVIT OF MOTHER.

UNITED STATES OF AMERICA, Indian Territory, }
Central District   DISTRICT.

I,   Josephine Payton , on oath state that I am   29   years of age and a citizen by   blood   , of the   Choctaw   Nation; that I am the lawful wife of   Ned Payton , who is a citizen, by   blood   of the   Choctaw   Nation; that a male   child was born to me on   24   day of   February , 1903; that said child has been named   Allen Payton , and was living March 4, 1905.

Josephine Payton

Witnesses To Mark:
{

Subscribed and sworn to before me this   1   day of   April , 1905

L. D. Horton
Notary Public.

AFFIDAVIT OF ATTENDING PHYSICIAN OR MID-WIFE.

UNITED STATES OF AMERICA, Indian Territory, }
Central District   DISTRICT.

I,   Minervia Dwight , a   Midwife , on oath state that I attended on Mrs.   Josephine Payton , wife of   Ned Payton   on the   24   day of   February , 1903; that there was born to her on said date a   male   child; that said child was living March 4, 1905, and is said to have been named   Allen Payton

her
Minervia x Dwight
mark

Witnesses To Mark:
{ *(Name Illegible)*
  V Branaugh

Subscribed and sworn to before me this   1   day of   April , 1905

L.D. Horton
Notary Public.

Applications for Enrollment of Choctaw Newborn
Act of 1905 Volume X

BIRTH AFFIDAVIT.

DEPARTMENT OF THE INTERIOR.
COMMISSION TO THE FIVE CIVILIZED TRIBES.

IN RE APPLICATION FOR ENROLLMENT, as a citizen of the Choctaw Nation, of Walter Payton, born on the 10 day of January, 1905

Name of Father: Ned Payton a citizen of the Choctaw Nation.
Name of Mother: Josephine Payton a citizen of the Choctaw Nation.
Postoffice Boswell, I.T.

AFFIDAVIT OF MOTHER.

UNITED STATES OF AMERICA, Indian Territory,
Central Judicial DISTRICT.

I, Josephine Payton, on oath state that I am 29 years of age and a citizen by blood, of the Choctaw Nation; that I am the lawful wife of Ned Payton, who is a citizen, by blood of the Choctaw Nation; that a male child was born to me on 10 day of January, 1905; that said child has been named Walter Payton, and was living March 4, 1905.

Josephine Payton

Witnesses To Mark:

Subscribed and sworn to before me this 1 day of April, 1905

L. D. Horton
Notary Public.

AFFIDAVIT OF ATTENDING PHYSICIAN OR MID-WIFE.

UNITED STATES OF AMERICA, Indian Territory,
Central Judicial DISTRICT.

I, Minervia Dwight, a Midwife, on oath state that I attended on Mrs. Josephine Payton, wife of Ned Payton on the 10 day of January, 1905; that there was born to her on said date a male child; that said child was living March 4, 1905, and is said to have been named Walter Payton

her
Minervia x Dwight
mark

Witnesses To Mark:
 (Name Illegible)
 V Branaugh

Applications for Enrollment of Choctaw Newborn
Act of 1905 Volume X

Subscribed and sworn to before me this 1 day of April , 1905

L.D. Horton
Notary Public.

Choc New Born 606
    Charlie Risener b. 8-31-03

BIRTH AFFIDAVIT.

DEPARTMENT OF THE INTERIOR.
COMMISSION TO THE FIVE CIVILIZED TRIBES.

IN RE APPLICATION FOR ENROLLMENT, as a citizen of the Choctaw Nation, of Charlie Risener , born on the 31st day of August , 1903

Name of Father: William Risener   a citizen of the Choctaw Nation.
Name of Mother: Lucy Risener   a citizen of the Choctaw Nation.

        Postoffice   Bennington

AFFIDAVIT OF MOTHER.

UNITED STATES OF AMERICA, Indian Territory,
    Cent   **DISTRICT.**

    I, Lucy Risener , on oath state that I am 36 years of age and a citizen by blood , of the Choctaw Nation; that I am the lawful wife of Wm Risener , who is a citizen, by blood of the Choctaw Nation; that a male child was born to me on 31st day of August , 1903; that said child has been named Charlie Risener , and was living March 4, 1905.

                                    her
                            Lucy x Risener
Witnesses To Mark: mark
  { Gertie Frazier
    Lizzie Burnside

    Subscribed and sworn to before me this 1st day of April , 1905

                            B.W. Williams
                                Notary Public.

Applications for Enrollment of Choctaw Newborn
Act of 1905   Volume X

AFFIDAVIT OF ATTENDING PHYSICIAN OR MID-WIFE.

UNITED STATES OF AMERICA, Indian Territory, }
   Cent   DISTRICT.

    I,   B.C. Rutherford   , a   Physician   , on oath state that I attended on Mrs.   Lucy Risener   , wife of   Wm Risener   on the   31st day of   August   , 1903; that there was born to her on said date a   male   child; that said child was living March 4, 1905, and is said to have been named   Charlie

                                      B.C. Rutherford M.D.
Witnesses To Mark:

{

    Subscribed and sworn to before me this   1st day of   April   , 1905

                                      B.W. Williams
                                          Notary Public.

NEW-BORN AFFIDAVIT.

                Number..............

Choctaw Enrolling Commission.

    IN THE MATTER OF THE APPLICATION FOR ENROLLMENT, as a citizen of the   Choctaw   Nation, of   Charlie Risener

born on the   31   day of   August   1903

Name of father   William Risener   a citizen of   Choctaw
Nation final enrollment Nov..............
Name of mother   Lucy Risener   a citizen of   Choctaw
Nation final enrollment No   10258

                        Postoffice   Bennington, I.T.

AFFIDAVIT OF MOTHER.

UNITED STATES OF AMERICA, }
    INDIAN TERRITORY,
   Central   DISTRICT

    I   Lucy Risener   on oath state that I am   38   years of age and a citizen by   ——   of the   ——   Nation, and as such have been placed upon the final roll of the   Choctaw   Nation, by the Honorable Secretary of the Interior my final enrollment number being   10258 ; that I am the lawful wife of   William Risener   , who is a citizen of the   Choctaw   Nation, and as such has been placed upon the final

Applications for Enrollment of Choctaw Newborn
Act of 1905   Volume X

roll of said Nation by the Honorable Secretary of the Interior, his final enrollment number being _____ and that a   male   child was born to me on the   31   day of   August   190 3 ; that said child has been named   Charles Risener   , and is now living.

                                                                                                  her

WITNESSETH: Lucy Risener   x

Must be two Witnesses who are Citizens.   }   TW Hunter   mark

             E.T. Dwight

        Subscribed and sworn to before me this   19   day of   Jany   190 5

                                          W.T. Glenn
                                                      Notary Public.

My commission expires   1907

AFFIDAVIT OF ATTENDING PHYSICIAN OR MIDWIFE

UNITED STATES OF AMERICA }
INDIAN TERRITORY
  Central   DISTRICT

    I,   B.C. Rutherford   a   Practicing Physician on oath state that I attended on Mrs.   Lucy Risener   wife of   William Risener on the   31   day of   August   , 190 3, that there was born to her on said date a   Male child, that said child is now living, and is said to have been named   Charlie Risener

                                          B.C. Rutherford   M.D.
    Subscribed and sworn to before me this, the   20th   day of   (Illegible)   190 5

                                          B.W. Williams
                                               Notary Public.

WITNESSETH:

Must be two witnesses who are citizens and know the child.   {   TW Hunter

                            E.T. Dwight

    We hereby certify that we are well acquainted with   B.C. Rutherford   a   practicing Physician   and know   him   to be reputable and of good standing in the community.

                                          TW Hunter

                                          E.T. Dwight

Applications for Enrollment of Choctaw Newborn
Act of 1905   Volume X

Choc New Born 607
   Gladys Burnside   b. 6-26-04

New-Born Affidavit

Number..................

Choctaw Enrolling Commission.

IN THE MATTER OF THE APPLICATION FOR ENROLLMENT, as a citizen of the Choctaw   Nation, of   Gladys Burnside

born on the   26th   day of   June   190 4

Name of father   DE Burnside   a citizen of   America
Nation final enrollment No ——   *(nee Risener)*
Name of mother   Lizzie Burnside   a citizen of   Choctaw
Nation final enrollment No   10259

                              Postoffice   Bennington I.T.

AFFIDAVIT OF MOTHER.

UNITED STATES OF AMERICA, }
   INDIAN TERRITORY,
   Cent   DISTRICT

   I   Lizzie Burnside (nee Risener)   on oath state that I am   19   years of age and a citizen by   Blood   of the   Choctaw   Nation, and as such have been placed upon the final roll of the   Choctaw   Nation, by the Honorable Secretary of the Interior my final enrollment number being   10259   ; that I am the lawful wife of   D.E. Burnside   , who is a citizen of the   United States   Nation, and as such has *not* been placed upon the final roll of said Nation by the Honorable Secretary of the Interior, his final enrollment number being —— and that a   Female   child was born to me on the   26th   day of   June   190 4 ; that said child has been named   Gladys Burnside   , and is now living.   *Risener*

                              Lizzie Burnside

WITNESSETH:
   Must be two   } WH Loring
   Witnesses who
   are Citizens.   J.N. Jones

       Subscribed and sworn to before me this   31st   day of   June   190 5

                              B.W. Williams
                                 Notary Public.

My commission expires Oct 16th 1907

Applications for Enrollment of Choctaw Newborn
Act of 1905 Volume X

Affidavit of Attending Physician or Midwife.

UNITED STATES OF AMERICA }
INDIAN TERRITORY
   Cent   DISTRICT

I, B.C. Rutherford a Physician on oath state that I attended on Mrs. Lizzie Burnside (nee Risener) wife of D.E. Burnside on the 26th day of June , 190 4 , that there was born to her on said date a Female child, that said child is now living, and is said to have been named Gladys Burnside

                                B C Rutherford   M.D.

Subscribed and sworn to before me this, the 31st day of Jan 190 5

                                BW Williams
                                       Notary Public.

WITNESSETH:
Must be two witnesses who are citizens and know the child.
    W.H. Loring
    Ross Frazier

We hereby certify that we are well acquainted with B.C. Rutherford a Physician and know him to be reputable and of good standing in the community.

                          W.H. Loring
                          Ross Frazier

BIRTH AFFIDAVIT.

DEPARTMENT OF THE INTERIOR.
COMMISSION TO THE FIVE CIVILIZED TRIBES.

IN RE APPLICATION FOR ENROLLMENT, as a citizen of the Choctaw Nation, of Gladys Burnside , born on the 26th day of June , 1904

Name of Father: D.E. Burnside a citizen of the Choctaw Nation.
Name of Mother: Lizzie Burnside (nee Risener) a citizen of the Choctaw Nation.

                          Postoffice   Bennington IT

Applications for Enrollment of Choctaw Newborn
Act of 1905 Volume X

AFFIDAVIT OF MOTHER.

UNITED STATES OF AMERICA, Indian Territory, }
Cent DISTRICT.

I, Lizzie Burnside, on oath state that I am 19 years of age and a citizen by blood, of the Choctaw Nation; that I am the lawful wife of D.E. Burnside, who is a citizen, by Intermarriage of the Choctaw Nation; that a Female child was born to me on 26th day of June, 1904; that said child has been named Gladys Burnside, and was living March 4, 1905.

Lizzie Burnside

Witnesses To Mark:
{

Subscribed and sworn to before me this ~~26th~~ 1st day of April, 1905

B.W. Williams
Notary Public.

AFFIDAVIT OF ATTENDING PHYSICIAN OR MID-WIFE.

UNITED STATES OF AMERICA, Indian Territory, }
Cent DISTRICT.

I, B.C. Rutherford, a Physician, on oath state that I attended on Mrs. Lizzie Burnside, wife of D E Burnside on the 26th day of June, 1904; that there was born to her on said date a Female child; that said child was living March 4, 1905, and is said to have been named Gladys Burnside

B.C. Rutherford MD

Witnesses To Mark:
{

Subscribed and sworn to before me this 1st day of April, 1905

B.W. Williams
Notary Public.

Applications for Enrollment of Choctaw Newborn
Act of 1905 Volume X

Choc New Born 608
    Minnie May Spain b. 7-10-03
    Jimmie B. Spain b. 1-12-05

COPY

7- 119.

Muskogee, Indian Territory, March 28, 1905.

Minnie Lee Spain,
    Care Sidney B. Spain,
        Harrisburg, Indian Territory.

Dear Madam:

    There is enclosed you herewith for execution application for the enrollment of your infant child, Minnie May Spain, born July 10, 1903.

    The affidavits heretofore filed with the Commission show the child was living October 13, 1904. It is necessary, for the child to be enrolled, that she was living on March 4, 1905.

    In having these affidavits executed care should be exercised to see that all names are written in full, as they appear in the body of the affidavit, and in the event that either of the persons signing the affidavit are unable to write, signatures by mark must be attested by two witnesses. Each affidavit must be executed before a Notary Public and the notarial seal and signature of the officer must be attached to each separate affidavit.

                Respectfully,

SIGNED
Tams Bixby
P.T. 1/28   Chairman.

COPY

7-119

Muskogee, Indian Territory, October 19, 1904.

Sidney D. Spain,
    Harrisburg, Indian Territory.

Dear Sir:-

    Receipt is hereby acknowledged of the affidavits of Minnie L. Spain and J. W. McHenry relative to the birth of your infant daughter Minnie May Spain July 10, 1903,

Applications for Enrollment of Choctaw Newborn
Act of 1905   Volume X

which it is presumed have been forwarded to this office as an application for the enrollment of said child as a citizen by blood of the Choctaw Nation.

The act of Congress approved July 1, 1902, which was ratified by the citizens of the Choctaw and Chickasaw Nations September 25, 1902, among other things provides that no child born to a citizen of the Choctaw or Chickasaw Nation subsequent to the date of said ratification shall be entitled to enrollment or to participate in the distribution of the tribal property of the Choctaw and Chickasaws.

Respectfully,

SIGNED

Tams Bixby
Chairman.

BIRTH AFFIDAVIT.

DEPARTMENT OF THE INTERIOR,
COMMISSION TO THE FIVE CIVILIZED TRIBES.

In Re Application for Enrollment, as a citizen of the Choctaw Nation, of Minnie May Spain , born on the 10 day of July , 1903

Name of Father: Sidney D[sic]. Spain   a citizen of the Choctaw Nation.
Name of Mother: Minnie L Spain   a citizen of the Choctaw Nation.

Post-office   Harrisburg Ind Ter

AFFIDAVIT OF MOTHER.

UNITED STATES OF AMERICA, ⎫
   INDIAN TERRITORY, ⎬
  Southern   District. ⎭

I, Minnie L Spain , on oath state that I am Eighteen years of age and a citizen by intermarriage , of the Choctaw Nation; that I am the lawful wife of Sidney D[sic] Spain , who is a citizen, by blood of the Choctaw Nation; that a female child was born to me on 10 day of July , 1903 , that said child has been named Minnie May Spain , and is now living.

Minnie L Spain

WITNESSES TO MARK:

Applications for Enrollment of Choctaw Newborn
Act of 1905   Volume X

Subscribed and sworn to before me this   13   day of   October , 1904

EH Bond
NOTARY PUBLIC.

AFFIDAVIT OF ATTENDING PHYSICIAN OR MID-WIFE.

UNITED STATES OF AMERICA, }
  INDIAN TERRITORY,
  Southern   District.

I,   J.W. McHenry , a   Physician   , on oath state that I attended on Mrs. Minnie L. Spain , wife of Sidney D[sic] Spain on the 10 day of July , 1903 ; that there was born to her on said date a   female   child; that said child is now living and is said to have been named Minnie May Spain

J.W. McHenry

WITNESSES TO MARK:

{

Subscribed and sworn to before me this   13   day of   October , 1904

EH Bond
NOTARY PUBLIC.

BIRTH AFFIDAVIT.

DEPARTMENT OF THE INTERIOR.
COMMISSION TO THE FIVE CIVILIZED TRIBES.

IN RE APPLICATION FOR ENROLLMENT, as a citizen of the   Choctaw   Nation, of Jimmie B Spain   , born on the   12th day of   January   , 1905

Name of Father: Sidney B. Spain   a citizen of the   Choctaw   Nation.
Name of Mother: Minnie Lee Spain   a citizen of the   Choctaw   Nation.

Postoffice   Ara, I.T.

AFFIDAVIT OF MOTHER.

UNITED STATES OF AMERICA, Indian Territory, }
  Southern   **DISTRICT.**

I,   Minnie Lee Spain   , on oath state that I am   19   years of age and a citizen by   marriage   , of the   Choctaw   Nation; that I am the lawful wife of

Applications for Enrollment of Choctaw Newborn
Act of 1905 Volume X

Sidney B Spain, who is a citizen, by blood of the Choctaw Nation; that a male child was born to me on 12th day of January, 1905; that said child has been named Jimmie B Spain, and was living March 4, 1905.

Minnie Lee Spain

Witnesses To Mark:
{

Subscribed and sworn to before me this 10th day of April, 1905

JE Williams
Notary Public.

AFFIDAVIT OF ATTENDING PHYSICIAN OR MID-WIFE.

UNITED STATES OF AMERICA, Indian Territory,
Southern DISTRICT.

I, J.W. McHenry, a ———, on oath state that I attended on Mrs. Minnie Lee Spain, wife of Sidney B Spain on the 12 day of January, 1905; that there was born to her on said date a male child; that said child was living March 4, 1905, and is said to have been named Jimmie B Spain

J W McHenry

Witnesses To Mark:
{

Subscribed and sworn to before me this 10th day of April, 1905

JE Williams
Notary Public.

BIRTH AFFIDAVIT.

DEPARTMENT OF THE INTERIOR.
COMMISSION TO THE FIVE CIVILIZED TRIBES.

IN RE APPLICATION FOR ENROLLMENT, as a citizen of the Choctaw Nation, of Minnie May Spain, born on the 10th day of July, 1903

Name of Father: Sidney B. Spain   a citizen of the Choctaw Nation.
Name of Mother: Minnie Lee Spain   a citizen of the Choctaw Nation.

Postoffice   Harrisburg Ind Ter

Applications for Enrollment of Choctaw Newborn
Act of 1905 Volume X

AFFIDAVIT OF MOTHER.

UNITED STATES OF AMERICA, Indian Territory, }
    Southern   DISTRICT. }

    I, Minnie Lee Spain, on oath state that I am 18 years of age and a citizen by intermarriage, of the Choctaw Nation; that I am the lawful wife of Sidney B Spain, who is a citizen, by blood of the Choctaw Nation; that a female child was born to me on 10th day of July, 1903; that said child has been named Minnie May Spain, and was living March 4, 1905.

                                      Minnie Lee Spain

Witnesses To Mark:
{

    Subscribed and sworn to before me this 10th day of April, 1905

                                      JE Williams
                                              Notary Public.

AFFIDAVIT OF ATTENDING PHYSICIAN OR MID-WIFE.

UNITED STATES OF AMERICA, Indian Territory, }
    Southern   DISTRICT. }

    I, J.W. McHenry, a ...., on oath state that I attended on Mrs. Minnie Lee Spain, wife of Sidney B Spain on the 10th day of July, 1903; that there was born to her on said date a female child; that said child was living March 4, 1905, and is said to have been named Minnie May Spain

                                      J W McHenry

Witnesses To Mark:
{

    Subscribed and sworn to before me this 10th day of April, 1905

                                        JE Williams
                                           Notary Public.

Applications for Enrollment of Choctaw Newborn
Act of 1905   Volume X

<u>Choc New Born 609</u>
    Carrie Dorset[sic]   b. 6-6[sic]-04

7-3818

Muskogee, Indian Territory, April 7, 1905.

John Dorset[sic],
    Caddo, Indian Territory.

Dear Sir:

    Receipt is hereby acknowledged of the affidavits of Ida Dorsett and Emily Edmond to the birth of Carrie Dorsett daughter of John and Ida Dorsett, June 26, 1904, and the same have been filed with our records as an application for the enrollment of said child.

                        Respectfully,

                                      Commissioner in Charge.

---

7 N. B. 609

COPY

Muskogee, Indian Territory, April 11, 1905.

John Dorset,
    Caddo, Indian Territory.

Dear Sir:

    You are hereby advised that before the application for the enrollment of your infant child, Carrie Dorset, can be finally disposed of, it will be necessary that you furnish either the original or a certified copy of the license and certificate of your marriage to Ida Dorset.

    Please give this matter your immediate attention.

                        Respectfully,

                  SIGNED *T. B. Needles.*
LM   Commissioner in Charge.

Applications for Enrollment of Choctaw Newborn
Act of 1905 Volume X

Choctaw N.B. 609.
COPY
Muskogee, Indian Territory, April 21, 1905.

John Dorset,
    Caddo, Indian Territory.

Dear Sir:

    Receipt is hereby acknowledged of your letter of recent date transmitting marriage certificate between yourself and Ida Umber which you offer in support of the application for the enrollment of your child, Carrie Dorset, and the same has been filed with our records in this case.

    The communication of the Commission of December 3, 1903, enclosed in your letter is herewith returned.

                        Respectfully,

                        SIGNED   *Tams Bixby*
                                    Chairman.

DeB-1-21.

Sub

                                             7-NB-609.

Muskogee, Indian Territory, May 27, 1905.

John Dorsett,
    Caddo, Indian Territory.

Dear Sir:

    There is enclosed you herewith for execution application for the enrollment of your infant child, Carrie Dorsett.

    In the affidavits of February 11, 1905, heretofore filed in this office, the date of the applicant's birth is given as June 6, 1903, while in those of March 27, 1905 it is given as June 26, 1904. In the enclosed application the date of birth is left blank. Please insert the correct date and, when the affidavits are properly executed, return them to this office.

    In having these affidavits executed care should be exercised to see that all names are written in full, as they appear in the body of the affidavit, and in the event that either of the persons signing the affidavit are unable to write, signatures by mark must be attested by two witnesses. Each affidavit must be executed before a Notary Public and the notarial seal and signature of the officer must be attached to each separate affidavit.

Applications for Enrollment of Choctaw Newborn
Act of 1905 Volume X

Respectfully,

VR 26-9.

Chairman.

---

7 NB 609

Muskogee, Indian Territory, June 21, 1905.

John Dorset,
    Caddo, Indian Territory.

Dear Sir:

    Receipt is hereby acknowledged of the affidavits of Ida Dorsett and Emily Edmond to the birth of Carrie Dorsett, daughter of John Dorsett and Ida Dorsett (Umber), June 6, 1903, and the same have been filed with our records in the matter of the enrollment of said child.

Respectfully,

Chairman.

7-NB-609

Muskogee, Indian Territory, October 19, 1905

John Dorsett,
    Caddo, Indian Territory.

Dear Sir:

    Receipt is hereby acknowledged of your letter of October 11, 1905, asking if you can file for your baby.

    In reply to your letter you are advised that on August 22, 1905, the Secretary of the Interior approved the enrollment of your child Carrie Dorset[sic] as a citizen by blood of the Choctaw Nation and selection of allotment may now be made in her behalf in accordance with the rules and regulations governing the selection of allotments and the designation of homesteads in the Choctaw and Chickasaw Nations.

Respectfully,

Commissioner.

Applications for Enrollment of Choctaw Newborn
Act of 1905 Volume X

Choctaw Nation.
County of Blue.

CERTIFICATE OF MARRIAGE.

Know All Men By These Present, That I, J. H. Goforth, County and Probate Judge of Blue County, Choctaw Nation, by virtue of the power and authority invested in me as such Judge, did on the 18th, day of August, 1902, solemnize the rites of matrimony between John Dorsey[sic], a Citizen of the Choctaw Nation, and Ida Umber, also a Choctaw Indian, in manner and form required by law.
In witness whereof I hereunto set my hand this the 19th, day of Aug. 1903.

J H Goforth
County & Probate Judge.

NEW BORN AFFIDAVIT

No

CHOCTAW ENROLLING COMMISSION

IN THE MATTER OF THE APPLICATION FOR ENROLLMENT as a citizen of the Choctaw Nation, of Carrey[sic] Dowset[sic] born on the 6th [sic] day of June 190 3[sic]

Name of father John Dowset a citizen of Choctaw Nation, final enrollment No. 14377 Dowset
Name of mother Ida Umbra[sic] now a citizen of Choctaw Nation, final enrollment No. 807

Caddo I.T. Postoffice.

AFFIDAVIT OF MOTHER

UNITED STATES OF AMERICA
INDIAN TERRITORY
DISTRICT Central

I Ida Umbra now Dowset , on oath state that I am 21 years of age and a citizen by blood of the Choctaw Nation, and as such have been placed upon the final roll of the Choctaw Nation, by the Honorable Secretary of the Interior my final enrollment number being 807 ; that I am the lawful wife of John Dowset , who is a citizen of the Choctaw Nation, and as such has been placed

Applications for Enrollment of Choctaw Newborn
Act of 1905   Volume X

upon the final roll of said Nation by the Honorable Secretary of the Interior, his final enrollment number being   14377   and that a   Female   child was born to me on the 6th day of   June   190 3; that said child has been named   Carrey Dowset   , and is now living.

                                                              her

WITNESSETH: Ida Umbra x now Dowset
  Must be two witnesses   { Henry Byington   mark
  who are citizens   Luvena Byington

      Subscribed and sworn to before me this, the   11th   day of   Feb   , 190 5

                                        A.E. Folsom
                                                 Notary Public.

My Commission Expires:
Jan 9-1909

Affidavit of Attending Physician or Midwife

UNITED STATES OF AMERICA,   }
   INDIAN TERRITORY,
  Central   DISTRICT

    I,   Emily Edmond   a   Mid wife
on oath state that I attended on Mrs. Ida Umbra Now Dowset   wife of   John Dowset   on the   6th   day of   June   , 190 3, that there was born to her on said date a   Female   child, that said child is now living, and is said to have been named   Carrey Dowset

                                            her
                                     Emily x Edmond   M.D.
                                            mark
       Subscribed and sworn to before me this the   11th   day of   February   1905

                                        A.E. Folsom
                                             Notary Public.

WITNESSETH:
  Must be two witnesses   { Henry Byington
  who are citizens and
  know the child.   Luvena Byington

    We hereby certify that we are well acquainted with   Emily Edmonds[sic]
a   Mid Wife   and know   her   to be reputable and of good standing in the community.

                                  Must be two citizen { Henry Byington
                                    witnesses.   Luvena Byington

Applications for Enrollment of Choctaw Newborn
Act of 1905   Volume X

BIRTH AFFIDAVIT.

DEPARTMENT OF THE INTERIOR.
COMMISSION TO THE FIVE CIVILIZED TRIBES.

IN RE APPLICATION FOR ENROLLMENT, as a citizen of the   Choctaw   Nation, of   Carrie Dorsett   , born on the 6th day of   June   , 1903

Name of Father: John Dorsett   a citizen of the   Choctaw   Nation.
Name of Mother: Ida Dorsett (Umber)   a citizen of the   Choctaw   Nation.

Postoffice   Caddo, Ind. Ter.

AFFIDAVIT OF MOTHER.

UNITED STATES OF AMERICA, Indian Territory,
Central   DISTRICT.

I,   Ida Dorsett (Umber)   , on oath state that I am   24   years of age and a citizen by   blood   , of the (Mississippi)   Choctaw   Nation; that I am the lawful wife of   John Dorsett   , who is a citizen, by blood   of the   Choctaw Nation; that a   female   child was born to me on   6th day of   June   , 1903; that said child has been named   Carrie Dorsett   , and was living March 4, 1905.

         her
     Ida x Dorsett
Witnesses To Mark: mark
  { Marion Moses
   (Name Illegible)

Subscribed and sworn to before me this 17th day of   June   , 1905

(Name Illegible)
Notary Public.

AFFIDAVIT OF ATTENDING PHYSICIAN OR MID-WIFE.

UNITED STATES OF AMERICA, Indian Territory,
Central   DISTRICT.

I,   Emily Edmond   , a   Midwife   , on oath state that I attended on Mrs.   Ida Dorsett   , wife of   John Dorsett   on the 6th day of   June   , 1903; that there was born to her on said date a   female   child; that said child was living March 4, 1905, and is said to have been named   Carrie Dorsett

     her
Emily x Edmond
    mark

Applications for Enrollment of Choctaw Newborn
Act of 1905   Volume X

Witnesses To Mark:
{ Marion Moses
{ *(Name Illegible)*

Subscribed and sworn to before me this 17th day of June , 1905

(Name Illegible)
Notary Public.

BIRTH AFFIDAVIT.

DEPARTMENT OF THE INTERIOR.
COMMISSION TO THE FIVE CIVILIZED TRIBES.

IN RE APPLICATION FOR ENROLLMENT, as a citizen of the   Choctaw   Nation, of Carrie Dorsett   , born on the 26th day of June , 1904

Name of Father: John Dorsett   a citizen of the   Choctaw   Nation.
Name of Mother: Ida Dorsett   a citizen of the   Choctaw   Nation.

Postoffice   Caddo, Ind. Ter.

AFFIDAVIT OF MOTHER.

UNITED STATES OF AMERICA, Indian Territory, }
   Central   DISTRICT. }

Enrolled as Ida Umber

I,   Ida Dorsett   , on oath state that I am 24   years of age and a citizen by Blood   , of the   Choctaw   Nation; that I am the lawful wife of   John Dorsett , who is a citizen, by Blood   of the   Choctaw   Nation; that a   Female   child was born to me on 26th day of June   , 1904; that said child has been named Carrie Dorsett   , and was living March 4, 1905.

                                    her
                              Ida x Dorsett
Witnesses To Mark: mark
{ Ben Byington
{ Marcus Washington

Subscribed and sworn to before me this 27th day of March , 1905

CH Ewing
Notary Public.

43

Applications for Enrollment of Choctaw Newborn
Act of 1905 Volume X

AFFIDAVIT OF ATTENDING PHYSICIAN OR MID-WIFE.

UNITED STATES OF AMERICA, Indian Territory,
   Central   DISTRICT.

    I,   Emily Edmond   , a   Midwife   , on oath state that I attended on Mrs. Carrie[sic] Dorsett , wife of   John Dorsett   on the 26th day of   June , 1904; that there was born to her on said date a   Female   child; that said child was living March 4, 1905, and is said to have been named   Carrie Dorsett

                                      her
                             Emily x Edmond
                                mark

Witnesses To Mark:
   { Ben Byington
     Marcus Washington

    Subscribed and sworn to before me this 27th day of   March   , 1905

                              CH Ewing
                                  Notary Public.

Choc New Born 610
      Dovey Rabon   b. 12-2-03

$W^m O.B.$

COMMISSIONERS:
TAMS BIXBY,
THOMAS B. NEEDLES,
C.R. BRECKINBRIDGE.

DEPARTMENT OF THE INTERIOR,
COMMISSIONER TO THE FIVE CIVILIZED TRIBES.

REFER IN REPLY TO THE FOLLOWING:

7-2545

WM. O. BEALL
Secretary

        ADDRESS ONLY THE
COMMISSION TO THE FIVE CIVILIZED TRIBES.

                          Muskogee, Indian Territory, April 7, 1905.

Minnie Rabon,
      Whitefield, Indian Territory.

Dear Madam:

    Receipt is hereby acknowledged of the affidavits of Minnie Forest[sic] and Annie Forrest to the birth of Dovey Rabon, daughter of William Rabon and Minnie Forrest

Applications for Enrollment of Choctaw Newborn
Act of 1905   Volume X

December 2, 1903, and the same have been filed with our records as an application for the enrollment of said child.

                    Respectfully,

                              T B Needles
                              Commissioner in Charge.

                                        7-NB-610.

                  Muskogee, Indian Territory, May 27, 1905.

Minnie Forrest,
      Whitefield, Indian Territory.

Dear Madam:

      There is enclosed you herewith for execution application for the enrollment of your infant child, Dovey Rabon.

      In your affidavit of January 3, 1905, the date of the applicant's birth is given as December 2, 1902, while in the affidavits of March 27, 1905, the date of birth is given as December 7, 1903. In the enclosed application the date of birth is left bland. Please insert the correct date and, when the affidavits are properly executed, return them to this office.

      In having these affidavits executed care should be exercised to see that all names are written in full, as they appear in the body of the affidavit, and in the event that either of the persons signing the affidavit are unable to write, signatures by mark must be attested by two witnesses. Each affidavit must be executed before a Notary Public and the notarial seal and signature of the officer must be attached to each separate affidavit.

                    Respectfully,

VR 26-11.   Chairman.

7-NB-610

                  Muskogee, Indian Territory, July 29, 1905.

Minnie Forrest,
      Whitefield, Indian Territory.

Dear Madam:

      Your attention is called to a communication addressed to you by the Commission to the Five Civilized Tribes, under date of May 27, 1905, with which there

Applications for Enrollment of Choctaw Newborn
Act of 1905   Volume X

was inclosed for execution, application for the enrollment of your infant child, Dovey Rabon.

In said letter you were advised that in your affidavit of June 3, 1905, heretofore filed in this office, the date of applicant's birth is given as December 2, 1902, while in the affidavit of March 27, 1905, the date of birth was given as December 2, 1903. You were requested to have said application properly executed and return to this office. No reply to this letter has been received.

The matter should receive your immediate attention as no further action can be taken relative to the enrollment of your said child until the evidence requested is supplied.

                        Respectfully,

                                                Commissioner.

NEW-BORN AFFIDAVIT.

            Number..............

...Choctaw Enrolling Commission...

IN THE MATTER OF THE APPLICATION FOR ENROLLMENT, as a citizen of the Chocktaw[sic] Nation, of Devie[sic] Rabon

born on the 2 day of ____December____ 190 2

Name of father Will Rabon	a citizen of	White
Nation final enrollment No. ———		
Name of mother Minie[sic] Forrest	a citizen of	Choctaw
Nation final enrollment No. 7389		
	Postoffice	Whitefield IT

AFFIDAVIT OF MOTHER.

UNITED STATES OF AMERICA
INDIAN TERRITORY
   Central   DISTRICT

        I   Minie Forresy   , on oath state that I am 23 years of age and a citizen by blood of the Choctaw Nation, and as such have been placed upon the final roll of the Choctaw Nation, by the Honorable Secretary of the Interior my final enrollment number being 7389 ; ~~that I am the~~ *not married* lawful wife of .... who is a citizen of the White Nation, and as such has been placed upon the final roll of said Nation by the Honorable Secretary of the

Applications for Enrollment of Choctaw Newborn
Act of 1905 Volume X

Interior, his final enrollment number being .... and that a Female child was born to me on the 2 day of December 190 2; that said child has been named Devie Rabon , and is now living.

Minnie Forret[sic]

Witnesseth.

Must be two Witnesses who are Citizens. } James Cooper
Wm Martin

Subscribed and sworn to before me this 3 day of Jan 190 5

James Bower
Notary Public.

My commission expires:
Sept 23-1907

AFFIDAVIT OF ATTENDING PHYSICIAN OR MIDWIFE

UNITED STATES OF AMERICA
INDIAN TERRITORY
Central DISTRICT

I, A.B. Callaway a Physician on oath state that I attended on Mrs. Minnie Forrest wife of .... on the 2^d day of December , 190 2 , that there was born to her on said date a Female child, that said child is now living, and is said to have been named Devie[sic] Rabon

A.B. Callaway

Subscribed and sworn to before me this, the .... day of .... 190 ....

.... Notary Public.

WITNESSETH:

Must be two witnesses who are citizens { James Cooper
Wm Martin

We hereby certify that we are well acquainted with ....
a .... and know .... to be reputable and of good standing in the community.

James Cooper   _____

Wm Martin   _____

Applications for Enrollment of Choctaw Newborn
Act of 1905   Volume X

BIRTH AFFIDAVIT.

DEPARTMENT OF THE INTERIOR.
COMMISSION TO THE FIVE CIVILIZED TRIBES.

  IN RE APPLICATION FOR ENROLLMENT, as a citizen of the   Choctaw   Nation, of Dovey Rabon , born on the 2nd   day of December , 1903

Name of Father: William Rabon   a citizen of the   ——————Nation.
Name of Mother: Minnie Forrest   a citizen of the   Choctaw   Nation.

         Postoffice   Whitefield IT

AFFIDAVIT OF MOTHER.

UNITED STATES OF AMERICA, Indian Territory,
   Western   **DISTRICT.**

  I, Minnie Forrest , on oath state that I am 23   years of age and a citizen by   blood , of the   Choctaw   Nation; that I am the lawful wife of ——————, who is a citizen, by —— of the —————— Nation; that a   female   child was born to me on   2nd   day of   December , 1903; that said child has been named   Dovey Rabon , and was living March 4, 1905.

            Minnie Forret[sic]

Witnesses To Mark:
{

  Subscribed and sworn to before me this 27th day of   March , 1905

          (Name Illegible)
          Notary Public.

AFFIDAVIT OF ATTENDING PHYSICIAN OR MID-WIFE.

UNITED STATES OF AMERICA, Indian Territory,
   Western   **DISTRICT.**

  I,   Annie Forrest , a   midwife , on oath state that I attended on ~~Mrs.~~   Minnie Forrest , ~~wife of~~   Single Woman   on the   2nd   day of December , 1903; that there was born to her on said date a   female   child; that said child was living March 4, 1905, and is said to have been named   Dovey Rabon

           Annie Forrest

Applications for Enrollment of Choctaw Newborn
Act of 1905 Volume X

Witnesses To Mark:

{

Subscribed and sworn to before me this 27th day of March , 1905

(Name Illegible)
Notary Public.

My Com expires March 4th 1907

BIRTH AFFIDAVIT.

DEPARTMENT OF THE INTERIOR.
COMMISSION TO THE FIVE CIVILIZED TRIBES.

IN RE APPLICATION FOR ENROLLMENT, as a citizen of the Choctaw Nation, of Dovey Rabon , born on the 2nd day of December , 1902

Name of Father: William Rabon   a citizen of the U.S. Nation.
Name of Mother: Minnie Forrest   a citizen of the Choctaw Nation.

Postoffice   Whitefield Ind Ter

AFFIDAVIT OF MOTHER.

UNITED STATES OF AMERICA, Indian Territory, }
     Western   DISTRICT.

I, Minnie Rabon , on oath state that I am 23 years of age and a citizen by blood , of the Choctaw Nation; ~~that I am the lawful wife of , who is a citizen, by~~ Whitefield of the Choctaw Nation; that a female child was born to me on 2nd day of December , 1902; that said child has been named Dovey Rabon , and was living March 4, 1905.

                                     Minnie Forrest

Witnesses To Mark:
{ Annie Forrest

Subscribed and sworn to before me this 22 day of July , 1905

                                     John H Oliver
                                     Notary Public.

my com expires April 10-1909

Applications for Enrollment of Choctaw Newborn
Act of 1905   Volume X

AFFIDAVIT OF ATTENDING PHYSICIAN OR MID-WIFE.

UNITED STATES OF AMERICA, Indian Territory,
  Central   DISTRICT.

    I, A.B. Callaway, a physician, on oath state that I attended on Mrs. Minnie Forrest, ~~wife of~~ on the 2nd day of December, 1902; that there was born to her on said date a female child; that said child was living March 4, 1905, and is said to have been named Dovey Rabon

                               A.B. Callaway

Witnesses To Mark:

{

    Subscribed and sworn to before me this 8th day of June, 1905

                              Edwin O Clark
                                  Notary Public.

My Commission expires
  Jan. 17, 1909.

Choc New Born 611
    James Benjamin   b. 6-12-03

7- 11493 - 7-11492

BIRTH AFFIDAVIT.

DEPARTMENT OF THE INTERIOR.
COMMISSION TO THE FIVE CIVILIZED TRIBES.

    IN RE APPLICATION FOR ENROLLMENT, as a citizen of the   Choctaw   Nation, of James Benjamin, born on the 12 day of June, 1903

Name of Father: Simeon Benjamin *(deceased)*   a citizen of the   Choctaw   Nation.
Name of Mother: Katie Benjamin   a citizen of the   Choctaw   Nation.

                        Postoffice   Herbert, I.T.

Applications for Enrollment of Choctaw Newborn
Act of 1905   Volume X

AFFIDAVIT OF MOTHER.

UNITED STATES OF AMERICA, Indian Territory, }
   Central   DISTRICT. }

      I, Katie Benjamin, on oath state that I am 38 years of age and a citizen by blood, of the Choctaw Nation; that I am the lawful wife of Simeon Benjamin, who is a citizen, by blood of the Choctaw Nation; that a male child was born to me on 12 day of June, 1903; that said child has been named James Benjamin, and was living March 4, 1905.

                                             Katie Benjamin

Witnesses To Mark:
{

      Subscribed and sworn to before me this 24 day of April, 1905

                                             OL Johnson
                                             Notary Public.

AFFIDAVIT OF ATTENDING PHYSICIAN OR MID-WIFE.

UNITED STATES OF AMERICA, Indian Territory, }
   Central   DISTRICT. }

      I, Josephine Benjamin, a midwife, on oath state that I attended on Mrs. Katie Benjamin, wife of Simeon Benjamin on the 12 day of June, 1903; that there was born to her on said date a male child; that said child was living March 4, 1905, and is said to have been named James Benjamin

                                            Josephine Bengeman[sic]

Witnesses To Mark:
{

      Subscribed and sworn to before me this 24 day of April, 1905

                                             OL Johnson
                                             Notary Public.

Applications for Enrollment of Choctaw Newborn
Act of 1905 Volume X

BIRTH AFFIDAVIT.

DEPARTMENT OF THE INTERIOR.
COMMISSION TO THE FIVE CIVILIZED TRIBES.

IN RE APPLICATION FOR ENROLLMENT, as a citizen of the Choctaw Nation, of James Benjamin, born on the 12th day of June, 1903

Name of Father: Simeon Benjamin   a citizen of the Choctaw Nation.
Name of Mother: Katie Benjamin   a citizen of the Choctaw Nation.

Postoffice Herbert, I.T.

AFFIDAVIT OF MOTHER.

UNITED STATES OF AMERICA, Indian Territory,
Central   DISTRICT.

I, Katie Benjamin, on oath state that I am 38 years of age and a citizen by blood, of the Choctaw Nation; that I am the lawful wife of Simeon Benjamin, who is a citizen, by blood of the Choctaw Nation; that a male child was born to me on 12th day of June, 1903; that said child has been named James Benjamin, and was living March 4, 1905.

Katie Benjamin

Witnesses To Mark:

Subscribed and sworn to before me this 3rd day of April, 1905

W.H. Angell
Notary Public.

AFFIDAVIT OF ATTENDING PHYSICIAN OR MID-WIFE.

UNITED STATES OF AMERICA, Indian Territory,
Central   DISTRICT.

I, Betsy Benjamin, a midwife, on oath state that I attended on Mrs. Katie Benjamin, wife of Simeon Benjamin on the 12th day of June, 1903; that there was born to her on said date a male child; that said child was living March 4, 1905, and is said to have been named James Benjamin

her
Betsy x Benjamin
mark

Applications for Enrollment of Choctaw Newborn
Act of 1905   Volume X

Witnesses To Mark:
  { M? Martin
  { Wm Martin

Subscribed and sworn to before me this 3rd   day of   April   , 1905

W.H. Angell
Notary Public.

Choc New Born 612
   Emmett Leroy Barnett   b. 1-9-04

A. M. Cummings, President   *F. O. Harriss, Vice President*   *W. L. Orear, Cashier*

First Bank of Allen

Allen, I.T.   April 1st   *190* 5

This is to certify, that I   Mary A Miller   a Mid-wife do solemnly swear that I attended on Mrs. Sarah A. Barnett, wife of W. W. Barnett the 9th day of January 1904, and there was born to her on said date a male child, said to have been named Emmett Leroy Barnett, and that said child is still living.
   This 1st day of April 1905.

Mary A Miller

Subscribed and sworn to before me this 1st day of April 1905.

R E Brians
Notary Public.

Commission expires Jan 20-1909

Applications for Enrollment of Choctaw Newborn
Act of 1905 Volume X

BIRTH AFFIDAVIT.

DEPARTMENT OF THE INTERIOR.
COMMISSION TO THE FIVE CIVILIZED TRIBES.

IN RE APPLICATION FOR ENROLLMENT, as a citizen of the Choctaw Nation, of Emmett Leroy Barnett, born on the 9th day of January, 1904

Name of Father: William W. Barnett   a citizen of the Choctaw Nation.
Name of Mother: Sarah A. "   a citizen of the " Nation.

Postoffice   Allen I T

AFFIDAVIT OF MOTHER.

UNITED STATES OF AMERICA, Indian Territory,
Central   DISTRICT.

I, Sarah A Barnett, on oath state that I am 35 years of age and a citizen by Intermarriage, of the Choctaw Nation; that I am the lawful wife of William A Barnett, who is a citizen, by blood of the Choctaw Nation; that a male child was born to me on 9th day of January, 1904; that said child has been named Emmett Leroy Barnett, and was living March 4, 1905.

Sarah A Barnett

Witnesses To Mark:
{

Subscribed and sworn to before me this 3rd day of April, 1905.

E Crosthwait
Notary Public.

AFFIDAVIT OF ATTENDING PHYSICIAN OR MIDWIFE

UNITED STATES OF AMERICA
INDIAN TERRITORY
Central   DISTRICT

I, Mary A Miller   a   Midwife on oath state that I attended on Mrs. Sarah A Barnett wife of William W Barnett on the 9 day of Jan., 190 4, that there was born to her on said date a male child, that said child is now living, and is said to have been named Emmett Leroy Barnett

Mary A Miller   *m.w.*

Applications for Enrollment of Choctaw Newborn
Act of 1905   Volume X

    Subscribed and sworn to before me this, the   17   day of Jan.   190 5

WITNESSETH: J. L. Cart   Notary Public.

Must be two witnesses who are citizens { A M Cummings
(Name Illegible)

  We hereby certify that we are well acquainted with   Mary A Miller a   Midwife   and know   her   to be reputable and of good standing in the community.

  A M Cummings   *(Illegible)* Brians

  (Name Illegible)   Lucy Miller

NEW-BORN AFFIDAVIT.

    Number............

...Choctaw Enrolling Commission...

  IN THE MATTER OF THE APPLICATION FOR ENROLLMENT, as a citizen of the Choctaw   Nation, of   Emmett Leroy Barnett

born on the   9   day of ____January____ 190 4

Name of father   William W. Barnett   a citizen of   Choctaw
Nation final enrollment No.   9570
Name of mother   Sarah A Barnett   a citizen of   Choctaw
Nation final enrollment No.   315

              Postoffice   Allen, I.T.

AFFIDAVIT OF MOTHER.

UNITED STATES OF AMERICA
INDIAN TERRITORY
  Central   DISTRICT

      I   Sarah A. Barnett   , on oath state that I am   35   years of age and a citizen by   Inter   of the   Choctaw   Nation, and as such have been placed upon the final roll of the   Choctaw   Nation, by the Honorable Secretary of the Interior my final enrollment number being   315 ; that I am the lawful wife of   William W. Barnett   , who is a citizen of the   Choctaw   Nation, and as such has been placed upon the final roll of said Nation by the Honorable Secretary of the Interior, his final enrollment number being   9570   and that a   Male   child was born to me on

Applications for Enrollment of Choctaw Newborn
Act of 1905 Volume X

the 9 day of January 190 4; that said child has been named Emmett Leroy Bennett , and is now living.

Sarah A Barnett

Witnesseth.

Must be two Witnesses who are Citizens. } A M Cummings

(Name Illegible)

Subscribed and sworn to before me this 17 day of Jan 190 5

J.L. Cart

Notary Public.

My commission expires: June 27-1908

Choc New Born 613
  Agnes Pusley b. 5-13-04

NEW-BORN AFFIDAVIT.

Number............

Choctaw Enrolling Commission.

IN THE MATTER OF THE APPLICATION FOR ENROLLMENT, as a citizen of the Choctaw Nation, of Agnes Pusley

born on the 13# day of May 190 4

Name of father Abner B. Pusley   a citizen of Choctaw
Nation final enrollment No 9618
Name of mother Sedalia Pusley   a citizen of Choctaw
Nation final enrollment No 9619

Postoffice Albany I.T.

AFFIDAVIT OF MOTHER.

UNITED STATES OF AMERICA,
  INDIAN TERRITORY,
  Central   DISTRICT }

I Sedalia Pusley   on oath state that I am 29 years of age and a citizen by blood   of the Choctaw   Nation, and as such have been

56

Applications for Enrollment of Choctaw Newborn
Act of 1905   Volume X

placed upon the final roll of the   Choctaw   Nation, by the Honorable Secretary of the Interior my final enrollment number being   9619   ; that I am the lawful wife of   Abner Pusley   , who is a citizen of the   Choctaw   Nation, and as such has been placed upon the final roll of said Nation by the Honorable Secretary of the Interior, his final enrollment number being   9618   and that a   female   child was born to me on the   13$^{\#}$ day of   May   190 4; that said child has been named   Agnes Pusley   , and is now living.

Sedlie[sic] Pusley

WITNESSETH:
Must be two Witnesses who are Citizens.   } Dennis Carr
                                            Jane Carr

Subscribed and sworn to before me this   17$^{\#}$ day of   January   190 5

P.L. Cain
Notary Public.

My commission expires   March 11-1907

AFFIDAVIT OF ATTENDING PHYSICIAN OR MIDWIFE

UNITED STATES OF AMERICA }
INDIAN TERRITORY
  Central   DISTRICT

I,   Nancy L Capshaw   a   Midwife   on oath state that I attended on Mrs.   Sedalie Pusley   wife of   Abner Pusley   on the   13$^{\#}$ day of   May   , 190 4, that there was born to her on said date a   female   child, that said child is now living, and is said to have been named   Agnes Pusley

Nancy L Capshaw   M.D.

Subscribed and sworn to before me this, the   17 day of   January   190 5

P.L. Cain
Notary Public.

WITNESSETH:
Must be two witnesses who are citizens and know the child.   { Dennis Carr
                                                                Jane Carr

We hereby certify that we are well acquainted with   Mrs. N. L. Capshaw   a   Midwife   and know   her   to be reputable and of good standing in the community.

{ Dennis Carr
Jane Carr

Applications for Enrollment of Choctaw Newborn
Act of 1905   Volume X

BIRTH AFFIDAVIT.

DEPARTMENT OF THE INTERIOR,
COMMISSION TO THE FIVE CIVILIZED TRIBES.

IN RE Application for Enrollment, as a citizen of the   Choctaw   Nation, of   Agnes Pusley , born on the $13^{\#}$ day of   May   , 1904

Name of Father: Abner Pusley   a citizen of the Choctaw   Nation.
Name of Mother: Sedalia Pusley   a citizen of the Choctaw   Nation.

Post-Office: Albany I.T.

AFFIDAVIT OF MOTHER.

UNITED STATES OF AMERICA,
   INDIAN TERRITORY.
Central   District.

I,   Sedalia Pusley   , on oath state that I am 29   years of age and a citizen by blood , of the Choctaw Nation; that I am the lawful wife of Abner Pusley , who is a citizen, by   blood   of the Choctaw Nation; that a   female   child was born to me on $13^{\#}$ day of   May   , 1904 , that said child has been named   Agnes Pusley , and is now living.

                       Sedalie Pusley

WITNESSES TO MARK:

Subscribed and sworn to before me this $27^{\#}$ day of   March   , 1905.

                       P.L. Cain
                           NOTARY PUBLIC.

AFFIDAVIT OF ATTENDING PHYSICIAN OR MID-WIFE.

UNITED STATES OF AMERICA,
   INDIAN TERRITORY.
Central   District.

I,   Nancy L Capshaw   , a   midwife   , on oath state that I attended on Mrs. Sedalie Pusley , wife of   Abner Pusley   on the $13^{\#}$ day of   May   , 1904 ; that there was born to her on said date a   female   child; that said child is now living and is said to have been named   Agnes Pusley

                       Nancy L Capshaw

Applications for Enrollment of Choctaw Newborn
Act of 1905   Volume X

WITNESSES TO MARK:

{

    Subscribed and sworn to before me this 27$^{\#}$ *day of* March , 1905.

                                            P.L. Cain
                                          NOTARY PUBLIC.

Choc New Born 614
      Julian Pusley b. 8-7-03
      Vivian Eloise Pusley b. 6-28-04

                        COPY   7-N. B. 614

                        Muskogee, Indian Territory, April 11, 1905.

William W. Pusley,
      McAlester, Indian Territory.

Dear Sir:

    There is inclosed you herewith for execution application for the enrollment of your infant child, Julian Pusley and Vivian Eloise Pusley, born August 7, 1903, and June 28, 1904.

    In having these affidavits executed care should be exercised to see that all names are written in full, as they appear in the body of the affidavit, and in the event that either of the persons signing the affidavit are unable to write, signatures by mark must be attested by two witnesses. Each affidavit must be executed before a Notary Public and the notarial seal and signature of the officer must be attached to each separate affidavit.

                        Respectfully,

                    SIGNED   *T. B. Needles.*
LM 11-24   Commissioner in Charge.

Applications for Enrollment of Choctaw Newborn
Act of 1905   Volume X

BIRTH AFFIDAVIT.

DEPARTMENT OF THE INTERIOR.
COMMISSION TO THE FIVE CIVILIZED TRIBES.

IN RE APPLICATION FOR ENROLLMENT, as a citizen of the   Ch_octaw[sic]   Nation, of   Vivian Eloise Pusley   , born on the   28th   day of   June   , 1904 blood I2930)
Name of Father: William W. Pusley (choc. by   a citizen of the   Choctaw   Nation.
Name of Mother: Lelan Pusley (choc. Inter.849) a citizen of the   Choctaw   Nation.

Postoffice   McAlester Ind. Ter.

AFFIDAVIT OF MOTHER.

UNITED STATES OF AMERICA, Indian Territory,
Central   DISTRICT.

I,   Lelan Pusley   , on oath state that I am   18   years of age and a citizen by Inter.   , of the   Choctaw   Nation; that I am the lawful wife of   William Pusley   , who is a citizen, by blood   of the   Choctaw   Nation; that a   female   child was born to me on   28th   day of   June   , 1904; that said child has been named Vivian Eloise Pusley   , and was living March 4, 1905.

Lelan Pusley

Witnesses To Mark:
{

Subscribed and sworn to before me this 1st   day of   April   , 1905

Harry L Baker
Notary Public.

AFFIDAVIT OF ATTENDING PHYSICIAN OR MID-WIFE.

UNITED STATES OF AMERICA, Indian Territory,
Central   DISTRICT.

I,   Harriet Sennett   , a   Mid-wife   , on oath state that I attended on Mrs.   Lelan Pusley   , wife of   William W Pusley   on the 28th day of   June , 1904; that there was born to her on said date a   female   child; that said child was living March 4, 1905, and is said to have been named   Vivian Eloise Pusley

Harriet Sennett

Witnesses To Mark:
{

Applications for Enrollment of Choctaw Newborn
Act of 1905   Volume X

Subscribed and sworn to before me this 1st day of   April   , 1905

                        Harry L Baker
                        Notary Public.

BIRTH AFFIDAVIT.

DEPARTMENT OF THE INTERIOR.
COMMISSION TO THE FIVE CIVILIZED TRIBES.

    IN RE APPLICATION FOR ENROLLMENT, as a citizen of the   Choctaw   Nation, of   Julian Pusley   , born on the   7th day of August   , 1903

Name of Father: William W. Pusley (Roll #I2930)   a citizen of the   Choctaw   Nation.
Name of Mother: Lelan Pusley (Inter 849)   a citizen of the   Choctaw   Nation.

                Postoffice   McAlester Indian Terr

AFFIDAVIT OF MOTHER.

UNITED STATES OF AMERICA, Indian Territory,
    Central   DISTRICT.

    I,   Lelan Pusley   , on oath state that I am   18   years of age and a citizen by Inter   , of the   Choctaw   Nation; that I am the lawful wife of   William W Pusley, who is a citizen, by Blood   of the   Choctaw   Nation; that a   Male   child was born to me on   7th   day of   August   , 1903; that said child has been named   Julian Pusley   , and was living March 4, 1905.

                    Lelan Pusley

Witnesses To Mark:

Subscribed and sworn to before me this 1st day of   April   , 1905

                      Harry L Baker
                      Notary Public.

AFFIDAVIT OF ATTENDING PHYSICIAN OR MID-WIFE.

UNITED STATES OF AMERICA, Indian Territory,
    Central   DISTRICT.

    I,   Harriet Sennett   , a   Mid-wife   , on oath state that I attended on Mrs.   Lelan Pusley   , wife of   William W Pusley   on the 7th day of August,

Applications for Enrollment of Choctaw Newborn
Act of 1905 Volume X

1903; that there was born to her on said date a   Male   child; that said child was living March 4, 1905, and is said to have been named   Julian Pusley

Harriet Sennett

Witnesses To Mark:

{ Subscribed and sworn to before me this 1st day of April , 1905

Harry L Baker
Notary Public.

BIRTH AFFIDAVIT.

DEPARTMENT OF THE INTERIOR.
COMMISSION TO THE FIVE CIVILIZED TRIBES.

IN RE APPLICATION FOR ENROLLMENT, as a citizen of the   Choctaw   Nation, of   Vivian Eloise Pusley   , born on the 28th day of June , 1904

Name of Father: William W. Pusley   a citizen of the   Choctaw   Nation.
Name of Mother: Lelan Pusley   a citizen of the   Choctaw   Nation.

Postoffice   McAlester Ind. Ter.

AFFIDAVIT OF MOTHER.

UNITED STATES OF AMERICA, Indian Territory, }
  15th Recording   DISTRICT.

I, Lelan Pusley   , on oath state that I am   Nineteen   years of age and a citizen by   Marriage   , of the   Choctaw   Nation; that I am the lawful wife of William W. Pusley , who is a citizen, by Blood   of the   Choctaw   Nation; that a   Female   child was born to me on 28th day of   June   , 1904; that said child has been named   Vivian Eloise Pusley   , and was living March 4, 1905.

Lelan Pusley

Witnesses To Mark:
{
  Subscribed and sworn to before me this 11th day of April   , 1905

R.S. Coleman
Notary Public.

My commission expires Feb 4th 1908

Applications for Enrollment of Choctaw Newborn
Act of 1905 Volume X

AFFIDAVIT OF ATTENDING PHYSICIAN OR MID-WIFE.

UNITED STATES OF AMERICA, Indian Territory,
15th Recording DISTRICT.

I, Harriette Senate, a Midwife, on oath state that I attended on Mrs. Lelan Pusley, wife of William W Pusley on the 28th day of June, 1904; that there was born to her on said date a Female child; that said child was living March 4, 1905, and is said to have been named Vivian Eloise

                her
              Harriette x Senate
Witnesses To Mark: mark
 { J M Green
   Mattie Senate

Subscribed and sworn to before me this 11th day of April, 1905

          R.S. Coleman
            Notary Public.

My commission expires Feb 4th 1908

BIRTH AFFIDAVIT.

DEPARTMENT OF THE INTERIOR.
COMMISSION TO THE FIVE CIVILIZED TRIBES.

IN RE APPLICATION FOR ENROLLMENT, as a citizen of the Choctaw Nation, of Julian Pusley, born on the 7th day of August, 1903

Name of Father: William W. Pusley   a citizen of the Choctaw Nation.
Name of Mother: Lelan Pusley   a citizen of the Choctaw Nation.

       Postoffice   McAlester, Indian Territory

AFFIDAVIT OF MOTHER.

UNITED STATES OF AMERICA, Indian Territory,
15th Recording DISTRICT.

I, Lelan Pusley, on oath state that I am Nineteen years of age and a citizen by Marriage, of the Choctaw Nation; that I am the lawful wife of William W. Pusley, who is a citizen, by Blood of the Choctaw Nation; that a Male child was born to me on 7th day of August, 1903; that said child has been named Julian Pusley, and was living March 4, 1905.

Applications for Enrollment of Choctaw Newborn
Act of 1905 Volume X

Lelan Pusley

Witnesses To Mark:
{

Subscribed and sworn to before me this 11th day of April , 1905

R.S. Coleman
Notary Public.

My commission expires Feb 4th 1908

AFFIDAVIT OF ATTENDING PHYSICIAN OR MID-WIFE.

UNITED STATES OF AMERICA, Indian Territory,
15th Recording DISTRICT. }

I, Harriette Senate , a Midwife , on oath state that I attended on Mrs. Lelan Pusley , wife of William W Pusley on the 7th day of August, 1903; that there was born to her on said date a Male child; that said child was living March 4, 1905, and is said to have been named Julian Pusley

her
Harriette x Senate
mark

Witnesses To Mark:
{ J M Green
  Mattie Senate

Subscribed and sworn to before me this 11th day of April , 1905

R.S. Coleman
Notary Public.

My commission expires Feb 4th 1908

7-4684

Muskogee, Indian Territory, April 19, 1905.

William W. Pusley,
    McAlester, Indian Territory.

Dear Sir:

Receipt is hereby acknowledged of the affidavits of Lelan Pusley and Harriette Senate to the birth of Julian Pusley and Vivian Eloise Pusley, children of William W. and Lelan Pusley, August 7, 1903, and June 28, 1904, and the same have been filed with our records as an application for the enrollment of said children.

Applications for Enrollment of Choctaw Newborn
Act of 1905   Volume X

Respectfully,

Chairman.

7-NB-614

Muskogee, Indian Territory, May 26, 1905.

Commissioner in Charge. Charge,
Choctaw Land Office,
Atoka, Indian Territory.

Dear Sir:

There are enclosed herewith applications for the enrollment of Julian Pusley and Vivian Eloise Pusley, born August 7, 1903 and June 28, 1904, respectively, which were executed in your office before Harry L. Baker, Notary Public, an employee in your office, from which the notarial seal has been omitted.

Please have the above mentioned Notary Public attach his seal to these affidavits and then return them to this office.

Respectfully,

2 Enclosures.

Chairman.

9 NB 614

Muskogee, Indian Territory, June 8, 1905.

William W. Pusley,
McAlester, Indian Territory.

Dear Sir:

Receipt is hereby acknowledged of your letter of June 3, 1905, asking if the names of your children have been placed on the roll so that you can now file for them.

In reply to your letter you are advised that the names of your children Julian and Vivian Eloise Pusley have been placed upon a schedule of citizens by blood of the Choctaw Nation prepared for forwarding to the Secretary of the Interior but pending the approval of their enrollment by him no selection of allotment can be made in their behalf.

The Matter[sic] of the land referred to in your letter will be made the subject of another communication.

Applications for Enrollment of Choctaw Newborn
Act of 1905   Volume X

Respectfully,

Chairman.

7-NB-614

Muskogee, Indian Territory, July 14, 1905.

William W. Pusley,
McAlester, Indian Territory.

Dear Sir:

Receipt is hereby acknowledged of your letter of July 10, 1905, asking what disposition has been made of the application for the enrollment of your two minor children Julian and Vivian Eloise Pusley.

In reply to your letter you are advised that the names of your children Julian and Vivian Pusley have been placed upon a schedule of citizens by blood of the Choctaw Nation which has been forwarded the Secretary of the Interior and you will be notified when their enrollment is approved.

The matter of the land referred to in your letter has been made the subject of another communication.

Respectfully,

Commissioner.

Choc New Born 615
      Pearl Butler   b. 8-24-04

Applications for Enrollment of Choctaw Newborn
Act of 1905   Volume X

NEW-BORN AFFIDAVIT.

Number................

...Choctaw Enrolling Commission...

IN THE MATTER OF THE APPLICATION FOR ENROLLMENT, as a citizen of the Choctaw Nation, of Pearl Butler

born on the 24 day of ___August___ 190 4

Name of father   Jno M Butler   a citizen of   Choctaw
Nation final enrollment No. ....
Name of mother   Delia Butler   a citizen of   Choctaw
Nation final enrollment No. 6729

Postoffice   Cameron I.T.

AFFIDAVIT OF MOTHER.

UNITED STATES OF AMERICA
INDIAN TERRITORY
 Central   DISTRICT

I   Delia Butler   , on oath state that I am 24 years of age and a citizen by Blood of the Choctaw Nation, and as such have been placed upon the final roll of the Choctaw Nation, by the Honorable Secretary of the Interior my final enrollment number being 6729 ; that I am the lawful wife of Jno M Butler , who is a non citizen of the ——— Nation, and as such has been placed upon the final roll of said Nation by the Honorable Secretary of the Interior, his final enrollment number being ——— and that a female child was born to me on the 24 day of August 190 4; that said child has been named Pearl Butler , and is now living.

Delia Butler

Witnesseth.
  Must be two ⎫ J T Reynolds
  Witnesses who ⎬
  are Citizens. ⎭ Clyde McMurtrey

Subscribed and sworn to before me this 14 day of Feb 190 5

Hascot Pilgreen
Notary Public.

My commission expires: Dec 9-07

Applications for Enrollment of Choctaw Newborn
Act of 1905 Volume X

AFFIDAVIT OF ATTENDING PHYSICIAN OR MIDWIFE

UNITED STATES OF AMERICA
INDIAN TERRITORY
   Central   DISTRICT

I, I.T. Harbour a Physician on oath state that I attended on Mrs. Delia Butler wife of Jno M Butler on the 24 day of August, 190 4, that there was born to her on said date a female child, that said child is now living, and is said to have been named Pearl Butler

                      I.T. Harbour   M.D.

WITNESSETH:
Must be two witnesses who are citizens and know the child.
   J T Reynolds
   Clyde McMurtrey

Subscribed and sworn to before me this, the 14 day of January 190 5

        Hascot Pilgreen   Notary Public.

We hereby certify that we are well acquainted with I.T. Harbour a Physician and know him to be reputable and of good standing in the community.

       J T Reynolds
       Clyde McMurtrey

BIRTH AFFIDAVIT.

DEPARTMENT OF THE INTERIOR.
COMMISSION TO THE FIVE CIVILIZED TRIBES.

IN RE APPLICATION FOR ENROLLMENT, as a citizen of the Choctaw Nation, of Pearl Butler, born on the 24 day of Aug, 1904

Name of Father: Jno M Butler   a citizen of the Choctaw Nation.
Name of Mother: Delia Butler   a citizen of the Choctaw Nation.

        Postoffice   Cameron I.T.

Applications for Enrollment of Choctaw Newborn
Act of 1905   Volume X

AFFIDAVIT OF MOTHER.

UNITED STATES OF AMERICA, Indian Territory, }
Central   DISTRICT.

I, Delia Butler, on oath state that I am 24 years of age and a citizen by blood, of the Choctaw Nation; that I am the lawful wife of John M. Butler, who is a citizen, ~~by~~ .... of the United States Nation; that a female child was born to me on 24th day of August, 1904, that said child has been named Pearl Butler, and is now living.

Delia Butler

Witnesses To Mark:
{

Subscribed and sworn to before me this 31st day of March, 1905.

Wirt Franklin
Notary Public.

AFFIDAVIT OF ATTENDING PHYSICIAN OR MID-WIFE.

UNITED STATES OF AMERICA, Indian Territory, }
Central   DISTRICT.

I, I.T. Harbour, a Physician, on oath state that I attended on Mrs. Delia Butler, wife of Jno M Butler on the 24 day of Aug, 1904; that there was born to her on said date a female child; that said child is now living and is said to have been named Pearl Butler

I T Harbour M.D.

Witnesses To Mark:
{

Subscribed and sworn to before me this 30 day of March, 1905.

Hascot Pilgreen
Notary Public.

My Com expires Dec 9-07

Applications for Enrollment of Choctaw Newborn
Act of 1905   Volume X

Choc New Born 616
    Simon Johnson   b. 7-17-03

7-4489

Muskogee, Indian Territory, April 7, 1905.

Alexander Johnson,
    Iron bridge[sic], Indian Territory.

Dear Sir:

    Receipt is hereby acknowledged of the affidavits of Alex Johnson and Elizabeth Johnson to the birth of Simon Johnson, son of Alex and Elizabeth Johnson, July 17, 1903, and the same have been filed with our records as an application for the enrollment of said child.

        Respectfully,

                Commissioner in Charge.

7 N. B. 616

COPY

Muskogee, Indian Territory, April 11, 1905.

Alex Johnson,
    Ironbridge, Indian Territory.

Dear Sir:

    Referring to the affidavits heretofore filed with the Commission relative to the enrollment of your infant child, Simon Johnson, it is noted that the midwife, Lida Bille, and the only one in attendance, is dead. It will therefore be necessary that you secure the affidavits of two persons who have actual knowledge of the facts, that the child was born, the date of his birth, that he was living on March 4, 1905, and that Elizabeth Johnson is his mother.

    Prompt attention should be given this matter.

        Respectfully,
        SIGNED
        T. B. Needles.
LM   Commissioner in Charge.

Applications for Enrollment of Choctaw Newborn
Act of 1905   Volume X

7-NB-616
7-NB-691

Muskogee, Indian Territory, July 24, 1905.

G. A. Holley,
    Attorney at law,
        Stigler, Indian Territory.

Dear Sir:

    Receipt is hereby acknowledged of your letter of July 18, 1905, asking if Clarence Martin, son of James and Maggie Martin has been enrolled; also the two year old son of Alex and Elizabeth Johnson.

    In reply to your letter you are advised that the name of Simon Johnson, son of Alexander and Elizabeth Johnson and Clarence Martin, son of James and Maggie Martin, have been placed upon a schedule of citizens by blood of the Choctaw Nation which has been forwarded the Secretary of the Interior but this office has not yet been notified of Departmental action thereon.

Respectfully,

Commissioner.

United States of America   }   In the Matter of the application for enrollment
Ind Tery Central Dist   }   as a citizen of the Choctaw Nation by Blood of Simon Johnson born on the 17th day of July 1903 I Dixon Billie on oath state that I am about 45 years of age that I am a citizen of the Choctaw Nation by Blood that I have personal knowledge of the birth of the above named child Simon Johnson on or about the 17th day of July 1903. That Elizabeth Johnson Wife of Alex Johnson is the mother of said child and that the said Elizabeth Johnson is a citizen of the Choctaw Nation by Blood and that said child is now living.

                                                      his
                                         Dixon x Billie
Witnesses   mark
John William
Joe McCain

    Sworn to and subscribed before me this the 17th day of April 1903.

M.W. Newman
Notary Public

My Commission Expires
Jan the 17th 1909

Applications for Enrollment of Choctaw Newborn
Act of 1905   Volume X

United States of America } In the Matter of the application for enrollment
Ind Tery Central Dist   } as a citizen of the Choctaw Nation by Blood of
Simon Johnson born on the 17th day of July 1903 I Milton Smith on oath state that I am 18 years old, that I am a citizen by blood of the Choctaw Nation that I have personal knowledge of the birth of the above named child Simon Johnson on or about the 17th day of July 1903. That Elizabeth Johnson, wife of Alex Johnson is the mother of said child and that the said Elizabeth Johnson is a citizen of the Choctaw Nation by blood and that said child is now living.

Witness   Milton Smith

Sworn to and subscribed before me this the 17th day of April 1905.

M.W. Newman
Notary Public

My Commission Expires
Jan the 17th 1909

In Re Application for enrollment, as a citizen of the Choctaw Nation, of Simon Johnson, born on the 17th day of July, 1903.
United States of America, Indian Territory,
Central District.

I, Alex Johnson, on oath state that I am 37 years of age and a citizen by blood of the Choctaw Nation. That Elizabeth Johnson is my lawful wife, and is also a citizen by blood of the Choctaw Nation.

That there was born to us on the 17th day of July 1903 a male child which was named Simon Johnson, and that said child is yet living.

That there was no physician in attendance at the birth of said child, and that the only woman in attendance, Lida Bille, wife of Dixie Bille, a Choctaw Indian by blood, is now dead.

Alex Johnson

Subscribed and sworn to before me this 31, day of March 1905.

A.L. Beckett
Notary Public

My Commission expires May 21, 1907.

Applications for Enrollment of Choctaw Newborn
Act of 1905   Volume X

BIRTH AFFIDAVIT.

DEPARTMENT OF THE INTERIOR.
COMMISSION TO THE FIVE CIVILIZED TRIBES.

IN RE APPLICATION FOR ENROLLMENT, as a citizen of the Choctaw Nation, of Simon Johnson, born on the 17 day of July, 1903

Name of Father: Alex Johnson   a citizen of the Choctaw Nation.
Name of Mother: Elizabeth Johnson   a citizen of the Choctaw Nation.

Postoffice ~~Stig~~ Iron Bridge, I.T.

AFFIDAVIT OF MOTHER.

UNITED STATES OF AMERICA, Indian Territory,
Central   **DISTRICT.**

I, Elizabeth Johnson, on oath state that I am 30 years of age and a citizen by Blood, of the Choctaw Nation; that I am the lawful wife of Alex Johnson, who is a citizen, by Blood of the Choctaw Nation; that a male child was born to me on 17 day of July, 1903; that said child has been named Simon Johnson, and was living March 4, 1905.

Elizabeth Johnson

Witnesses To Mark:

Subscribed and sworn to before me this 31 day of March, 1905
My Comm expires
May 21, 1907.   A.L. Beckett
Notary Public.

Choc New Born 617
    Wesley James   b. 12-30-02

Applications for Enrollment of Choctaw Newborn
Act of 1905   Volume X

7-2937

Muskogee, Indian Territory, April 7, 1905.

Joseph James,
    Redoak, Indian Territory.

Dear Sir:

    Receipt is hereby acknowledged of the affidavits of Mrs. Nellie James and Joseph James to the birth of Wesley James, son of Joseph and Nellie James, December 30, 1902, and the same have been filed with our records as an application for the enrollment of said child.

        Respectfully,

                Commissioner in Charge.

COPY   7N. B. 617

Muskogee, Indian Territory, April 13, 1905.

Joseph James,
    Redoak, Indian Territory.

Dear Sir:

    It appears from the application heretofore forwarded to the Commission for the enrollment of your infant child, Wesley James, that the mid-wife in attendance at the birth of said child, is dead. It is, therefore, necessary that you secure the affidavits of two persons who have actual knowledge of the fact, that the child was born, the date of his birth, that he was living on March 4, 1905, and that Nellie James is his mother.

    Please attend to the matter at once.

        Respectfully,
        SIGNED
          T. B. Needles.
          Commissioner in Charge.

Applications for Enrollment of Choctaw Newborn
Act of 1905   Volume X

COPY

Choctaw N.B. 617.

Muskogee, Indian Territory, April 29, 1905.

Joseph James,
    Red Oak, Indian Territory.

Dear Sir:

    Receipt is hereby acknowledged of the joint affidavit of Elum Baker and Johnson Coley to the birth of Wesley James, son of Joseph and Nellie James, December 30, 1902, and the same have been filed with our records in the matter of the enrollment of said child.

                      Respectfully,
                        SIGNED

                        Tams Bixby
                        Chairman.

NEW-BORN AFFIDAVIT.

                Number............

...Choctaw Enrolling Commission...

IN THE MATTER OF THE APPLICATION FOR ENROLLMENT, as a citizen of the Choctaw Nation, of Wesley James

born on the 30 day of __December__ 190 2

Name of father   Joseph James   a citizen of   Choctaw
Nation final enrollment No. 8636
Name of mother   Nellie James   a citizen of   Choctaw
Nation final enrollment No. 8637

                        Postoffice   Red Oak Ind. Ter.

AFFIDAVIT OF MOTHER.

UNITED STATES OF AMERICA
INDIAN TERRITORY
    Central   DISTRICT

         I   Nellie James   , on oath state that I am 34 years of age and a citizen by blood of the Choctaw Nation, and as such have been placed upon the final roll of the Choctaw Nation, by the Honorable

Applications for Enrollment of Choctaw Newborn
Act of 1905   Volume X

Secretary of the Interior my final enrollment number being 8637 ; that I am the lawful wife of Joseph James , who is a citizen of the Choctaw Nation, and as such has been placed upon the final roll of said Nation by the Honorable Secretary of the Interior, his final enrollment number being 8636 and that a Male child was born to me on the 30 day of December 190 2; that said child has been named Wesley James , and is now living.

       J. D. Yandell   her
               x Nellie James
Witnesseth.   his   mark
 Must be two } mark Joseph Laflore
 Witnesses who
 are Citizens. Dennis Wade

  Subscribed and sworn to before me this 17 day of Jan 190 5

             J.D. Yandell
                 Notary Public.

My commission expires: Jan 14 1907

AFFIDAVIT OF ATTENDING PHYSICIAN OR MIDWIFE

UNITED STATES OF AMERICA
INDIAN TERRITORY
 Central   DISTRICT

  I, Mary Jefferson a Mid Wife on oath state that I attended on Mrs. Nellie James wife of Joseph James on the 30 day of December , 190 2 , that there was born to her on said date a male child, that said child is now living, and is said to have been named Wesley James
           her
           x
        mark Mary Jefferson

  Subscribed and sworn to before me this, the 17 day of January 190 5

WITNESSETH: *J.D. Yandell*   J D Yandell Notary Public.
 Must be two witnesses } mark Joseph Leflore
 who are citizens
 Witness *W. B. M Carley* Dennis Wade
  J.D. Yandell

  We hereby certify that we are well acquainted with Joseph James a Citizen of Chocktaw[sic] Nation and know him to be reputable and of good standing in the community.

 his
 mark Joseph Laflore   J.D. Yandell

   Dennis Wade   N.P.

Applications for Enrollment of Choctaw Newborn
Act of 1905   Volume X

Know all men by these presents:
  Know Ye:

That we   Elum Baker   and   Johnson Coley   who are citizens by blood of the Choctaw Nation do hereby certify that   Mary Jefferson   the attendant upon   Nellie James   at the birth of her infant child Wesley James is dead and we further certify that Wesley James infant son of Nellie James and Joseph James was born on the   30 day of   Dec.   1902 and that he was living on the 4th day of March 1905.

Elum Baker
Johnson Coley

Sworn and subscribed to before me this the 26th day of April 1905.

J.D. Yandell
N.P.

My commission expires January 1907

BIRTH AFFIDAVIT.

DEPARTMENT OF THE INTERIOR.
COMMISSION TO THE FIVE CIVILIZED TRIBES.

IN RE APPLICATION FOR ENROLLMENT, as a citizen of the   Choctaw   Nation, of   Wesley James   , born on the 30   day of Dec   , 1902

Name of Father: Joseph James   a citizen of the   Choctaw   Nation.
Name of Mother: Nellie James   a citizen of the   Choctaw   Nation.

Postoffice   Red Oak, Ind. Ter.

AFFIDAVIT OF MOTHER.

UNITED STATES OF AMERICA, Indian Territory,
  Central   DISTRICT.

  I,   Mrs. Nellie James   , on oath state that I am   34   years of age and a citizen by   blood   , of the   Choctaw   Nation; that I am the lawful wife of   Joseph James   , who is a citizen, by blood   of the   Choctaw   Nation; that a   male   child was born to me on 30   day of   December   , 1902; that said child has been named   Wesley James   , and was living March 4, 1905.

her
x Mrs. Nellie James
mark

Witnesses To Mark:
  { Nelson Thompson
  { Robin Jacks

Applications for Enrollment of Choctaw Newborn
Act of 1905   Volume X

Subscribed and sworn to before me this 31 day of   March   , 1905

J.D. Yandell
Notary Public.

Husband
AFFIDAVIT OF ~~ATTENDING PHYSICIAN OR MID-WIFE~~.

UNITED STATES OF AMERICA, Indian Territory,
.... DISTRICT.

am the husband of

I,   Joseph James   , ~~a~~   , on oath state that I ~~attended on~~ Mrs. Nellie James   , ~~wife of~~   that   on the 30 day of Dec   , 1902; that there was born to her on said date a   male   child; that said child was living March 4, 1905, and is said to have been named   Wesley James; *and that the midwife who attended on my said wife on 30 day of Dec 19- - is deceased.*

Joseph James

Witnesses To Mark:

Subscribed and sworn to before me this 31   day of   March   , 1905

J.D. Yandell
My Com Expires Jan 1907.   Notary Public.

Choc New Born 618
   Meda Jones   b. 2-18-03

7-3526

Muskogee, Indian Territory, April 7, 1905.

J. N. Jones,
   Bennington, Indian Territory.

Dear Sir:

   Receipt is hereby acknowledged of the affidavits of Dovie Jones and Jocie Rogers to the birth of Meda Jones, daughter of J. N. and Dovie Jones, February 18, 1903,

Applications for Enrollment of Choctaw Newborn
Act of 1905 Volume X

and the same have been filed with our records as an application for the enrollment of said child.

Respectfully,

Commissioner in Charge.

BIRTH AFFIDAVIT.

DEPARTMENT OF THE INTERIOR.
COMMISSION TO THE FIVE CIVILIZED TRIBES.

IN RE APPLICATION FOR ENROLLMENT, as a citizen of the Choctaw Nation, of Meda Jones, born on the 18th day of Feby, 1903

Name of Father: J N Jones   a citizen of the Choctaw Nation.
Name of Mother: Dovie Jones   a citizen of the Choctaw Nation.

Postoffice   Bennington I.T.

AFFIDAVIT OF MOTHER.

UNITED STATES OF AMERICA, Indian Territory,
    Cent   DISTRICT.

I, Dovie Jones, on oath state that I am 23 years of age and a citizen by Intermarriage, of the Choctaw Nation; that I am the lawful wife of J.N. Jones, who is a citizen, by blood of the Choctaw Nation; that a Female child was born to me on 18th day of Feby, 1903; that said child has been named Meda Jones, and was living March 4, 1905.

Dovie Jones

Witnesses To Mark:

Subscribed and sworn to before me this 30th day of Mch, 1905

B.W. Williams
Notary Public.

Applications for Enrollment of Choctaw Newborn
Act of 1905   Volume X

AFFIDAVIT OF ATTENDING PHYSICIAN OR MID-WIFE.

UNITED STATES OF AMERICA, Indian Territory,
    Cent   DISTRICT.

I,   Josie Rogers   , a   Midwife   , on oath state that I attended on Mrs.   Dovie Jones   , wife of   J.N. Jones   on the   18th day of   Feby   , 1903; that there was born to her on said date a   Female   child; that said child was living March 4, 1905, and is said to have been named   Meda Jones

                                  Jocie[sic] Rogers

Witnesses To Mark:

Subscribed and sworn to before me this   30th   day of   Mch   , 1905

                                  B.W. Williams
                                  Notary Public.

<u>Choc New Born 619</u>
      Frank Davis Folsom   b. 10-2-03
      Fletcher Daniel Folsom   b. 2-2-05

7-6671   7-184
BIRTH AFFIDAVIT.

DEPARTMENT OF THE INTERIOR.
COMMISSION TO THE FIVE CIVILIZED TRIBES.

IN RE APPLICATION FOR ENROLLMENT, as a citizen of the   Choctaw   Nation, of   Frank David Folsom   , born on the   2nd   day of   October   , 1903

Name of Father: Frank D. Folsom   a citizen of the   Choctaw   Nation.
Name of Mother: Mary G. Folsom   a citizen of the   Choctaw   Nation.

                        Postoffice   Ward, Ind. Ter.

Applications for Enrollment of Choctaw Newborn
Act of 1905   Volume X

AFFIDAVIT OF MOTHER.

UNITED STATES OF AMERICA, Indian Territory, }
Central   DISTRICT.

I, Mary G. Folsom , on oath state that I am 39 years of age and a citizen by intermarriage , of the Choctaw Nation; that I am the lawful wife of Frank D. Folsom , who is a citizen, by blood of the Choctaw Nation; that a male child was born to me on 2nd day of October , 1903; that said child has been named Frank Davis Folsom , and was living March 4, 1905.

Mary G. Folsom

Witnesses To Mark:
{

Subscribed and sworn to before me this 3rd day of April , 1905

OL Johnson
Notary Public.

AFFIDAVIT OF ATTENDING PHYSICIAN OR MID-WIFE.

UNITED STATES OF AMERICA, Indian Territory, }
Central   DISTRICT.

I, Netty[sic] Thomas , a midwife , on oath state that I attended on Mrs. Mary G. Folsom , wife of Frank D. Folsom on the 2nd day of October , 1903; that there was born to her on said date a male child; that said child was living March 4, 1905, and is said to have been named Frank Davis Folsom

Nettie Tomas[sic]

Witnesses To Mark:
{

Subscribed and sworn to before me this 3rd day of April , 1905

OL Johnson
Notary Public.

Applications for Enrollment of Choctaw Newborn
Act of 1905 Volume X

7-184   7-6671
BIRTH AFFIDAVIT.
DEPARTMENT OF THE INTERIOR.
COMMISSION TO THE FIVE CIVILIZED TRIBES.

IN RE APPLICATION FOR ENROLLMENT, as a citizen of the   Choctaw   Nation, of Fletcher Daniel Folsom   , born on the 2nd   day of February , 1905

Name of Father: Frank D. Folsom   a citizen of the   Choctaw   Nation.
Name of Mother: Mary G. Folsom   a citizen of the   Choctaw   Nation.

Postoffice   Ward, Ind. Ter.

AFFIDAVIT OF MOTHER.

UNITED STATES OF AMERICA, Indian Territory, }
     Central   DISTRICT.

I,   Mary G. Folsom   , on oath state that I am 39   years of age and a citizen by   intermarriage   , of the   Choctaw   Nation; that I am the lawful wife of Frank D. Folsom   , who is a citizen, by blood   of the   Choctaw   Nation; that a   male   child was born to me on 2nd   day of   February   , 1905; that said child has been named   Fletcher Daniel Folsom   , and was living March 4, 1905.

Mary G. Folsom

Witnesses To Mark:
{

Subscribed and sworn to before me this 3rd   day of   April   , 1905

OL Johnson
Notary Public.

AFFIDAVIT OF ATTENDING PHYSICIAN OR MID-WIFE.

UNITED STATES OF AMERICA, Indian Territory, }
     Central   DISTRICT.

I,   Netty[sic] Thomas   , a   midwife   , on oath state that I attended on Mrs.   Mary G. Folsom   , wife of Frank D. Folsom   on the 2nd day of February   , 1905; that there was born to her on said date a   male   child; that said child was living March 4, 1905, and is said to have been named   Fletcher Daniel Folsom

Nettie Tomas[sic]

Applications for Enrollment of Choctaw Newborn
Act of 1905   Volume X

Witnesses To Mark:
{

Subscribed and sworn to before me this 3rd day of April , 1905

OL Johnson
Notary Public.

Choc New Born 620
    Harvey Andrew Gollihare   b. 6-24-03
    Hurbert Gollihare   b. 2-21-05

BIRTH AFFIDAVIT.

DEPARTMENT OF THE INTERIOR.
COMMISSION TO THE FIVE CIVILIZED TRIBES.

IN RE APPLICATION FOR ENROLLMENT, as a citizen of the   Choctaw   Nation, of Harvey Andrew Gollihare   , born on the 24 day of June , 1903

Name of Father: Andrew Jackson Gollihare   a citizen of the   U.S.   Nation.
Name of Mother: Harriett Cordelia Gollihare   a citizen of the   Choctaw   Nation.

Postoffice   Panama, Ind. Ter.

AFFIDAVIT OF MOTHER.

UNITED STATES OF AMERICA, Indian Territory,
    Central   **DISTRICT.**
}

    I,   Harriett Cordelia Gollihare   , on oath state that I am   23   years of age and a citizen by   Blood   , of the   Choctaw   Nation; that I am the lawful wife of Andrew Jackson Gollihare   , who is a citizen, by —— of the   U.S.   ~~Nation~~; that a   male   child was born to me on   24   day of   June   , 1903; that said child has been named   Harvey Andrew Gollihare   , and was living March 4, 1905.

                      Harriett Cordelia Gollihare

Witnesses To Mark:
  { EG Goodnight
    A M Goforth

Applications for Enrollment of Choctaw Newborn
Act of 1905   Volume X

Subscribed and sworn to before me this 31 day of March, 1905

My com expires 1/19/08

John H Goodnight
Notary Public.

AFFIDAVIT OF ATTENDING PHYSICIAN OR MID-WIFE.

UNITED STATES OF AMERICA, Indian Territory,
Central   DISTRICT.

I, Mary Ann Daily, a Midwife, on oath state that I attended on Mrs. Harriett Cordelia Gollihare, wife of Andrew Jackson Gollihare on the 24 day of June, 1903; that there was born to her on said date a male child; that said child was living March 4, 1905, and is said to have been named Harvey Andrew Gollihare

Maryann Daily

Witnesses To Mark:
{ J H Hickman
  EG Goodnight

Subscribed and sworn to before me this 31 day of March, 1905

John H. Goodnight
Notary Public.

BIRTH AFFIDAVIT.

DEPARTMENT OF THE INTERIOR.
COMMISSION TO THE FIVE CIVILIZED TRIBES.

IN RE APPLICATION FOR ENROLLMENT, as a citizen of the Choctaw Nation, of Hurbert Gollihare, born on the 21st day of Feb, 1905

Name of Father: Andrew Jackson Gollihare   a citizen of the U.S. Nation.
Name of Mother: Harriett Cordelia Gollihare   a citizen of the Choctaw Nation.

Postoffice   Panama, Ind. Ter.

AFFIDAVIT OF MOTHER.

UNITED STATES OF AMERICA, Indian Territory,
Central   DISTRICT.

I, Harriett Cordelia Gollihare, on oath state that I am 23 years of age and a citizen by Blood, of the Choctaw Nation; that I am the lawful wife of

Applications for Enrollment of Choctaw Newborn
Act of 1905   Volume X

Andrew Jackson Gollihare , who is a citizen, by ....of the U.S. ~~Nation~~; that a male child was born to me on 21st day of Feb , 1905; that said child has been named Hurbert Gollihare , and was living March 4, 1905.

                                        Harriett Cordelia Gollihare

Witnesses To Mark:
{ EG Goodnight
  A M Goforth

      Subscribed and sworn to before me this 30th day of Mch , 1905

My com expires 1/19/08   John H Goodnight
                                              Notary Public.

AFFIDAVIT OF ATTENDING PHYSICIAN OR MID-WIFE.

UNITED STATES OF AMERICA, Indian Territory,
   Central   DISTRICT.

      I, Eliza Adams , a Midwife , on oath state that I attended on Mrs. Harriett Cordelia Gollihare , wife of Andrew Jackson Gollihare on the 21st day of Feb , 1905; that there was born to her on said date a male child; that said child was living March 4, 1905, and is said to have been named Hurbert Gollihare

                                      her
                            Eliza Adams x
Witnesses To Mark: mark
{ EG Goodnight
  A.M. Goforth

      Subscribed and sworn to before me this 30th day of March , 1905

My com expires 1/19/08   John H Goodnight
                                              Notary Public.

7-NB-620

                              Muskogee, Indian Territory, August 3, 1905.

Harriet Cordelia Gollihare,
      Panama, Indian Territory.

Dear Madam:

      Replying to that portion of your letter in which you ask when yo can file for your new born children, you are advised that on July 22, 1905, the Secretary of the

Applications for Enrollment of Choctaw Newborn
Act of 1905 Volume X

Interior approved the enrollment of Harvey Andrew and Hurbert Gollihare as citizens by blood of the Choctaw Nation and selection of allotment may now be made in their behalf in accordance with the rules and regulation governing the selection of allotments and the designation of homesteads in the Choctaw and Chickasaw Nations.

Respectfully,

Commissioner.

NEW-BORN AFFIDAVIT.

Number

...Choctaw Enrolling Commission...

IN THE MATTER OF THE APPLICATION FOR ENROLLMENT, as a citizen of the Choctaw Nation, of Harvie[sic] Andrew Gollihare

born on the 24 day of June 190 3

Name of father Andrew J. Gollihare   a citizen of   Choctaw
Nation final enrollment No.
Name of mother   Harriett Cordelia Gollihare   a citizen of   Choctaw
Nation final enrollment No. 7458

Postoffice   Panama ?.T.

AFFIDAVIT OF MOTHER.

UNITED STATES OF AMERICA
INDIAN TERRITORY
  Central   DISTRICT

I Harriett Cordelia Gollihare   , on oath state that I am 23   years of age and a citizen by   Blood   of the   Choctaw   Nation, and as such have been placed upon the final roll of the   Choctaw   Nation, by the Honorable Secretary of the Interior my final enrollment number being   7458 ; that I am the lawful wife of   Andrew J Gollihare   , who is a citizen of the   United States   Nation, and as such has been placed upon the final roll of said Nation by the Honorable Secretary of the Interior, his final enrollment number being   and that a   Male   child was born to me on the   24   day of June   190 3; that said child has been named   Harvie Andrew Gollihare   , and is now living.

Harriett Cordelia Gollihare

Applications for Enrollment of Choctaw Newborn
Act of 1905   Volume X

Witnesseth.
  Must be two Witnesses who are Citizens. } J H Hickman

  Minnie Hickman

Subscribed and sworn to before me this   4   day of   Feb   190 5

John H. Goodnight
Notary Public.

My commission expires:
January the 19th..1908

AFFIDAVIT OF ATTENDING PHYSICIAN OR MIDWIFE

UNITED STATES OF AMERICA
INDIAN TERRITORY
  Central   DISTRICT

I,   Mary Daily   a   Midwife on oath state that I attended on Mrs.   Harriett Cordelia Gollihare   wife of   Andrew J Gollihare   on the   24   day of   June   , 190 3, that there was born to her on said date a male   child, that said child is now living, and is said to have been named   Harvie[sic] Andrew Gollihare

her
x
Mary Daily   mark   M.D.

WITNESSETH:
  Must be two witnesses who are citizens and know the child. { J H Hickman

  Minnie Hickman

Subscribed and sworn to before me this, the   4   day of   February   190 5

John H Goodnight   Notary Public.

We hereby certify that we are well acquainted with   Mary Daily   a   Midwife   and know   her   to be reputable and of good standing in the community.

{ J H Hickman
  Minnie Hickman

Applications for Enrollment of Choctaw Newborn
Act of 1905   Volume X

<u>Choc New Born 621</u>
    Lois Annie Bowman   b. 2-26-05

BIRTH AFFIDAVIT.

DEPARTMENT OF THE INTERIOR.
COMMISSION TO THE FIVE CIVILIZED TRIBES.

IN RE APPLICATION FOR ENROLLMENT, as a citizen of the   Choctaw   Nation, of Lois Annie Bowman   , born on the 26   day of   February   , 1905

Name of Father: Edward S Bowman   a citizen of the   Choctaw   Nation.
Name of Mother: Gertrude Bowman   a citizen of the   Choctaw   Nation.

        Postoffice   Oak Lodge I.T.

AFFIDAVIT OF MOTHER.

UNITED STATES OF AMERICA, Indian Territory, }
    Central   DISTRICT. }

    I,   Gertrude Bowman   , on oath state that I am   33   years of age and a citizen by   blood   , of the   Choctaw   Nation; that I am the lawful wife of   Edward S Bowman   , who is a citizen, by   blood   of the   Choctaw   Nation; that a   female   child was born to me on   26   day of   February   , 1905; that said child has been named   Lois Annie Bowman   , and was living March 4, 1905.

                          Gertrude Bowman
Witnesses To Mark:
{
    Subscribed and sworn to before me this   27   day of   March   , 1905

                          James Bower
                              Notary Public.

AFFIDAVIT OF ATTENDING PHYSICIAN OR MID-WIFE.

UNITED STATES OF AMERICA, Indian Territory, }
    Central   DISTRICT. }

    I,   W. O.~~issie~~ Hartshorne   , a   Physician   , on oath state that I attended on Mrs.   Gertrude Bowman   , wife of   Edward S Bowman   on the 26   day of   February   , 1905; that there was born to her on said date a   female   child; that said child was living March 4, 1905, and is said to have been named Lois Annie Bowman

Applications for Enrollment of Choctaw Newborn
Act of 1905 Volume X

W.O. Hartshorne

Witnesses To Mark:
{

Subscribed and sworn to before me this 31th[sic] day of March , 1905

Wirt Franklin
Notary Public.

Choc New Born 622
    Henry Monroe Collins b. 12-23-02
    Ollie Belle Collins b. 2-18-05

BIRTH AFFIDAVIT.
DEPARTMENT OF THE INTERIOR.
COMMISSION TO THE FIVE CIVILIZED TRIBES.

IN RE APPLICATION FOR ENROLLMENT, as a citizen of the Choctaw Nation, of Ollie Belle Collins , born on the 18th day of February , 1905

Name of Father: Miles S Collins   a citizen of the Choctaw Nation.
Name of Mother: Gracie A Collins   a citizen of the Choctaw Nation.

Postoffice   Spiro, Indian Territory

AFFIDAVIT OF MOTHER.

UNITED STATES OF AMERICA, Indian Territory,
    Central   **DISTRICT.** }

    I, Gracie A Collins , on oath state that I am 29 years of age and a citizen by marriage , of the Choctaw Nation; that I am the lawful wife of Miles S Collins , who is a citizen, by blood of the Choctaw Nation; that a female child was born to me on 18th day of February , 1905; that said child has been named Ollie Belle Collins , and was living March 4, 1905. *and that said child died on March 29, 1905*

                                         Gracie A Collins

Witnesses To Mark:
{

Applications for Enrollment of Choctaw Newborn
Act of 1905 Volume X

Subscribed and sworn to before me this 31st day of March, 1905

Wirt Franklin
Notary Public.

AFFIDAVIT OF ATTENDING PHYSICIAN OR MID-WIFE.

UNITED STATES OF AMERICA, Indian Territory, }
Central   DISTRICT.

I, W.O. Hartshorne, a physician, on oath state that I attended on Mrs. Gracie A Collins, wife of Miles S Collins on the 18th day of February, 1905; that there was born to her on said date a female child; that said child was living March 4, 1905, and is said to have been named Ollie Belle Collins; *and that said child died March 29, 1905.*

W.O. Hartshorne

Witnesses To Mark:
{

Subscribed and sworn to before me this 31st day of March, 1905

Wirt Franklin
Notary Public.

BIRTH AFFIDAVIT.

DEPARTMENT OF THE INTERIOR.
COMMISSION TO THE FIVE CIVILIZED TRIBES.

IN RE APPLICATION FOR ENROLLMENT, as a citizen of the Choctaw Nation, of Henry Monroe Collins, born on the 23rd day of December, 1902

Name of Father: Miles S Collins   a citizen of the Choctaw Nation.
Name of Mother: Gracie A Collins   a citizen of the Choctaw Nation.

Postoffice Spiro, Ind. Territory

AFFIDAVIT OF MOTHER.

UNITED STATES OF AMERICA, Indian Territory, }
Central   DISTRICT.

I, Gracie A Collins, on oath state that I am 29 years of age and a citizen by marriage, of the Choctaw Nation; that I am the lawful wife of Miles S Collins, who is a citizen, by blood of the Choctaw Nation; that a

Applications for Enrollment of Choctaw Newborn
Act of 1905 Volume X

male   child was born to me on 23rd   day of   December   , 1902; that said child has been named   Henry Monroe Collins   , and was living March 4, 1905.

                                      Gracie A Collins

Witnesses To Mark:

{ Subscribed and sworn to before me this 31st   day of   March   , 1905

                                      Wirt Franklin
                                        Notary Public.

AFFIDAVIT OF ATTENDING PHYSICIAN OR MID-WIFE.

UNITED STATES OF AMERICA, Indian Territory, }
   Central   DISTRICT. }

I,   A. P. Thompson   , a physician   , on oath state that I attended on Mrs.   Gracie A Collins   , wife of   Miles S Collins   on the   23rd day of December   , 1902; that there was born to her on said date a   male   child; that said child was living March 4, 1905, and is said to have been named   Henry Monroe Collins .

                                      A. P. Thompson

Witnesses To Mark:

{ Subscribed and sworn to before me this 30th   day of   March   , 1905

                                      Wirt Franklin
                                        Notary Public.

Choc New Born 623
        Gibson James   b. 5-29-04

Applications for Enrollment of Choctaw Newborn
Act of 1905   Volume X

BIRTH AFFIDAVIT.

DEPARTMENT OF THE INTERIOR.
COMMISSION TO THE FIVE CIVILIZED TRIBES.

IN RE APPLICATION FOR ENROLLMENT, as a citizen of the Choctaw Nation, of Gibson James, born on the 5th ~~Sunday~~ ~~day~~ of May, 1904

Name of Father: Ben James   a citizen of the Choctaw Nation.
Name of Mother: Rhoda James   a citizen of the Choctaw Nation.

Postoffice   Brazil, Ind. Ter.

AFFIDAVIT OF MOTHER.

UNITED STATES OF AMERICA, Indian Territory, }
  Central   DISTRICT.

I, Rhoda James, on oath state that I am 36 years of age and a citizen by blood, of the Choctaw Nation; that I am the lawful wife of Ben James, who is a citizen, by blood of the Choctaw Nation; that a male child was born to me on 5th ~~day of~~ *Sunday of May*, 1904; that said child has been named Gibson James, and was living March 4, 1905. *and that no physician or midwife attended me at the birth of said child*

                                          her
                                  Rhoda x James
Witnesses To Mark: mark
  { Victor M Locke JR
  { Vester W Rose

Subscribed and sworn to before me this 31st day of March, 1905

                          Wirt Franklin
                              Notary Public.

AFFIDAVIT OF ATTENDING PHYSICIAN OR MID-WIFE.

UNITED STATES OF AMERICA, Indian Territory, }
  Central   DISTRICT.

                                    was acquainted with
I, Emily James, ~~a~~ ...., on oath state that I ~~attended on~~ Mrs. Rhoda James, wife of Ben James on the 5th ~~day of~~ *Sunday of May*, 1904; that there was born to her on said date a male child; that said child was living March 4, 1905, and is said to have been named Gibson James

                              Emily James

Applications for Enrollment of Choctaw Newborn
Act of 1905   Volume X

Witnesses To Mark:

{

    Subscribed and sworn to before me this 31st day of   March   , 1905

                                    Wirt Franklin
                                    Notary Public.

(The affidavit below typed as given.)

                            Sutter Indian Territory, June 27th 1905

I Noel Folsom of Sutter I.T. know that on or about the 29 day of May 1904 that a child was born to Rhoda James and that the said child was living on March the 4th 1905, and the said child was named Gibson James and the Father of said child was Ben James.

                                    Noel Folsom

Central District Indian Territory

                        Personaly appeared before me a Notary Public for the central district of the Indian Territory, Noel Folsom to me personaly well known as the one who signed the above ,
Subscribed and sworn to before me this the 27th day of June 1905

                                    Frank Lewis
                                    Notay Public

---

                                                  7 NB 623

                      Muskogee, Indian Territory, July 1, 1905.

Ben James,
    Brazil, Indian Territory.

Dear Sir:

    Receipt is hereby acknowledged of the affidavit of Noel Folsom to the birth of Gibson James, son of Rhoda and Ben James, May 29, 1904, and the same has been filed with our records in the matter of the enrollment of said child.

                                Respectfully,

                                                Commissioner.

Applications for Enrollment of Choctaw Newborn
Act of 1905   Volume X

7-NB-623

Muskogee, Indian Territory, July 3, 1905.

Ben James,
  Brazil, Indian Territory.

Dear Sir:

  Receipt is hereby acknowledged of the affidavit of Noel Folsom to the birth of Gibson James, son of Rhoda and Ben James, May 29, 1904, and the same has been filed with our records in the matter of the enrollment of said child.

      Respectfully,

           Commissioner.

Choc New Born 624
  Oslin Folsom   b. 1-29-03

7- 5388 card   7- 13636 Roll
BIRTH AFFIDAVIT.

Department of the Interior,
COMMISSION TO THE FIVE CIVILIZED TRIBES.

IN RE APPLICATION FOR ENROLLMENT, as a citizen of the   Choctaw   Nation, of   Oslin Folsom   , born on the 29   day of   January   , 190 3

Name of Father: Arnold Folsom   a citizen of the   Choctaw   Nation.
Name of Mother: Lizzie Folsom   a citizen of the   Choctaw   Nation.

      Post-Office: Stigler I.T.

AFFIDAVIT OF MOTHER.

UNITED STATES OF AMERICA,
 INDIAN TERRITORY,
  Central   District.

  I,   Lizzie Folsom   , on oath state that I am   36   years of age and a citizen by   Intermarriage   , of the   Choctaw   Nation; that I am the lawful wife of

Applications for Enrollment of Choctaw Newborn
Act of 1905 Volume X

Arnold Folsom, who is a citizen, by Blood of the Choctaw Nation; that a male child was born to me on 29 day of January, 190 3, that said child has been named Oslin Folsom, and is now living.

Lizzie Folsom

WITNESSES TO MARK:
{

Subscribed and sworn to before me this 31 day of March, 190 6

C C Jones
Notary Public.

AFFIDAVIT OF ATTENDING PHYSICIAN OR MID-WIFE.

UNITED STATES OF AMERICA, }
INDIAN TERRITORY,
Central District. }

I, C C Jones, a Physician, on oath state that I attended on Mrs. Lizzie Folsom, wife of Arnold Folsom on the 29 day of January, 190 3; that there was born to her on said date a male child; that said child is now living and is said to have been named Oslin Folsom

C C Jones

WITNESSES TO MARK:
{

Subscribed and sworn to before me this 31 day of March, 190 6

J N Jones
Notary Public.

NEW-BORN AFFIDAVIT.

Number..................

...Choctaw Enrolling Commission...

IN THE MATTER OF THE APPLICATION FOR ENROLLMENT, as a citizen of the Choctaw Nation, of Oslin Folsom

born on the 29th day of ___January___ 190 3

Applications for Enrollment of Choctaw Newborn
Act of 1905   Volume X

Name of father   Arnold Folsom   a citizen of   Choctaw
Nation final enrollment No.   13636
Name of mother   Lizzie Folsom   a citizen of   Choctaw
Nation final enrollment No.   7-5388

Postoffice   Stigler IT

AFFIDAVIT OF MOTHER.

UNITED STATES OF AMERICA
INDIAN TERRITORY
Central   DISTRICT

I   Lizzie Folsom   , on oath state that I am 36 years of age and a citizen by marriage *approved by Sec Ind Dec 13, 04* of the Choctaw Nation, and as such have been placed upon the final roll of the Choctaw Nation, by the Honorable Secretary of the Interior my final enrollment number being   13636; that I am the lawful wife of   Arnold Folsom   , who is a citizen of the Choctaw Nation, and as such has been placed upon the final roll of said Nation by the Honorable Secretary of the Interior, his final enrollment number being   7-5388   and that a   Male child was born to me on the   29   day of   January   190 3; that said child has been named   Oslin Folsom   , and is now living.

Lizzie Folsom

Witnesseth.
Must be two Witnesses who are Citizens.   } Annie Rose
   Maurice Cass

Subscribed and sworn to before me this 3   day of   Jan   190 5

James Bower
Notary Public.

My commission expires:
Sept 23 - 1907

AFFIDAVIT OF ATTENDING PHYSICIAN OR MIDWIFE

UNITED STATES OF AMERICA
INDIAN TERRITORY
Central   DISTRICT

I,   Dr. C.C. Jones   a   physician on oath state that I attended on Mrs.   Lizzie Folsom   wife of   Arnold Folsom   on the   29th   day of   January   , 190 3 , that there was born to her on said date a   male child, that said child is now living, and is said to have been named   Oslin Folsom

C.C. Jones

Subscribed and sworn to before me this, the   9th   day of   January   190 5

Applications for Enrollment of Choctaw Newborn
Act of 1905 Volume X

WITNESSETH: *My Commission Expires May 7th 1907*   Chas T Walker   Notary Public.

Must be two witnesses who are citizens { Josiah Garland

Ida Garland

We hereby certify that we are well acquainted with   Dr C C Jones   a   Physician   and know   him   to be reputable and of good standing in the community.

Josiah Garland   _____

Ida Garland   _____

Choc New Born 625
    William Gibson   b. 11-6-04

BIRTH AFFIDAVIT.

DEPARTMENT OF THE INTERIOR.
COMMISSION TO THE FIVE CIVILIZED TRIBES.

IN RE APPLICATION FOR ENROLLMENT, as a citizen of the   Choctaw   Nation, of William Gibson   , born on the 6th   day of November , 1904

Name of Father: Wesley Gibson   a citizen of the   Choctaw   Nation.
Name of Mother: Jennie Gibson nee Jennie Wade   a citizen of the   Choctaw   Nation.

             Postoffice   Lehigh Ind Ter

AFFIDAVIT OF MOTHER.

UNITED STATES OF AMERICA, Indian Territory,
     Central   **DISTRICT.**

I,   Jennie Gibson   , on oath state that I am   25   years of age and a citizen by   blood   , of the   Choctaw   Nation; that I am the lawful wife of   Wesley Gibson   , who is a citizen, by blood   of the   Choctaw   Nation; that a male   child was born to me on   6th   day of   November   , 1904; that said child has been named   William Gibson   , and was living March 4, 1905.

Applications for Enrollment of Choctaw Newborn
Act of 1905   Volume X

                                            her
                                    Jennie x Gibson

Witnesses To Mark: mark
  { EA Newman
    Richard Shanafelt

Subscribed and sworn to before me this 4th day of April, 1905

                                    EA Newman
                                          Notary Public.

Husband
AFFIDAVIT OF ~~ATTENDING PHYSICIAN OR MID-WIFE.~~

UNITED STATES OF AMERICA, Indian Territory, }
   Central   **DISTRICT.** }

    I, Wesley Gibson, ~~a~~_____, on oath state that I attended on Mrs. Jennie Gibson *enrolled as Jennie Wade (7.4158)*, ~~wife of~~_____ on the 6th day of November, 1904; that there was born to her on said date a male child; that said child was living March 4, 1905, and is said to have been named William Gibson *and that there was no one present at the birth of said child except the mother and myself*

                                    Wesley Gibson

Witnesses To Mark:
  { EA Newman
    Richard Shanafelt

Subscribed and sworn to before me this 4th day of April, 1905

                                    EA Newman
                                          Notary Public.

BIRTH AFFIDAVIT.
                              DEPARTMENT OF THE INTERIOR.
              COMMISSION TO THE FIVE CIVILIZED TRIBES.

    IN RE APPLICATION FOR ENROLLMENT, as a citizen of the Choctaw Nation, of William Gibson, born on the 6th day of Nov, 1904

Name of Father: Wesley Gibson   a citizen of the Choctaw Nation.
Name of Mother: Jennie Gibson (nee Wade)   a citizen of the Choctaw Nation.

                         Postoffice   Lehigh I.T.

Applications for Enrollment of Choctaw Newborn
Act of 1905   Volume X

AFFIDAVIT OF MOTHER.

UNITED STATES OF AMERICA, Indian Territory,
Central   DISTRICT.

I, Vicey Williams, on oath state that I am 60 years of age and a citizen by blood, of the Choctaw Nation; ~~that I am~~ *that I am personally acquainted with Jennie Gibson nee Wade, who is* the lawful wife of Wesley Gibson, who is a citizen, by blood of the Choctaw Nation; that a male child was born to ~~me~~ *said Jennie Gibson* on 6th day of November, 1904; that said child has been named William Gibson, and was living March 4, 1905.

                         her
                     Vicey x Williams
Witnesses To Mark: mark
{ HH Martin
{ James Culberson

Subscribed and sworn to before me this 15 day of May, 1905

                     W.H. Angell
                         Notary Public.

AFFIDAVIT OF ATTENDING PHYSICIAN OR MID-WIFE.

UNITED STATES OF AMERICA, Indian Territory,
Central   DISTRICT.

                              was personally acquainted with
I, Austin Williams, ~~a~~, on oath state that I ~~attended on~~ Mrs. Jennie Gibson, nee Wade, wife of Wesley Gibson *and* on the 6th day of Nov, 1904; that there was born to her on said date a male child; that said child was living March 4, 1905, and is said to have been named William Gibson

                       his
                   Austin x Williams
Witnesses To Mark: mark
{ HH Martin
{ James Culberson

Subscribed and sworn to before me this 15th day of May, 1905

                     W.H. Angell
                         Notary Public.

Applications for Enrollment of Choctaw Newborn
Act of 1905 Volume X

COMMISSIONERS:
TAMS BIXBY,
THOMAS B. NEEDLES,
C.R. BRECKINBRIDGE.

WM. O. BEALL
Secretary

DEPARTMENT OF THE INTERIOR,
COMMISSIONER TO THE FIVE CIVILIZED TRIBES.

$W^m O.B.$

REFER IN REPLY TO THE FOLLOWING:

7 N. B. 625

ADDRESS ONLY THE
COMMISSION TO THE FIVE CIVILIZED TRIBES.

Muskogee, Indian Territory, April 11, 1905.

Wesley Gibson,
    Lehigh, Indian Territory.

Dear Sir:

    Referring to the application heretofore forwarded to the Commission for the enrollment of your infant child, William Gibson, you state therein that there was no on in attendance at the birth of said child execpting[sic] yourself. It will, therefore, be necessary that you secure the affidavits of two persons who have actual knowledge of the facts, that the child was born, the date of his birth, that he was living on March 4, 1905, and that Jennie Gibson is his mother.

                    Respectfully,
                        T.B. Needles
                              Commissioner in Charge.

Choctaw N B 625

Muskogee, Indian Territory, May 19, 1905.

Wesley Gibson,
    Lehigh, Indian Territory.

Dear Sir:

    Receipt is hereby acknowledged of the affidavits of Vicy Williams and Austin Williams to the birth of William Gibson, child of Wesley Gibson and Jennie Gibson (Wade) November 6, 1904, and the same have been filed with the record in the matter of the enrollment of said child.

                    Respectfully,

                              Chairman.

Applications for Enrollment of Choctaw Newborn
Act of 1905   Volume X

Choc New Born 626
   Henry Jackson Airington   b. 11-6-03

COPY

Choctaw N.B. 626.

Muskogee, Indian Territory, April 19, 1905.

Jackson Airington,
   Graham, Indian Territory.

Dear Sir:

   Receipt is hereby acknowledged of the affidavits of Elmina Airington, Lou Clegg and Elizabeth Crowell to the birth of Henry Jackson Airington, son of Jackson and Elmina Airington, November 6, 1903, and the same have been filed with our records in the matter of the enrollment of said child.

                              Respectfully,
                              SIGNED

                              Tams Bixby
                              Chairman.

7-260.
COPY
Muskogee, Indian Territory, March 29, 1905.

Elmina Airington,
   Care Jackson Airington,
      Graham, Indian Territory.

Dear Madam:

   There is enclosed you herewith for execution application for the enrollment of your infant child, Henry Jackson Airington, born November 6, 1903.

   The affidavits heretofore filed with the Commission show the child was living January 16, 1905. It is necessary, for the child to be enrolled, that she was living on March 4, 1905.

   It is also noted from the above mentioned affidavits that there was neither a physician or midwife in attendance on you at the time of the birth of the applicant. If this is the case it will be necessary that you secure the affidavits of two persons who have actual knowledge that the child was born, was living on the 4th day of March 1905, and that you are his mother.

Applications for Enrollment of Choctaw Newborn
Act of 1905 Volume X

In having these affidavits executed care should be exercised to see that all names are written in full, as they appear in the body of the affidavit, and in the event that either of the persons signing the affidavit are unable to write, signatures by mark must be attested by two witnesses. Each affidavit must be executed before a Notary Public and the notarial seal and signature of the officer must be attached to each separate affidavit.

Respectfully,
SIGNED

Tams Bixby
Chairman.

P.T. 9/29

BIRTH AFFIDAVIT.

DEPARTMENT OF THE INTERIOR.
COMMISSION TO THE FIVE CIVILIZED TRIBES.

IN RE APPLICATION FOR ENROLLMENT, as a citizen of the Choctaw Nation, of Henry Jackson Airington, born on the 6th day of Nov, 1903

Name of Father: Jackson Airington   a citizen of the Choctaw Nation.
Name of Mother: Elmina Airington   a citizen of the Intermarried Nation.

Postoffice   Graham Ind Ter

AFFIDAVIT OF MOTHER.

UNITED STATES OF AMERICA, Indian Territory, }
    Southern   DISTRICT.

I, Elmina Airington, on oath state that I am forth three years of age and a citizen by marriage, of the Choctaw Nation; that I am the lawful wife of Jackson Airington, who is a citizen, by birth of the Choctaw Nation; that a male child was born to me on 6th day of November, 1903, that said child has been named Henry Jackson Airington, and is now living.

                                          her
                              Elmina x Airington
Witnesses To Mark: mark
   { M.D. Butler
     M.E. Airington

Subscribed and sworn to before me this 16th day of January, 1905.

                         M.D. Butler
                             Notary Public.

Applications for Enrollment of Choctaw Newborn
Act of 1905 Volume X

AFFIDAVIT OF ATTENDING PHYSICIAN OR MID-WIFE.

UNITED STATES OF AMERICA, Indian Territory, }
    Southern   DISTRICT.}

    I, Jackson Airington, a mid-wife, on oath state that I attended on Mrs. Elmina Airington, wife of mine *(had no physician)* on the 6th day of Nov., 1903; that there was born to her on said date a male child; that said child is now living and is said to have been named Henry Jackson Airington

                                      Jackson Airington

Witnesses To Mark:
{

    Subscribed and sworn to before me this 16th day of January, 1905.

                              M.D. Butler
                                    Notary Public.

BIRTH AFFIDAVIT.
DEPARTMENT OF THE INTERIOR.
COMMISSION TO THE FIVE CIVILIZED TRIBES.

    IN RE APPLICATION FOR ENROLLMENT, as a citizen of the Choctaw Nation, of Henry Jackson Airington, born on the 6th day of November, 1903

Name of Father: Jackson Airington   a citizen of the Choctaw Nation.
Name of Mother: Elmina Airington   a citizen of the Choctaw Nation.

                        Postoffice   Graham, Ind Ter

AFFIDAVIT OF MOTHER.

UNITED STATES OF AMERICA, Indian Territory, }
    Southern   DISTRICT.}

    I, Elmina Airington, on oath state that I am 43 years of age and a citizen by intermarriage, of the Choctaw Nation; that I am the lawful wife of Jackson Airington, who is a citizen, by blood of the Choctaw Nation; that a male child was born to me on 6th day of November, 1903; that said child has been named Henry Jackson Airington, and was living March 4, 1905.

Applications for Enrollment of Choctaw Newborn
Act of 1905   Volume X

                                        her
                              Elmina x Airington
Witnesses To Mark: mark
  { Chas A. Bennett
    Jackson Airington

Subscribed and sworn to before me this 13th day of April , 1905

                                      Chas A. Bennett
                                            Notary Public.

United States of America,)
   Indian Territory,   (Affidavit of Witness.
.. Southern District.   )

      I, Mrs. Lou Clegg   on oath state that I was with Mrs. Elmina Airington, wife of Jackson Airington, on or about the 7th day of November, 1903: that to the best of my knowledge and belief, there was born to her on the 6th day of November, 1903, a male child, that said child was living on March 4, 1905, and is said to have been named Henry Jackson Airington.

                                          Lou Clegg

Subscribed and sworn to before me this the 13th day of April, 1905.

                                    Chas A. Bennett
                                    Notary Public, Southern District,
                                        Indian Territory.

United States of America,)
   Indian Territory,   (Affidavit of Witness.
   Southern District.   )

      I, Mrs.   Elizabeth Crowell   on oath state that I was with Mrs. Elmina Airington, wife of Jackson Airington, on or about the 7th day of November, 1903: that to the best of my knowledge and belief, there was born to her on the 6th day of November, 1903, a male child, that said child was living on March 4, 1905, and is said to have been named Henry Jackson Airington.

                                        Elizabeth Crowell

Subscribed and sworn to before me this the 13th day of April, 1905.

                                    Chas A. Bennett
                                    Notary Public, Southern District,
                                        Indian Territory.

Applications for Enrollment of Choctaw Newborn
Act of 1905   Volume X

Choc New Born 627
        Agnes Taylor   b. 10-2-04

7-1453

Muskogee, Indian Territory, March 30, 1905.

Selin Taylor,
        Corrine, Indian Territory.

Dear Sir:

        Receipt is hereby acknowledged of the affidavits of Ellen Taylor and Margaret Taylor to the birth of Agnes Taylor, infant daughter of Selin and Ellen Taylor, October 2, 1904.

        For the purpose of identifying your wife Ellen Taylor upon our records you are requested to state the names of her parents and her brothers and sisters if any.

Respectfully,

Chairman.

NEW-BORN AFFIDAVIT.

                Number_____

...Choctaw Enrolling Commission...

        IN THE MATTER OF THE APPLICATION FOR ENROLLMENT, as a citizen of the Choctaw   Nation, of   Agnes Taylor

born on the 2^d day of ___October___ 190 4

Name of father   Selin Taylor   a citizen of   Choctaw
Nation final enrollment No. 2709
Name of mother   Ellen Holman   a citizen of   Choctaw
Nation final enrollment No. 2402

                                Postoffice   Corrine

Applications for Enrollment of Choctaw Newborn
Act of 1905   Volume X

AFFIDAVIT OF MOTHER.

UNITED STATES OF AMERICA
INDIAN TERRITORY
Central   DISTRICT

I   Ellen Holman   , on oath state that I am 24 years of age and a citizen by Blood of the Choctaw Nation, and as such have been placed upon the final roll of the Choctaw Nation, by the Honorable Secretary of the Interior my final enrollment number being 2402 ; that I am the lawful wife of Selin Taylor , who is a citizen of the Choctaw Nation, and as such has been placed upon the final roll of said Nation by the Honorable Secretary of the Interior, his final enrollment number being 2709 and that a Female child was born to me on the 2^d day of October 190 4; that said child has been named Agnes Taylor , and is now living.

Ellen Holman

Witnesseth.

Must be two Witnesses who are Citizens.
James Thomas
John Taylor

Subscribed and sworn to before me this 18 day of Feb 190 5

Jno E. Talbert
Notary Public.

My commission expires:
Dec 12 1908

AFFIDAVIT OF ATTENDING PHYSICIAN OR MIDWIFE

UNITED STATES OF AMERICA
INDIAN TERRITORY
Central   DISTRICT

I,   Margred[sic] Taylor   a   Midwife on oath state that I attended on Mrs. Ellen Holman wife of Selin Taylor on the 2^d day of October , 190 4 , that there was born to her on said date a Female child, that said child is now living, and is said to have been named Agnes Taylor

Margred Taylor   𝑚.𝒟.

Subscribed and sworn to before me this, the 18 day of February 190 5

WITNESSETH:
Must be two witnesses who are citizens
James Thomas
John Taylor

Jno E Talbert   Notary Public.

Applications for Enrollment of Choctaw Newborn
Act of 1905   Volume X

We hereby certify that we are well acquainted with   Margred Taylor   a   Midwife   and know   him   to be reputable and of good standing in the community.

James Thomas   James Thomas

John Taylor   John Taylor

BIRTH AFFIDAVIT.

DEPARTMENT OF THE INTERIOR.
COMMISSION TO THE FIVE CIVILIZED TRIBES.

IN RE APPLICATION FOR ENROLLMENT, as a citizen of the   Choctaw   Nation, of Agnes Taylor   , born on the 2nd day of Oct , 1904

Name of Father: Selin Taylor   a citizen of the Choctaw Nation.
Name of Mother: Ellen Taylor   a citizen of the Choctaw Nation.

Postoffice   Corrine Ind Ter

AFFIDAVIT OF MOTHER.

UNITED STATES OF AMERICA, Indian Territory, }
     Central   DISTRICT. }

I,   Ellen Taylor   , on oath state that I am 24   years of age and a citizen by Blood   , of the   Choctaw   Nation; that I am the lawful wife of Selin Taylor   , who is a citizen, by Blood   of the   Choctaw   Nation; that a   Female   child was born to me on 2nd day of   October   , 1904; that said child has been named Agnes Taylor   , and was living March 4, 1905.

                                         her
                                Ellen x Taylor
Witnesses To Mark: mark
 { Claude P Spriggs
 { Thos Fennell

Subscribed and sworn to before me this 25th day of   March   , 1905

                                Thomas Fennell
                                   Notary Public.

107

Applications for Enrollment of Choctaw Newborn
Act of 1905   Volume X

AFFIDAVIT OF ATTENDING PHYSICIAN OR MID-WIFE.

UNITED STATES OF AMERICA, Indian Territory,
Central DISTRICT.

I, Margret Taylor, a midwife, on oath state that I attended on Mrs. Ellen Taylor, wife of Selin Taylor on the 2nd day of October, 1904; that there was born to her on said date a Female child; that said child was living March 4, 1905, and is said to have been named Agnes Taylor

                             her
                      Margret x Taylor
Witnesses To Mark: mark
   { Claude P Spriggs
    Thos Fennell

Subscribed and sworn to before me this 25th day of March, 1905

                          Thomas Fennell
                          Notary Public.

Choc New Born 628
     William B. Massey   b. 10-14-03

                                                       7-4452

                Muskogee, Indian Territory, April 8, 1905.

Oliver Massey,
     Massey, Indian Territory.

Dear Sir:

     Receipt is hereby acknowledged of the affidavits of Arizona C. Massey and H. E. Williams to the birth of William B. Massey, son of Oliver Massey and Arizona C. Massey, October 14, 1903, and the same have been filed with our records as an application for the enrollment of said child.

                      Respectfully,

                         Commissioner in Charge.

Applications for Enrollment of Choctaw Newborn
Act of 1905 Volume X

COPY 7 N.B. 628

Muskogee, Indian Territory, April 12, 1905.

Oliver Massey,
    Massey, Indian Territory.

Dear Sir:

    You are hereby advised that before the allication[sic] for the enrollment of your infant child, William B. Massey, can be finally disposed of, ti[sic] will be necessary for you to furnish the Commission with either the original or a certified copy of the license and certificate of your marriage to the child's mother, Arizona C. Massey.

    Please give this matter your immediate attention.

Respectfully,

SIGNED
T. B. Needles.
Commissioner in Charge.

BIRTH AFFIDAVIT.

DEPARTMENT OF THE INTERIOR.
COMMISSION TO THE FIVE CIVILIZED TRIBES.

    IN RE APPLICATION FOR ENROLLMENT, as a citizen of the Choctaw Nation, of William B. Massey, born on the 14th day of Oct., 1903

Name of Father: Oliver Massey   a citizen of the Choctaw Nation.
Name of Mother: Arizona C. Massey   a citizen of the Choctaw Nation.

Postoffice   Massey, I.T.

AFFIDAVIT OF MOTHER.

UNITED STATES OF AMERICA, Indian Territory, }
    Central   DISTRICT. }

    I, Arizona C. Massey, on oath state that I am 22 years of age and a citizen by marriage, of the Choctaw Nation; that I am the lawful wife of Oliver Massey, who is a citizen, by blood of the Choctaw Nation; that a male child was born to me on 14th day of October, 1903; that said child has been named William B. Massey, and was living March 4, 1905.

Applications for Enrollment of Choctaw Newborn
Act of 1905   Volume X

Arizona C Massey

Witnesses To Mark:
{

    Subscribed and sworn to before me this 23   day of   March   , 1905

O P Swisher
Notary Public.

My commission expires Jan 14-1908

AFFIDAVIT OF ATTENDING PHYSICIAN OR MID-WIFE.

UNITED STATES OF AMERICA, Indian Territory, }
   Central   DISTRICT.

I,   H.E. Williams   , a   physician   , on oath state that I attended on Mrs.   Arizona C Massey   , wife of   Oliver Massey   on the 14th   day of   October   , 1903; that there was born to her on said date a   male   child; that said child was living March 4, 1905, and is said to have been named William B. Massey

H E Williams

Witnesses To Mark:
{

    Subscribed and sworn to before me this   21st day of   March   , 1905

Wirt Franklin
Notary Public.

Choc New Born 629
    Lena Cecile Moore   b. 11-25[sic]-04

Applications for Enrollment of Choctaw Newborn
Act of 1905   Volume X

7-3835

Muskogee, Indian Territory, April 8, 1905.

R. F. Moore,
    Bokchito, Indian Territory.

Dear Sir:

    Receipt is hereby acknowledged of the affidavits of Rosa Moore and N. J. Hamilton to the birth of Lena Cecile Moore, daughter of R. F. and Rosa Moore, November 29, 1904, and the same have been filed with our records as an application for the enrollment of said child.

                    Respectfully,

                                      Commissioner in Charge.

NEW-BORN AFFIDAVIT.

Number

Choctaw Enrolling Commission.

IN THE MATTER OF THE APPLICATION FOR ENROLLMENT, as a citizen of the Choctaw   Nation, of   Lena Cecile Moore

born on the   29   day of   November   190 4

Name of father   Robert F Moore   a citizen of   United States
Nation final enrollment No
Name of mother   Rosa Moore   a citizen of   Choctaw
Nation final enrollment No   10821

                    Postoffice   Bokchito I.T.

AFFIDAVIT OF MOTHER.

UNITED STATES OF AMERICA,
    INDIAN TERRITORY,
Central   DISTRICT

    I   Rosa Moore   on oath state that I am   21   years of age and a citizen by   Blood   of the   Choctaw   Nation, and as such have been placed upon the final roll of the   Choctaw   Nation, by the Honorable Secretary of the Interior my final enrollment number being   10821   ; that I am the lawful wife of   Robert F Moore   , who is a citizen of the   Choctaw   Nation, and as such has been placed upon the final roll of said Nation by the Honorable Secretary of the Interior, his

Applications for Enrollment of Choctaw Newborn
Act of 1905   Volume X

final enrollment number being 10821[sic]   and that a   Female   child was born to me on the   29   day of   November   190 4 ; that said child has been named   Lena Cecile Moore   , and is now living.

Rosa Moore

WITNESSETH:
Must be two Witnesses who are Citizens. } John A. M. Impson
Jacob Thompson

Subscribed and sworn to before me this   16   day of   January   190 5

(Name Illegible)
Notary Public.

My commission expires   2/19/05

AFFIDAVIT OF ATTENDING PHYSICIAN OR MIDWIFE

UNITED STATES OF AMERICA
INDIAN TERRITORY
Central   DISTRICT

I,   N. J. Hamilton   a   Physician on oath state that I attended on Mrs.   Rosa Moore   wife of   Robert F Moore on the   29   day of   November , 190 4, that there was born to her on said date a   Female child, that said child is now living, and is said to have been named   Lena Cecile Moore

N.J. Hamilton   M.D.

WITNESSETH:
Must be two witnesses who are citizens and know the child. { John Impson
Jake Thompson

Subscribed and sworn to before me this, the   16   day of   January   190 5

(Name Illegible)
Notary Public.

We hereby certify that we are well acquainted with   U. J. Hamilton   a   Practicing Physician   and know   him   to be reputable and of good standing in the community.

{ John A.M. Impson
Jacob Thompson

Applications for Enrollment of Choctaw Newborn
Act of 1905   Volume X

BIRTH AFFIDAVIT.

DEPARTMENT OF THE INTERIOR.
COMMISSION TO THE FIVE CIVILIZED TRIBES.

IN RE APPLICATION FOR ENROLLMENT, as a citizen of the   Choctaw   Nation, of Lena Cecile Moore   , born on the 29   day of Nov , 1904

Name of Father: R. F. Moore   a citizen of the   U.S.   Nation.
Name of Mother: Rosa Moore   a citizen of the   Choctaw   Nation.

Postoffice   Bokchito I.T.

AFFIDAVIT OF MOTHER.

UNITED STATES OF AMERICA, Indian Territory, }
    Central   DISTRICT.   }

I, Rosa Moore   , on oath state that I am   21   years of age and a citizen by Blood   , of the   Choctaw   Nation; that I am the lawful wife of   R F Moore   , who is a citizen, by .... of the   United States   ~~Nation~~; that a   Female   child was born to me on   29   day of   Nov   , 1904; that said child has been named Lena Cecile Moore   , and was living March 4, 1905.

Rosa Moore

Witnesses To Mark:
{

Subscribed and sworn to before me this 1ˢᵗ   day of   April   , 1905

J.M. Moore
Notary Public.

AFFIDAVIT OF ATTENDING PHYSICIAN OR MID-WIFE.

UNITED STATES OF AMERICA, Indian Territory, }
    Central   DISTRICT.   }

I,   N J Hamilton   , a Physician   , on oath state that I attended on Mrs.   Rosa Moore   , wife of   R.F. Moore   on the 29   day of   Nov   , 1904; that there was born to her on said date a   Female   child; that said child was living March 4, 1905, and is said to have been named   Lena Cecile Moore

N J Hamilton

Witnesses To Mark:
{

Applications for Enrollment of Choctaw Newborn
Act of 1905   Volume X

Subscribed and sworn to before me this 1st day of   April   , 1905

                         J.M. Moore
                         Notary Public.

Choc New Born 630
    Orilla Spradlin   b. 8-4[sic]-04

NEW-BORN AFFIDAVIT.

      Number..............

Choctaw Enrolling Commission.

  IN THE MATTER OF THE APPLICATION FOR ENROLLMENT, as a citizen of the Choctaw   Nation, of   Arrilla Spradlin

born on the   1 day of   August   190 4

Name of father   Emmet J Spradlin   a citizen of   White
Nation final enrollment No ——
Name of mother   Jaunita[sic] Spradlin   a citizen of   Choctaw
Nation final enrollment No   13843

                Postoffice   Durant I.T.

            AFFIDAVIT OF MOTHER.

UNITED STATES OF AMERICA, }
   INDIAN TERRITORY,
  Central   DISTRICT

    I   Juanita Spradlin   on oath state that I am   17 years of age and a citizen by   blood   of the   Choctaw   Nation, and as such have been placed upon the final roll of the   Choctaw   Nation, by the Honorable Secretary of the Interior my final enrollment number being   13843   ; that I am the lawful wife of Emmet J Spradlin   , who is a citizen of the   White   Nation, and as such has been placed upon the final roll of said Nation by the Honorable Secretary of the Interior, his final enrollment number being ——and that a   Female   child was born to me on the 1 day of   August   190 4 ; that said child has been named   Arrilla Spradlin   , and is now living.

                       Jaunita[sic] Spradlin

Applications for Enrollment of Choctaw Newborn
Act of 1905 Volume X

WITNESSETH:
Must be two Witnesses who are Citizens. } J. J. Gardner
Thos. J. Sexton

Subscribed and sworn to before me this 14 day of January 190 5

James Bower
Notary Public.

My commission expires Sept 23 - 1907

AFFIDAVIT OF ATTENDING PHYSICIAN OR MIDWIFE

UNITED STATES OF AMERICA
INDIAN TERRITORY
Central DISTRICT

I, J. J. Stephens a Practicing Physician on oath state that I attended on Mrs. Juanita Spradlin wife of Emmet J Spradlin on the 1 day of August , 190 4 , that there was born to her on said date a Female child, that said child is now living, and is said to have been named Arrilla Spradlin

John J Stephens M.D.

Subscribed and sworn to before me this, the 14 day of January 190 5

James Bower
Notary Public.

WITNESSETH:
Must be two witnesses who are citizens and know the child. { J. J. Gardner
Thos J Sexton

We hereby certify that we are well acquainted with .... a .... and know .... to be reputable and of good standing in the community.

{ J J Gardner
Thos J. Sexton

Applications for Enrollment of Choctaw Newborn
Act of 1905 Volume X

BIRTH AFFIDAVIT.

DEPARTMENT OF THE INTERIOR.
COMMISSION TO THE FIVE CIVILIZED TRIBES.

IN RE APPLICATION FOR ENROLLMENT, as a citizen of the   Choctaw   Nation, of Orilla Spradlin   , born on the 1st   day of   August   , 1904

Name of Father: Emet[sic] Spradlin, a non-citizen   a citizen of the .... Nation.
Name of Mother: Juanita Durant Spradlin   a citizen of the   Choctaw   Nation.

Postoffice   Durant, Indian Territory.

AFFIDAVIT OF MOTHER.

UNITED STATES OF AMERICA, Indian Territory, }
Central District   DISTRICT.

I,   Juanita Durant Spradlin   , on oath state that I am   17   years of age and a citizen by   blood   , of the   Choctaw   Nation; that I am the lawful wife of   Emet Spradlin, who is a noncitizen   , who is a citizen, by .... of the .... Nation; that a   Female   child was born to me on   1st   day of   August   , 1904; that said child has been named   Orilla Spradlin   , and was living March 4, 1905.

Juanita Durant Spradlin

Witnesses To Mark:
{

Subscribed and sworn to before me this 1st   day of   April, 1905.   , 190......

A.H. Ferguson
Notary Public.

AFFIDAVIT OF ATTENDING PHYSICIAN OR MID-WIFE.

UNITED STATES OF AMERICA, Indian Territory, }
Central District   DISTRICT.

I,   J. J. Stephens   , a   Physician   , on oath state that I attended on Mrs.   Juanita Durant Spradlin   , wife of   Emet Spradlin   on the   1st day of   August   , 1904; that there was born to her on said date a   female   child; that said child was living March 4, 1905, and is said to have been named   Orilla Spradlin

J.J. Stephens

Witnesses To Mark:
{

Applications for Enrollment of Choctaw Newborn
Act of 1905   Volume X

Subscribed and sworn to before me this 1st day of   April   , 1905

A. H. Ferguson
Notary Public.

Choc New Born 631
 Joseph M. Wooley b. 8-6-04

7-3344

Muskogee, Indian Territory, April 8, 1905.

Samuel L. Wooley,
 Stewart, Indian Territory.

Dear Sir:

Receipt is hereby acknowledged of the affidavits of Lela Wooley and E. E. Whitaker to the birth of Joseph M. Wooley, son of Samuel L. and Lela Wooley, August 6, 1904, and the same have been filed with our records as an application for the enrollment of said child.

Respectfully,

Commissioner in Charge.

COPY   7 N.B. 631

Muskogee, Indian Territory, April 12, 1905.

Samuel L. Wooley,
 Stuart, Indian Territory.

Dear Sir:

You are hereby advised that before the application for the enrollment of your infant child, Joseph M. Wooley, can be finally disposed of, it will be necessary for you to furnish the Commission with either the original or a certified copy of the license and certificate of marriage of yourself and Lela Wolley[sic].

Please give this matter your immediate attention.

Applications for Enrollment of Choctaw Newborn
Act of 1905 Volume X

Respectfully,

SIGNED   *T. B. Needles.*

LM   Commissioner in Charge.

Choctaw N.B. 631.

Muskogee, Indian Territory, April 21, 1905.

Samuel L. Wooley,
    Stuart, Indian Territory.

Dear Sir:

    Receipt is hereby acknowledged of your letter of April 17, enclosing marriage license and certificate between Samuel L. Wooley and Lila[sic] Turner which you offer in support of the application for the enrollment of your child, Joseph Wooley, and the same have been filed with the records in this case.

Respectfully,

Chairman.

7-NB-631.

Muskogee, Indian Territory, May 27, 1905.

Samuel L. Wooley,
    Stuart, Indian Territory.

Dear Sir:

    There is enclosed you herewith for execution application for the enrollment of your infant child, Joseph M. Wooley, born August 6, 1904.

    In the affidavits, heretofore filed in this office, the physician failed to sign the affidavit purported to be executed by him. It will, therefore, be necessary that the enclosed application be executed and returned to this office.

    In having these affidavits executed care should be exercised to see that all names are written in full, as they appear in the body of the affidavit, and in the event that either of the persons signing the affidavit are unable to write, signatures by mark must be attested by two witnesses. Each affidavit must be executed before a Notary Public and the notarial seal and signature of the officer must be attached to each separate affidavit.

Applications for Enrollment of Choctaw Newborn
Act of 1905 Volume X

Respectfully,

Chairman.

VR 27-5.

7 N.B. 631.

Muskogee, Indian Territory, June 5, 1905.

Samuel L. Wooley,
    Stuart, Indian Territory.

Dear Sir:

    Receipt is hereby acknowledged of the affidavits of Lela Wooley and E. E. Whitaker to the birth of Joseph M. Wooley, son of Samuel L. and Lela Wooley, August 6, 1904, and the same have been filed with our records in the matter of the enrollment of said child.

Respectfully,

Commissioner in Charge.

7-NB-631

Muskogee, Indian Territory, August 25, 1906.

Samuel L. Wooley,
    Stuart, Indian Territory.

Dear Sir:

    Receipt is hereby acknowledged of your letter of August 17, 1906, in which you ask for the return of the marriage license which was filed in the matter of the application for the enrollment of your child Joseph M. Wooley.

    In reply to your letter you are advised that you marriage license and certificate was filed with the record in the matter of the application for enrollment of your child Joseph M. Wooley and this office has been directed by the Department to retain all papers filed with its records. It will therefore be impracticable to comply with your request for the return of your marriage license and certificate.

Respectfully,

Acting Commissioner.

Applications for Enrollment of Choctaw Newborn
Act of 1905   Volume X

No. 3939

Certificate of Record of Marriages.

United States of America,
The Indian Territory,   } sct.
CENTRAL District.

I, E. J. Fannin   Clerk
of the United States Court, in the Indian Territory and District aforesaid, do hereby CERTIFY, that the License for and Certificate of the Marriage of

Mr. Samuel L Wooley   and

M iss Lila[sic] Turner   was

filed in my office in said Territory and District the   14 day of Dec
A.D., 190 3 , and duly recorded in Book   11
of Marriage Record, Page   36

WITNESS my hand and Seal of said Court, at South McAlester.
this   14   day of Dec
A.D. 190 3

E. J. Fannin
                                Clerk.
By   WC Donnelly   Deputy.

P. O. ....

DEPARTMENT OF THE INTERIOR,
COMMISSION TO THE FIVE CIVILIZED TRIBES.

FILED

APR 20 1905

Tams Bixby   CHAIRMAN.

Applications for Enrollment of Choctaw Newborn
Act of 1905   Volume X

No. *3939*

MARRIAGE LICENSE

United States of America,   The Indian Territory,
                                                      Central DISTRICT, SS.

To any Person Authorized by Law to Solemnize Marriage, Greeting:

You are hereby commanded to Solemnize the Rite and publish the Banns of Matrimony between Mr.   Samuel L Wooley
of   Stuart   *in the Indian Territory, aged*   24   *years,*
and M iss Lila Turner   *of*   Stuart
in the Indian Territory., aged   20   *years, according to law, and do you officially sign and return this License to the parties therein named.*

                    WITNESS my hand and official seal, this   12   *day*
                    of   December   *A. D. 190* 3

                              (Name Illegible)
                              Clerk of the United States Court.

                    ....*Deputy*

Certificate of Marriage.

United States of America,
  The Indian Territory,   } ss.
  ....*District.*   I,   Joel H Elliott

a   Minister of the Gospel   *, do hereby certify, that on the*   13"   *day of*
Dec   *A. D. 190* 3 *, I did, duly and according to law, as commanded in the foregoing License, solemnize the Rite and publish the Banns of Matrimony between the parties therein named.*

              Witness my hand, this   14"   *day of*   Dec   *A. D. 190* 3

My credentials are recorded in the office of the Clerk of ⎫   Joel H Elliott
the United States Court in the Indian Territory,   ⎬
Central District, Book   9   *, Page*   92   ⎭   *a*   Minister of the Gospel

---

    Note—This License and Certificate of Marriage must be returned to the Office of the Clerk of the United States Court of the Indian Territory, from whence it was issued, within sixty days from the date thereof, or the party to whom the License was issued will be liable in the amount of the One Hundred Dollars ($100.00).

Applications for Enrollment of Choctaw Newborn
Act of 1905   Volume X

NEW BORN AFFIDAVIT

No ....

CHOCTAW ENROLLING COMMISSION

IN THE MATTER OF THE APPLICATION FOR ENROLLMENT as a citizen of the Choctaw Nation, of   Joseph M Wooley   born on the 6th day of August   1904

Name of father   Samuel L Wooley   a citizen of   Choctaw   Nation, final enrollment No.   9596
Name of mother   Lela Wooley   a citizen of   United States   final enrollment No. ....

Stuart I.T.   Postoffice.

AFFIDAVIT OF MOTHER

UNITED STATES OF AMERICA }
INDIAN TERRITORY }
DISTRICT .... }

I   Lela Wooley   , on oath state that I am   21   years of age and a citizen by ~~blood~~ of the   U.S.   ~~Nation~~, and as such have been placed upon the final roll of the ——— Nation, by the Honorable Secretary of the Interior my final enrollment number being ———; that I am the lawful wife of   Samuel L Wooley   , who is a citizen of the   Choctaw   Nation, and as such has been placed upon the final roll of said Nation by the Honorable Secretary of the Interior, his final enrollment number being   9596   and that a   boy   child was born to me on the   6   day of   August   1904; that said child has been named   Joseph M Wooley   , and is now living.

WITNESSETH: Lela Wooley

Must be two witnesses { Elias Wesley
who are citizens   { Mrs J H Bruce

Subscribed and sworn to before me this, the FEB 25 1905 day of .... , 190........

J H Elliott
Notary Public.

My Commission Expires: July 8th 1908

Applications for Enrollment of Choctaw Newborn
Act of 1905   Volume X

Affidavit of Attending Physician or Midwife

UNITED STATES OF AMERICA, }
INDIAN TERRITORY, }
............................DISTRICT }

I,   E.E. Whitaker   a   physician on oath state that I attended on Mrs.   Lela Wooley   wife of   S L Wooley on the   6th day of   August   , 190 4, that there was born to her on said date a   male child, that said child is now living, and is said to have been named   Joseph M.

E.E. Whitaker   M. D.

FEB 25 1905

Subscribed and sworn to before me this the .... day of 1905

J H Elliott

Notary Public.

WITNESSETH:

Must be two witnesses who are citizens and know the child. { Elias Wesley
Mrs J H Bruce

We hereby certify that we are well acquainted with   E.E. Whitaker a   Physician   and know   him   to be reputable and of good standing in the community.

Must be two citizen witnesses. { Elias Wesley
Jerome Ervin Quincy

BIRTH AFFIDAVIT.

DEPARTMENT OF THE INTERIOR.
COMMISSION TO THE FIVE CIVILIZED TRIBES.

IN RE APPLICATION FOR ENROLLMENT, as a citizen of the   Choctaw   Nation, of   Joseph M Wooley   , born on the   6th day of   August   , 1904

Name of Father: Samuel L Wooley   a citizen of the   Choctaw   Nation.
Name of Mother: Lela Wooley   a citizen of the United States Nation.

Postoffice   Stuart

Applications for Enrollment of Choctaw Newborn
Act of 1905 Volume X

AFFIDAVIT OF MOTHER.

UNITED STATES OF AMERICA, Indian Territory,
Central   DISTRICT.

I, Mrs Lela Wooley, on oath state that I am 21 years of age and a citizen by ...., of the United States ~~Nation~~; that I am the lawful wife of Samuel L Wooley, who is a citizen, by blood of the Choctaw Nation; that a male child was born to me on 6th day of August, 1904; that said child has been named Joseph M Wooley, and was living March 4, 1905.

Lela Wooley

Witnesses To Mark:
{ WG Webb
{ Mrs J H Bruce

APR 1- 1905
Subscribed and sworn to before me this............day of ...., 190......

JH Elliott
Notary Public.

AFFIDAVIT OF ATTENDING PHYSICIAN OR MID-WIFE.

UNITED STATES OF AMERICA, Indian Territory,
Central   DISTRICT.

I, E.E. Whitaker, a physician, on oath state that I attended on Mrs. Lela Wooley, wife of S.L. Wooley on the 6th day of August, 1~~and~~; that there was born to her on said date a male child; that said child was living March 4, 1905, and is said to have been named Joseph M Wooley

Witnesses To Mark:
{ SV Pryor
{ Clara Wooley

APR 1- 1905
Subscribed and sworn to before me this............day of ...., 190......

JH Elliott
Notary Public.

My com exp July 8" 1908

Applications for Enrollment of Choctaw Newborn
Act of 1905   Volume X

BIRTH AFFIDAVIT.

DEPARTMENT OF THE INTERIOR.
COMMISSION TO THE FIVE CIVILIZED TRIBES.

IN RE APPLICATION FOR ENROLLMENT, as a citizen of the Choctaw Nation, of Joseph M Wooley, born on the 6th day of August, 1904

Name of Father: Samuel L Wooley   a citizen of the Choctaw Nation.
Name of Mother: Lela Wooley   a citizen of the U.S. Nation.

Postoffice   Stuart Ind Ter

AFFIDAVIT OF MOTHER.

UNITED STATES OF AMERICA, Indian Territory, }
Central   DISTRICT. }

I, Lela Wooley, on oath state that I am 21 years of age and a citizen by ——————, of the United States ~~Nation~~; that I am the lawful wife of Samuel L Wooley, who is a citizen, by blood of the Choctaw Nation; that a male child was born to me on 6th day of August, 1904; that said child has been named Joseph M Wooley, and was living March 4, 1905.

                              Lela Wooley

Witnesses To Mark:
   { Kate Bruce (her)
   { Alice Elliott (mark)

MAY 31 1905
Subscribed and sworn to before me this........day of ...., 190....

                    JH Elliott
JUL 8 1908   Notary Public.

AFFIDAVIT OF ATTENDING PHYSICIAN OR MID-WIFE.

UNITED STATES OF AMERICA, Indian Territory, }
Central   DISTRICT. }

I, E.E. Whitaker, a physician & surgeon, on oath state that I attended on Mrs. Lela Wooley, wife of Samuel L. Wooley on the 6th day of August, 1904; that there was born to her on said date a male child; that said child was living March 4, 1905, and is said to have been named Joseph M Wooley

                             E.E. Whitaker

Applications for Enrollment of Choctaw Newborn
Act of 1905   Volume X

Witnesses To Mark:
  { Kate Bruce
    Alice Elliott

MAY 31 1905

Subscribed and sworn to before me this..............day of ...., 190......

JUL 8 1908

JH Elliott
        Notary Public.

Choc New Born 632
    Bernard Preston Pearson *(b. 11-5-04)*

7-4766

Muskogee, Indian Territory April 8, 1905.

Robert T. Piersol[sic],
    Indianola, Indian Territory.

Dear Sir:

    Receipt is hereby acknowledged of the affidavits of Amelia E. Pearson and Alic[sic] Hobby to the birth of Bernard Preston Pearson son of Robert T. and Amelia E. Pearson November 5, 1904, and the same have been filed with our records as an application for the enrollment of said child.

           Respectfully,

                Commissioner in Charge.

Applications for Enrollment of Choctaw Newborn
Act of 1905   Volume X

NEW-BORN AFFIDAVIT.

Number..................

...Choctaw Enrolling Commission...

IN THE MATTER OF THE APPLICATION FOR ENROLLMENT, as a citizen of the Choctaw Nation, of Bernard Preston Pearson

born on the 5th day of November 190 4

Name of father   Robert T. Pearson   a citizen of   Choctaw
Nation final enrollment No. 13155
Name of mother   Amelia E Pearson   a citizen of   Choctaw
Nation final enrollment No. 576

Postoffice   Indianola I.T.

AFFIDAVIT OF MOTHER.

UNITED STATES OF AMERICA
INDIAN TERRITORY
Western   DISTRICT

I   Amelia E. Pearson   , on oath state that I am 35 years of age and a citizen by Intermarriage of the Choctaw Nation, and as such have been placed upon the final roll of the Choctaw Nation, by the Honorable Secretary of the Interior my final enrollment number being   576 ; that I am the lawful wife of   Robert T Pearson   , who is a citizen of the   Choctaw   Nation, and as such has been placed upon the final roll of said Nation by the Honorable Secretary of the Interior, his final enrollment number being   13155   and that a   Male   child was born to me on the 5th   day of   November   190 4; that said child has been named   Bernard Preston Pearson   , and is now living.

Amelia E Pearson

Witnesseth.
Must be two Witnesses who are Citizens.   W.F. Choats
L.H. Perkins

Subscribed and sworn to before me this   22[d]   day of   Feb   190 5

S.M. Gold
Notary Public.

My commission expires: 2/19 - 1908

Applications for Enrollment of Choctaw Newborn
Act of 1905   Volume X

AFFIDAVIT OF ATTENDING PHYSICIAN OR MIDWIFE

UNITED STATES OF AMERICA
INDIAN TERRITORY
Western   DISTRICT

I, Mrs Alice Hobbs   a   Midwife on oath state that I attended on Mrs. Amelia E Pearson   wife of   Robert T Pearson on the 5th day of November, 190 4, that there was born to her on said date a   male child, that said child is now living, and is said to have been named   Bernard Preston Pearson

Mrs Alice Hobbs   M. D.

WITNESSETH:
Must be two witnesses who are citizens and know the child.
- W.F. Choats
- L.H. Perkins

Subscribed and sworn to before me this, the   22^{d} day of February   190 5

SM Gold   Notary Public.

We hereby certify that we are well acquainted with   Mrs Alice Hobbs a   Midwife   and know   her   to be reputable and of good standing in the community.

W.F. Choats
L.H. Perkins

BIRTH AFFIDAVIT.

DEPARTMENT OF THE INTERIOR.
COMMISSION TO THE FIVE CIVILIZED TRIBES.

IN RE APPLICATION FOR ENROLLMENT, as a citizen of the   Choctaw   Nation, of Bernard Preston Pearson   , born on the 5th day of November   , 1904

Name of Father: Robert T Pearson   a citizen of the   Choctaw   Nation.
Name of Mother: Amelia E Pearson   a citizen of the   Choctaw   Nation.

Postoffice   Indianola   I T

Applications for Enrollment of Choctaw Newborn
Act of 1905 Volume X

AFFIDAVIT OF MOTHER.

UNITED STATES OF AMERICA, Indian Territory, }
Western   DISTRICT.

I, Amelia E Pearson , on oath state that I am 35 years of age and a citizen by marriage , of the Choctaw Nation; that I am the lawful wife of Robert T Pearson , who is a citizen, by Blood of the Choctaw Nation; that a Male child was born to me on 5th day of November , 1904; that said child has been named Bernard Preston Pearson , and was living March 4, 1905.

Amelia E Pearson

Witnesses To Mark:
{

Subscribed and sworn to before me this 1st day of April , 1905

SM Gold
Notary Public.

AFFIDAVIT OF ATTENDING PHYSICIAN OR MID-WIFE.

UNITED STATES OF AMERICA, Indian Territory, }
Western   DISTRICT.

I, Alice Hobbs , a midwife , on oath state that I attended on Mrs. Amelia E Pearson , wife of Robert T Pearson on the 5th day of Nov , 1904; that there was born to her on said date a male child; that said child was living March 4, 1905, and is said to have been named Bernard Preston Pearson

Alice Hobbs

Witnesses To Mark:
{

Subscribed and sworn to before me this 1st day of April , 1905

SM Gold
Notary Public.

Applications for Enrollment of Choctaw Newborn
Act of 1905   Volume X

Choc New Born 633
    Houston Perry   b.   1-4-03

7-4449

Muskogee, Indian Territory, April 8, 1905.

Frank Perry,
    Stigler, Indian Territory.

Dear Sir:

    Receipt is hereby acknowledged of the affidavits of Sallie Perry and L. K. Stephens to the birth of Houston Perry, son of Frank and Sallie Perry, January 4, 1903, and the same have been filed with our records as an application for the enrollment of said child.

                      Respectfully,

                                      Commissioner in Charge.

NEW-BORN AFFIDAVIT.

            Number............

...Choctaw Enrolling Commission...

    IN THE MATTER OF THE APPLICATION FOR ENROLLMENT, as a citizen of the Choctaw   Nation, of   Houston Perry

born on the 11th day of ___January___ 190 3

Name of father   Frank Perry   a citizen of   Choctaw
Nation final enrollment No.   12362
Name of mother   Sallie Perry   a citizen of   Choctaw
Nation final enrollment No.   12363

                                  Postoffice   Stigler

Applications for Enrollment of Choctaw Newborn
Act of 1905 Volume X

AFFIDAVIT OF MOTHER.

UNITED STATES OF AMERICA
INDIAN TERRITORY
Central   DISTRICT

I   Sallie Perry   , on oath state that I am 22   years of age and a citizen by   Blood   of the   Choctaw   Nation, and as such have been placed upon the final roll of the   Choctaw   Nation, by the Honorable Secretary of the Interior my final enrollment number being   12363   ; that I am the lawful wife of   Frank Perry   , who is a citizen of the   Choctaw   Nation, and as such has been placed upon the final roll of said Nation by the Honorable Secretary of the Interior, his final enrollment number being   12362   and that a   Male   child was born to me on the 4th day of   January   190 3; that said child has been named   Houston Perry   , and is now living.

                                              her
                                  Sallie x Perry

Witnesseth.   mark

Must be two Witnesses who are Citizens.   }   Joseph Nelson
Abel Cooper

Subscribed and sworn to before me this   5th day of   Jan   190 5

G.A. Holley
Notary Public.

My commission expires: Nov 7, 1907

AFFIDAVIT OF ATTENDING PHYSICIAN OR MIDWIFE

UNITED STATES OF AMERICA
INDIAN TERRITORY
Central   DISTRICT

I,   Jancy Fulsom   a   Midwife on oath state that I attended on Mrs.   Sallie Perry   wife of   Frank Perry on the   4th day of   January   , 190 3 , that there was born to her on said date a   male child, that said child is now living, and is said to have been named   Houston Perry

                                          her
                              Jancy x Fulsom
                                mark

Subscribed and sworn to before me this, the   2   day of   January   190 5

WITNESSETH: James Bower   Notary Public.

Must be two witnesses who are citizens   {   Frank Folsom
Abel Cooper

Applications for Enrollment of Choctaw Newborn
Act of 1905   Volume X

We hereby certify that we are well acquainted with   Jancy Fulsom   a   Midwife   and know   her   to be reputable and of good standing in the community.

    Frank Folsom   _____

    Abel Cooper   _____

BIRTH AFFIDAVIT.

DEPARTMENT OF THE INTERIOR.
COMMISSION TO THE FIVE CIVILIZED TRIBES.

IN RE APPLICATION FOR ENROLLMENT, as a citizen of the   Choctaw   Nation, of   Houston Perry   , born on the   4" day of   Jany   , 1903

Name of Father: Frank Perry   a citizen of the   Choctaw   Nation.
Name of Mother: Sallie Perry   a citizen of the   Choctaw   Nation.

                    Postoffice   Stigler I.T.

AFFIDAVIT OF MOTHER.

UNITED STATES OF AMERICA, Indian Territory,
    Central   **DISTRICT.**

I,   Sallie Perry   , on oath state that I am   23   years of age and a citizen by Blood   , of the   Choctaw   Nation; that I am the lawful wife of   Frank Perry   , who is a citizen, by Blood   of the   Choctaw   Nation; that a   male   child was born to me on   4" day of   Jany   , 1903; that said child has been named   Houston Perry   , and was living March 4, 1905.

                                her
                           Sallie x Perry
Witnesses To Mark: mark
  { J S Stigler
    George L Wadley

Subscribed and sworn to before me this   3rd day of   April   , 1905

My com expires May 21" 1907   A.L. Beckett
                                  Notary Public.

Applications for Enrollment of Choctaw Newborn
Act of 1905 Volume X

AFFIDAVIT OF ATTENDING PHYSICIAN OR MID-WIFE.

UNITED STATES OF AMERICA, Indian Territory, }
  Central   DISTRICT.

I, L. K. Stephens , a Physician , on oath state that I attended on Mrs. Sallie Perry , wife of Frank Perry on the 4" day of Jany , 1903; that there was born to her on said date a male child; that said child was living March 4, 1905, and is said to have been named Houston Perry

                              Dr. L. K. Stephens
Witnesses To Mark:
{

Subscribed and sworn to before me this 3rd day of April , 1905

My com expires May 21" 1907   A.L. Beckett
                                    Notary Public.

Choc New Born 634
    Herman Newton Garland b. 1-3-03
    Clara Sterling Garland b. 11-20-04

NEW-BORN AFFIDAVIT.

Number..................

...Choctaw Enrolling Commission...

IN THE MATTER OF THE APPLICATION FOR ENROLLMENT, as a citizen of the Choctaw   Nation, of   Herman Newton Garland

born on the 13th day of ___January___ 190 3

Name of father   Davis Garland   a citizen of   Choctaw
Nation final enrollment No. 7072
Name of mother   Arizona Garland   a citizen of   Choctaw
Nation final enrollment No. 906

                              Postoffice   Garland I.T.

133

Applications for Enrollment of Choctaw Newborn
Act of 1905 Volume X

AFFIDAVIT OF MOTHER.

UNITED STATES OF AMERICA
INDIAN TERRITORY
Central DISTRICT

I Arizona Garland , on oath state that I am 32 years of age and a citizen by Intermarriage of the Choctaw Nation, and as such have been placed upon the final roll of the Choctaw Nation, by the Honorable Secretary of the Interior my final enrollment number being 906 ; that I am the lawful wife of Davis Garland , who is a citizen of the Choctaw Nation, and as such has been placed upon the final roll of said Nation by the Honorable Secretary of the Interior, his final enrollment number being 7072 and that a Male child was born to me on the 13th day of January 190 3; that said child has been named Herman Newton Garland , and is now living.

Witnesseth.

Must be two Witnesses who are Citizens. *(Name Illegible)*

Ward Garland

Subscribed and sworn to before me this 23 day of Jan 190 5

W. S. Jones
Notary Public.

My commission expires: Feb 23 - 1905

7-2442

Muskogee, Indian Territory, April 8, 1905.

Davis Garland,
Garland, Indian Territory.

Dear Sir:

Receipt is hereby acknowledged of the affidavits of Arizona Garland and A. T. Hill to the birth of Clara Stirling[sic] Garland, daughter of Davis and Arizona Garland, November 20, 1904; also the affidavits of Arizona Garland and C. C. Jones to the birth of Herman Newton Garland, son of Davis and Arizona Garland, January 13, 1903, and the same have been filed with our records as applications for the enrollment of said children.

Respectfully,

Commissioner in Charge.

Applications for Enrollment of Choctaw Newborn
Act of 1905 Volume X

BIRTH AFFIDAVIT.

DEPARTMENT OF THE INTERIOR.
COMMISSION TO THE FIVE CIVILIZED TRIBES.

IN RE APPLICATION FOR ENROLLMENT, as a citizen of the   Choctaw   Nation, of Herman Newton Garland   , born on the 13th day of   January , 1903

Name of Father: Davis Garland   a citizen of the   Choctaw   Nation.
Name of Mother: Arizona Garland   a citizen of the   Choctaw   Nation.

Postoffice   Garland I.T.

AFFIDAVIT OF MOTHER.

UNITED STATES OF AMERICA, Indian Territory, }
    Centreal[sic]   DISTRICT.

I,   Arizona Garland   , on oath state that I am Thirty two   years of age and a citizen by Inter-marriage , of the   Choctaw   Nation; that I am the lawful wife of Davis Garland   , who is a citizen, by Blood   of the   Choctaw   Nation; that a   male   child was born to me on 13th day of   January   , 1903; that said child has been named   Herman Newton Garland   , and was living March 4, 1905.

                    Arizona Garland

Witnesses To Mark:
{

Subscribed and sworn to before me this 29th day of   March   , 1905

                    C. C. Jones
                        Notary Public.

AFFIDAVIT OF ATTENDING PHYSICIAN OR MID-WIFE.

UNITED STATES OF AMERICA, Indian Territory, }
    Centeral[sic]   DISTRICT.

I,   C. C. Jones   , a   Physician   , on oath state that I attended on Mrs.   Arizona Garland   , wife of   Davis Garland   on the   13th day of January   , 1903; that there was born to her on said date a   male   child; that said child was living March 4, 1905, and is said to have been named Herman Newton

                    C. C. Jones

Witnesses To Mark:
{

Applications for Enrollment of Choctaw Newborn
Act of 1905 Volume X

Subscribed and sworn to before me this 29th day of March, 1905

J. N. Jones
Notary Public.

AFFIDAVIT OF ATTENDING PHYSICIAN OR MIDWIFE

UNITED STATES OF AMERICA
INDIAN TERRITORY
Central DISTRICT

I, C C Jones a Physician on oath state that I attended on Mrs. Arizona Garland wife of Davis Garland on the 13th day of January, 1903, that there was born to her on said date a Male child, that said child is now living, and is said to have been named Hermn Newton Garland

C.C. Jones

Subscribed and sworn to before me this, the 23 day of Jan 1905

W.S. Jones Notary Public.

WITNESSETH:
Must be two witnesses who are citizens
J.M. Scantlen
Ward Garland

We hereby certify that we are well acquainted with C C Jones a Physician and know him to be reputable and of good standing in the community.

J M Scantlen   _____

Ward Garland   _____

BIRTH AFFIDAVIT.

DEPARTMENT OF THE INTERIOR.
COMMISSION TO THE FIVE CIVILIZED TRIBES.

IN RE APPLICATION FOR ENROLLMENT, as a citizen of the Choctaw Nation, of Clara Stirling[sic] Garland, born on the 20th day of November, 1904

Name of Father: Davis Garland   a citizen of the Choctaw Nation.
Name of Mother: Arizona Garland   a citizen of the Choctaw Nation.

Postoffice Garland I.T.

Applications for Enrollment of Choctaw Newborn
Act of 1905   Volume X

AFFIDAVIT OF MOTHER.

UNITED STATES OF AMERICA, Indian Territory, }
Centreal[sic]   DISTRICT. }

I,   Arizona Garland   , on oath state that I am Thirty two   years of age and a citizen by Inter-marriage , of the   Choctaw   Nation; that I am the lawful wife of Davis Garland   , who is a citizen, by Blood   of the   Choctaw   Nation; that a   Female   child was born to me on   the 20th day of   November   , 1904; that said child has been named   Clara Stirling Garland   , and was living March 4, 1905.

Arizona Garland

Witnesses To Mark:
{

Subscribed and sworn to before me this 29th day of   March   , 1905

C. C. Jones
Notary Public.

AFFIDAVIT OF ATTENDING PHYSICIAN OR MID-WIFE.

UNITED STATES OF AMERICA, Indian Territory, }
Central   DISTRICT. }

I,   Arthur T Hill   , a   Physician   , on oath state that I attended on Mrs.   Arizona Garland   , wife of   Davis Garland   on the   20 day of   November   , 1904; that there was born to her on said date a   Female   child; that said child was living March 4, 1905, and is said to have been named Clara Stirling Garland

A.T. Hill M.D.

Witnesses To Mark:
{

Subscribed and sworn to before me this 30   day of   March   , 1905

My Commission }   W.B. Davidson
Expires May 1907 }   Notary Public.

137

Applications for Enrollment of Choctaw Newborn
Act of 1905   Volume X

Choc New Born 635
    Walter L. Crowder   b. 9-18-04

7-3547

Muskogee, Indian Territory, April 8, 1905.

Louis F. Crowder,
    Stringtown, Indian Territory.

Dear Sir:

    Receipt is hereby acknowledged of the affidavits of Lydia Ann Crowder and J. A. Dabney to the birth of Walter L. Crowder son of Loran F. and Lydia Ann Crowder September 19, 1904, and the same have been filed with our records as an application for the enrollment of said child.

                Respectfully,

                              Commissioner in Charge.

BIRTH AFFIDAVIT.

DEPARTMENT OF THE INTERIOR,
COMMISSION TO THE FIVE CIVILIZED TRIBES.

In Re Application for Enrollment, as a citizen of the   Choctaw   Nation, of   Walter L Crowder   , born on the   18th day of   Sept   , 1904

Name of Father: Loui[sic] F. Crowder   a citizen of the   Choctaw   Nation.
Name of Mother: Lydia A. Crowder   a citizen of the   Choctaw   Nation.

                Post-office   Stringtown, I.T.

AFFIDAVIT OF MOTHER.

UNITED STATES OF AMERICA,
    INDIAN TERRITORY,
    Central Judician   District.

    I, Lydia A Crowder   , on oath state that I am   33   years of age and a citizen by   marriage   , of the   Choctaw   Nation; that I am the lawful wife of Loran F. Crowder   , who is a citizen, by Blood of the   Choctaw   Nation; that a male   child was born to me on   18th day of   Sept   , 190 4, that said child has been named   Walter L Crowder   , and is now living.

Applications for Enrollment of Choctaw Newborn
Act of 1905 Volume X

Lydia A Crowder

WITNESSES TO MARK:

{

Subscribed and sworn to before me this 28th day of Nov , 1904

D.S. Kennedy
NOTARY PUBLIC.

AFFIDAVIT OF ATTENDING PHYSICIAN OR MID-WIFE.

UNITED STATES OF AMERICA,
INDIAN TERRITORY,
Central Judicial District.

I, J A Dabney , a Physician , on oath state that I attended on Mrs. Lydia A Crowder , wife of Loran F Crowder on the 18th day of Sept , 190 4; that there was born to her on said date a male child; that said child is now living and is said to have been named Walter L. Crowder

JA Dabney MD

WITNESSES TO MARK:

{

Subscribed and sworn to before me this 30th day of Nov , 1904

D.S. Kennedy
NOTARY PUBLIC.

NEW-BORN AFFIDAVIT.

Number............

...Choctaw Enrolling Commission...

IN THE MATTER OF THE APPLICATION FOR ENROLLMENT, as a citizen of the Choctaw Nation, of Walter Lee Crowder

born on the 18 day of __September__ 190 4

Name of father Loring F Crowder   a citizen of Choctaw
Nation final enrollment No. 10065
Name of mother Lydia Crowder   a citizen of white
Nation final enrollment No. ——

Applications for Enrollment of Choctaw Newborn
Act of 1905   Volume X

Postoffice   Stringtown IT

AFFIDAVIT OF MOTHER.

UNITED STATES OF AMERICA
INDIAN TERRITORY
Central   DISTRICT

I   Lydia Crowder   , on oath state that I am 34   years of age and a citizen by   marriage   of the   Choctaw   Nation, and as such have been placed upon the final roll of the   Choctaw   Nation, by the Honorable Secretary of the Interior my final enrollment number being —— ; that I am the lawful wife of Loring F Crowder   , who is a citizen of the   Choctaw   Nation, and as such has been placed upon the final roll of said Nation by the Honorable Secretary of the Interior, his final enrollment number being   10065   and that a   Male   child was born to me on the 18   day of   September   190 4; that said child has been named   Walter Lee Crowder   , and is now living.

Mrs Lydia Crowder

Witnesseth.
Must be two Witnesses who are Citizens.   J C Scott
James Self

Subscribed and sworn to before me this   16th day of   Jan   190 5

D.S. Kennedy
Notary Public.

My commission expires: Nov 1st 1905

AFFIDAVIT OF ATTENDING PHYSICIAN OR MIDWIFE

UNITED STATES OF AMERICA
INDIAN TERRITORY
Central   DISTRICT

I,   J.A. Dabney   a   Practicing Physician on oath state that I attended on Mrs. Lydia Crowder   wife of   Loring F Crowder on the   18   day of   September   , 190 4 , that there was born to her on said date a Male   child, that said child is now living, and is said to have been named   Walter Lee Crowder

J A Dabney   M.D.

Subscribed and sworn to before me this, the 20th day of   Jan   190 5

D S Kennedy
Notary Public.

Applications for Enrollment of Choctaw Newborn
Act of 1905   Volume X

WITNESSETH:

Must be two witnesses who are citizens and know the child.
{ J C Scott
James Self }

We hereby certify that we are well acquainted with J.A. Dabney a Practicing Physician and know him to be reputable and of good standing in the community.

{ J C Scott

James Self }

BIRTH AFFIDAVIT.

DEPARTMENT OF THE INTERIOR.
COMMISSION TO THE FIVE CIVILIZED TRIBES.

IN RE APPLICATION FOR ENROLLMENT, as a citizen of the Choctaw Nation, of Walter L Crowder , born on the 18th day of Sept , 1904

Name of Father: Loran F Crowder   a citizen of the Choctaw Nation.
Name of Mother: Lydia Ann Crowder   a citizen of the Choctaw Nation.

Postoffice   Stringtown, I.T.

AFFIDAVIT OF MOTHER.

UNITED STATES OF AMERICA, Indian Territory,
Central Judicial   DISTRICT.

I, Lydia Ann Crowder , on oath state that I am 34 years of age and a citizen by Marriage , of the Choctaw Nation; that I am the lawful wife of Loran F Crowder , who is a citizen, by blood of the Choctaw Nation; that a male child was born to me on 18th day of Sept , 1904; that said child has been named Walter L Crowder , and was living March 4, 1905.

Lydia Ann Crowder

Witnesses To Mark:
{

Subscribed and sworn to before me this 1st day of April , 1905

D.S. Kennedy
Notary Public.

Applications for Enrollment of Choctaw Newborn
Act of 1905   Volume X

AFFIDAVIT OF ATTENDING PHYSICIAN OR MID-WIFE.

UNITED STATES OF AMERICA, Indian Territory,
Central Judicial   DISTRICT.

I,   J.A. Dabney , a Physician , on oath state that I attended on Mrs.   Lydia Ann Crowder , wife of   Loran F Crowder   on the 18th day of Sept , 1904; that there was born to her on said date a   male   child; that said child was living March 4, 1905, and is said to have been named Walter L Crowder

J A Dabney M.D.

Witnesses To Mark:
{

Subscribed and sworn to before me this 1st day of   April , 1905

D.S. Kennedy
Notary Public.

*Evidence marriage
filed in Choc Jkt*
3547

Choc New Born 636
    July Neal   b. 10-14-03

BIRTH AFFIDAVIT.

DEPARTMENT OF THE INTERIOR.
COMMISSION TO THE FIVE CIVILIZED TRIBES.

IN RE APPLICATION FOR ENROLLMENT, as a citizen of the   Choctaw   Nation, of   July Neal , born on the 14 day of Oct , 1903

Name of Father: John W Neal	a citizen of the Choctaw	Nation.
Name of Mother: Susan Neal	a citizen of the Choctaw	Nation.

Postoffice   Brooken I.T.

Applications for Enrollment of Choctaw Newborn
Act of 1905   Volume X

AFFIDAVIT OF MOTHER.

UNITED STATES OF AMERICA, Indian Territory, }
Western   DISTRICT.

I,   Susan Neal   , on oath state that I am   37   years of age and a citizen by Blood   , of the   Choctaw   Nation; that I am the lawful wife of   John W Neal   , who is a citizen, by Intermarriage   of the   Choctaw   Nation; that a   gurl[sic] child was born to me on   14   day of   Oct   , 1903; that said child has been named   July Neal   , and was living March 4, 1905.

                                        Susan Neal

Witnesses To Mark:
{

Subscribed and sworn to before me this   30   day of   March   , 1905

                                        S P Davis
                                            Notary Public.

AFFIDAVIT OF ATTENDING PHYSICIAN OR MID-WIFE.

UNITED STATES OF AMERICA, Indian Territory, }
Western   DISTRICT.

I,   Martha Watkins   , a   mid wife   , on oath state that I attended on Mrs.   Susan Neal   , wife of   John W Neal   on the   14   day of   Oct   , 1903; that there was born to her on said date a   girl   child; that said child was living March 4, 1905, and is said to have been named July Neal

                                        her
                                Martha x Watkins
Witnesses To Mark: mark
{ James Watkins
  Jennie Walls

Subscribed and sworn to before me this   30   day of   March   , 1905

                                        S P Davis
                                            Notary Public.

my commish expir feb[sic] 9-07

Applications for Enrollment of Choctaw Newborn
Act of 1905 Volume X

NEW-BORN AFFIDAVIT.

Number................

...Choctaw Enrolling Commission...

IN THE MATTER OF THE APPLICATION FOR ENROLLMENT, as a citizen of the Choctaw Nation, of Julia[sic] Neal

born on the 14th day of __October__ 190 3

Name of father John W Neal   a citizen of   Choctaw
Nation final enrollment No. 1042
Name of mother Susan Neal   a citizen of   Choctaw
Nation final enrollment No. 13564

Postoffice   Brooken I.T.

AFFIDAVIT OF MOTHER.

UNITED STATES OF AMERICA
INDIAN TERRITORY
  Western   DISTRICT

I   Susan Neal   , on oath state that I am 37 years of age and a citizen by blood of the Choctaw Nation, and as such have been placed upon the final roll of the Choctaw Nation, by the Honorable Secretary of the Interior my final enrollment number being 13564 ; that I am the lawful wife of John W Neal , who is a citizen of the Choctaw Nation, and as such has been placed upon the final roll of said Nation by the Honorable Secretary of the Interior, his final enrollment number being   1042   and that a   female   child was born to me on the 14th day of October   190 3; that said child has been named Julia Neal , and is now living.

Susan Neal

Witnesseth.
  Must be two } T.J. Walls
  Witnesses who }
  are Citizens.   Jess Walls

Subscribed and sworn to before me this 5 day of Jan   190 5

John M Lenz
Notary Public.

My commission expires: Nov 27 1907

144

Applications for Enrollment of Choctaw Newborn
Act of 1905   Volume X

AFFIDAVIT OF ATTENDING PHYSICIAN OR MIDWIFE

UNITED STATES OF AMERICA
INDIAN TERRITORY
   Western   DISTRICT

I, Martha Watkins a midwife on oath state that I attended on Mrs. Susan Neal wife of John W Neal on the 14th day of October , 190 3 , that there was born to her on said date a female child, that said child is now living, and is said to have been named Julia[sic] Neal

                                            her
                             Martha Watkins x
                                     mark

Subscribed and sworn to before me this, the 5 day of January 190 5

WITNESSETH: John M Lenz   Notary Public.
Must be two witnesses { J M Walls
who are citizens   James Fitzer

We hereby certify that we are well acquainted with Martha Watkins a midwife and know .... to be reputable and of good standing in the community.

    T J Walls

    Jess Walls

                                                              7-5353

                        Muskogee, Indian Territory, April 8, 1905.

John W. Neal,
    Brooken, Indian Territory.

Dear Sir:

    Receipt is hereby acknowledged of the affidavits of Susan Neal and Martha Watkins to the birth of July Neal, daughter of John W. and Susan Neal, October 14, 1903, and the same have been filed with our records as an application for the enrollment of said child.

                              Respectfully,

                                          Commissioner in Charge.

Applications for Enrollment of Choctaw Newborn
Act of 1905   Volume X

<u>Choc New Born 637</u>
    Rupert Bernard Stigler   b. 11-2-04

7-5389

Muskogee, Indian Territory, April 8, 1905.

J. S. Stigler,
    Stigler, Indian Territory.

Dear Sir:

    Receipt is hereby acknowledged of the affidavits of Mary J. Stigler and S. E. Mitchell to the birth of Rupert Bernard Stigler, son of J. S. and Mary J. Stigler, November 2, 1904, and the same have been filed with our records as an application for the enrollment of said child.

                      Respectfully,

                      Commissioner in Charge.

7-NB-637

Muskogee, Indian Territory, August 3, 1905.

J. S. Stigler,
    Stigler, Indian Territory.

Dear Sir:

    Receipt is hereby acknowledged of your letter of July 27, asking if Rupert Bernard Stigler has been approved.

    In reply to your letter you are advised that on July 22, 1905, the Secretary of the Interior approved the enrollment of your child Rupert Bernard Stigler as a citizen by blood of the Choctaw Nation, and selection of allotment may now be made in his behalf in accordance with the rules and regulations governing the selection of allotments and the designation of homesteads in the Choctaw and Chickasaw Nations.

                      Respectfully,

                              Commissioner.

Applications for Enrollment of Choctaw Newborn
Act of 1905   Volume X

NEW-BORN AFFIDAVIT.

Number..............

...Choctaw Enrolling Commission...

IN THE MATTER OF THE APPLICATION FOR ENROLLMENT, as a citizen of the Choctaw Nation, of Rupert Bernard Stigler

born on the 2nd day of __November__ 190 4

Name of father   Joseph S Stigler   a citizen of   Choctaw
Nation final enrollment No. ....
Name of mother   Mary J Stigler   a citizen of   Choctaw
Nation final enrollment No. 13641

Postoffice   Stigler, I.T.

AFFIDAVIT OF MOTHER.

UNITED STATES OF AMERICA
INDIAN TERRITORY
    Central   DISTRICT

I   Mary J Stigler   , on oath state that I am   35   years of age and a citizen by   blood   of the   Choctaw   Nation, and as such have been placed upon the final roll of the   Choctaw   Nation, by the Honorable Secretary of the Interior my final enrollment number being   13641 ; that I am the lawful wife of   Joseph S Stigler   , who is a citizen of the   Choctaw   Nation, and as such has been placed upon the final roll of said Nation by the Honorable Secretary of the Interior, his final enrollment number being ....and that a   Male   child was born to me on the 2nd day of   November   190 4; that said child has been named   Rupert Bernard Stigler   , and is now living.

Mary J Stigler

Witnesseth.
Must be two Witnesses who are Citizens. } Walter Folsom
Arian Coleman

Subscribed and sworn to before me this   2nd day of   Jan   190 5

Wm O. Carr
Notary Public.

My commission expires: Feby 25th 1908

Applications for Enrollment of Choctaw Newborn
Act of 1905 Volume X

AFFIDAVIT OF ATTENDING PHYSICIAN OR MIDWIFE

UNITED STATES OF AMERICA
INDIAN TERRITORY
  Central   DISTRICT

I,   S E Mitchell   a   Physician on oath state that I attended on Mrs.   Mary J Stigler   wife of   Joseph S Stigler   on the   2nd day of   November , 190 4 , that there was born to her on said date a   male child, that said child is now living, and is said to have been named   Rupert Bernard Stigler

S. E. Mitchell   M.D.

Subscribed and sworn to before me this, the   2nd day of   January   190 5

W^m O Carr   Notary Public.

WITNESSETH:
Must be two witnesses who are citizens { Sarah Gaddy Coleman
Frank Folsom

We hereby certify that we are well acquainted with   S.E. Mitchell   a   practicing physician   and know   him   to be reputable and of good standing in the community.

Frank Folsom   A.L. Coleman

Henry Cooper   G A Holley

BIRTH AFFIDAVIT.

DEPARTMENT OF THE INTERIOR.
COMMISSION TO THE FIVE CIVILIZED TRIBES.

IN RE APPLICATION FOR ENROLLMENT, as a citizen of the   Choctaw   Nation, of   Rupert Bernard Stigler   , born on the 2" day of Nov , 1904

Name of Father: J.S. Stigler   a citizen of the Choctaw Nation.
Name of Mother: Mary J Stigler   a citizen of the Choctaw Nation.

Postoffice   Stigler, I.T.

Applications for Enrollment of Choctaw Newborn
Act of 1905 Volume X

AFFIDAVIT OF MOTHER.

UNITED STATES OF AMERICA, Indian Territory, }
Central   DISTRICT.

I, Mary J Stigler , on oath state that I am 36 years of age and a citizen by Blood , of the Choctaw Nation; that I am the lawful wife of J.S. Stigler , who is a citizen, by marriage of the Choctaw Nation; that a male child was born to me on 2" day of Nov , 1904; that said child has been named Rupert Bernard Stigler , and was living March 4, 1905.

Mary J Stigler

Witnesses To Mark:
{

Subscribed and sworn to before me this 31 day of March , 1905

A.L. Beckett
Notary Public.

AFFIDAVIT OF ATTENDING PHYSICIAN OR MID-WIFE.

UNITED STATES OF AMERICA, Indian Territory, }
Central   DISTRICT.

I,............................., a Physician , on oath state that I attended on Mrs. Mary J Stigler , wife of S.J.[sic] Stigler on the 2 day of November, 1904; that there was born to her on said date a male child; that said child was living March 4, 1905, and is said to have been named Rupert Bernard Stigler

SE Mitchell MD

Witnesses To Mark:
{

Subscribed and sworn to before me this 1st day of April , 1905

A L Beckett
Notary Public.
My com exp 4/28/07

Applications for Enrollment of Choctaw Newborn
Act of 1905   Volume X

Choc New Born 638
   Eunice Melvina Turner   b. 11-8-03

7-5365

Muskogee, Indian Territory, April 8, 1905.

Albert P. Turner,
   Tupelo, Indian Territory.

Dear Sir:

   Receipt is hereby acknowledged of the affidavits of Artie M. Turner and Maggie Grist to the birth of Eunice Melvina Turner, daughter of Albert P. and Artie M. Turner, November 18, 1903, and the same have been filed with our records as an application for the enrollment of said child.
                     Respectfully,

                                             Commissioner in Charge.

BIRTH AFFIDAVIT.
DEPARTMENT OF THE INTERIOR.
COMMISSION TO THE FIVE CIVILIZED TRIBES.

   IN RE APPLICATION FOR ENROLLMENT, as a citizen of the   Choctaw   Nation, of Eunice Melvina Turner   , born on the   18   day of   Nov   , 1903

Name of Father: Albert P. Turner   a citizen of the   Choctaw   Nation.
Name of Mother: Artie M. Turner   a citizen of the   Choctaw   Nation.

                     Postoffice   Tupelo I.T.

AFFIDAVIT OF MOTHER.

UNITED STATES OF AMERICA, Indian Territory,
   Cent   DISTRICT.

   I,   Artie M. Turner   , on oath state that I am   21   years of age and a citizen by   Marriage   , of the   Choctaw   Nation; that I am the lawful wife of   Albert P. Turner   , who is a citizen, by Blood   of the   Choctaw   Nation; that a Female   child was born to me on   18   day of   Nov   , 1903; that said child has been named   Eunice Melvina   , and was living March 4, 1905.

                        Artie M Turner

150

Applications for Enrollment of Choctaw Newborn
Act of 1905   Volume X

Witnesses To Mark:

{

Subscribed and sworn to before me this 1st day of   April   , 1905

R.T. Breedlove
Notary Public.

AFFIDAVIT OF ATTENDING PHYSICIAN OR MID-WIFE.

UNITED STATES OF AMERICA, Indian Territory, }
Cent   DISTRICT. }

I, Maggie Grist   , a   Midwife   , on oath state that I attended on Mrs. Artie M. Turner   , wife of Albert P. Turner   on the 18 day of   Nov , 1903; that there was born to her on said date a   Female   child; that said child was living March 4, 1905, and is said to have been named Eunice Melvina Turner

Maggie Grist

Witnesses To Mark:

{

Subscribed and sworn to before me this 1st day of   April   , 1905

R.T. Breedlove
Notary Public.

Choc New Born 639
    Lee O. Henderson   b. 10-4-03

Choctaw 2473.

Muskogee, Indian Territory, April 8, 1905.

W. L. Henderson,
    Shadypoint, Indian Territory.

Dear Sir:

Receipt is hereby acknowledged of the affidavits of Amanda Henderson and J. C. Lindsey to the birth of Lee O. Henderson, son of W. L. and Amanda Henderson, October

Applications for Enrollment of Choctaw Newborn
Act of 1905   Volume X

4, 1903, and the same have been filed with our records as an application for the enrollment of said child.

Respectfully,

Commissioner in Charge.

BIRTH AFFIDAVIT.

DEPARTMENT OF THE INTERIOR.
COMMISSION TO THE FIVE CIVILIZED TRIBES.

IN RE APPLICATION FOR ENROLLMENT, as a citizen of the   Choctaw   Nation, of   Lee O. Henderson   , born on the 4   day of   October   , 1903

Name of Father: W L Henderson   a citizen of the   Choctaw   Nation.
Name of Mother: Amanda Henderson   a citizen of the   Choctaw   Nation.

Postoffice   Shady Point I.T.

AFFIDAVIT OF MOTHER.

UNITED STATES OF AMERICA, Indian Territory, ⎫
   Central   DISTRICT.   ⎭

I,   Amanda Henderson   , on oath state that I am   39   years of age and a citizen by   Blood   , of the   Choctaw   Nation; that I am the lawful wife of W L Henderson   , who is a citizen, by marriage   of the   Choctaw   Nation; that a   male   child was born to me on   4th day of   October   , 1903; that said child has been named   Lee O Henderson   , and was living March 4, 1905.

Amanda Henderson

Witnesses To Mark:
{

Subscribed and sworn to before me this 1st day of   April   , 1905

WH Phillips
Notary Public.

Applications for Enrollment of Choctaw Newborn
Act of 1905   Volume X

AFFIDAVIT OF ATTENDING PHYSICIAN OR MID-WIFE.

UNITED STATES OF AMERICA, Indian Territory, }
.... DISTRICT. }

 I,   Dr J C Lindsey   , a   Physician   , on oath state that I attended on Mrs. Amanda Henderson   , wife of   W L Henderson   on the   4 day of October   , 1903; that there was born to her on said date a   male   child; that said child was living March 4, 1905, and is said to have been named Lee O Henderson

J.C. Lindsey M.D.

Witnesses To Mark:
{

 Subscribed and sworn to before me this 1   day of   April   , 1905

WH Phillips
Notary Public.

NEW-BORN AFFIDAVIT.

 Number................

...Choctaw Enrolling Commission...

 IN THE MATTER OF THE APPLICATION FOR ENROLLMENT, as a citizen of the Choctaw   Nation, of   Lee O Henderson

born on the 4 day of __October__   190 3

Name of father   Wilson L Henderson   a citizen of   Choc by Inter
Nation final enrollment No. 106
Name of mother   Amanda Henderson   a citizen of   Choctaw
Nation final enrollment No. 7172

                                    Postoffice   Shadypoint IT

AFFIDAVIT OF MOTHER.
UNITED STATES OF AMERICA
INDIAN TERRITORY
  Central   DISTRICT

 I   Amanda Henderson   , on oath state that I am   39   years of age and a citizen by   Blood   of the   Choctaw   Nation, and as such have been placed upon the final roll of the   Choctaw   Nation, by the Honorable Secretary of the Interior my final enrollment number being   7172 ; that I am the lawful wife

153

Applications for Enrollment of Choctaw Newborn
Act of 1905   Volume X

of   Wilson L Henderson   , who is a citizen of the   Choctaw   (by Intermarriage) Nation, and as such has been placed upon the final roll of said Nation by the Honorable Secretary of the Interior, his final enrollment number being   106   and that a   Male child was born to me on the   4th day of   October   190 3; that said child has been named   Lee O. Henderson   , and is now living.

Witnesseth.	her
Must be two Witnesses who are Citizens. { Lewis Sockey V.P. Trahan	Amanda x Henderson mark

Subscribed and sworn to before me this   21   day of   Jan   190 5

WH Phillips
Notary Public.

My commission expires: 19 day Jan 1907

AFFIDAVIT OF ATTENDING PHYSICIAN OR MIDWIFE

UNITED STATES OF AMERICA
INDIAN TERRITORY
  Central   DISTRICT

I,   J.C. Lindsay   a   Phician[sic] on oath state that I attended on Mrs.   Amanda Henderson   wife of   Wilson L Henderson on the   4th day of   October   , 190 3 , that there was born to her on said date a   male child, that said child is now living, and is said to have been named   Lee O Henderson

J.C. Lindsay   𝑀.𝒟.

Subscribed and sworn to before me this, the .... day of
  Feb 11th   190 5

WITNESSETH: WH Phillips   Notary Public.
  Must be two witnesses who are citizens { (Name Illegible)
  Lewis Sockey

We hereby certify that we are well acquainted with   J C Lindsay a   Phician   and know   him   to be reputable and of good standing in the community.

  (Name Illegible)   WH Phillips

  Lewis Sockey   Notary Public

Applications for Enrollment of Choctaw Newborn
Act of 1905 Volume X

Choc New Born 640
Julia Frazier b. 8-7-04

Choctaw 3263.

Muskogee, Indian Territory, April 8, 1905.

Thompson Frazier,
Citra, Indian Territory.

Dear Sir:

Receipt is hereby acknowledged of the affidavits of Lona Frazier and Lousa Mishontambe to the birth of Julia Frazier, daughter of Thompson and Lona Frazier, August 7, 1904, and the same have been filed with our records as an application for the enrollment of said child.

Respectfully,

Commissioner in Charge.

BIRTH AFFIDAVIT.
DEPARTMENT OF THE INTERIOR.
COMMISSION TO THE FIVE CIVILIZED TRIBES.

IN RE APPLICATION FOR ENROLLMENT, as a citizen of the   Choctaw   Nation, of Julia Frazier   , born on the 7 day of August , 1904

Name of Father: Thompson Frazier   a citizen of the Choctaw   Nation.
Name of Mother: Lona Frazier   a citizen of the Choctaw   Nation.

Postoffice   Citra I.T.

AFFIDAVIT OF MOTHER.

UNITED STATES OF AMERICA, Indian Territory,
    Central   DISTRICT.

I, Lona Frazier , on oath state that I am 22 years of age and a citizen by Blood , of the Choctaw Nation; that I am the lawful wife of Thompson Frazier , who is a citizen, by Blood of the Choctaw Nation; that a female child was born to me on 7 day of August , 1904; that said child has been named Julia Frazier , and was living March 4, 1905.

her
Lona x Frazier
mark

Applications for Enrollment of Choctaw Newborn
Act of 1905   Volume X

Witnesses To Mark:
{ M Ross
{ *(Name Illegible)*

    Subscribed and sworn to before me this 31 day of   March   , 1905

                                    WH Hudson
                                            Notary Public.

AFFIDAVIT OF ATTENDING PHYSICIAN OR MID-WIFE.

UNITED STATES OF AMERICA, Indian Territory, }
    Central   DISTRICT. }

    I, Louisa Mishontambe , a ...., on oath state that I attended on Mrs. Lona Frazier , wife of Thompson Frazier   on the 7 day of August , 1904; that there was born to her on said date a   female   child; that said child was living March 4, 1905, and is said to have been named Julia Frazier

                                      her
                             Louisa x Mishontambe
Witnesses To Mark: mark
{ M Ross
{ *(Name Illegible)*

    Subscribed and sworn to before me this 31 day of   March   , 1905

                                    WH Hudson
                                            Notary Public.
      My com exp March 14/1907

<u>Choc New Born 641</u>
        Leola Williams b. 3-11-04

Applications for Enrollment of Choctaw Newborn
Act of 1905 Volume X

7-NB-641

Muskogee, Indian Territory, August 1, 1905.

Jack Williams,
    Spiro, Indian Territory.

Dear Sir:

    Receipt is hereby acknowledged of your letter of July 27, 1905, asking if your child Leoler[sic] Williams has been approved.

    In reply to your letter you are advised that the name of your child Leola Williams has been placed upon a schedule of citizens by blood of the Choctaw Nation prepared for forwarding to the Secretary of the Interior and you will be notified when her enrollment is approved by the Department.

    The matter of the land referred to in your letter has been made the subject of another communication.

        Respectfully,

                Commissioner.

AFFIDAVIT OF ATTENDING PHYSICIAN OR MIDWIFE

UNITED STATES OF AMERICA
INDIAN TERRITORY
  Central   DISTRICT

    I,   Emma Frazier   a   midwife
on oath state that I attended on Mrs. Mary Jane Williams   wife of   Jack Williams
on the   11   day of   March   , 190 4 , that there was born to her on said date a   Female child, that said child is now living, and is said to have been named   Leola Williams

                              her
                        Emma x Frazier   *M.D.*
                            mark

        Subscribed and sworn to before me this, the   25   day of
        January   190 5

                                                    ....Notary Public.

WITNESSETH:
  Must be two witnesses   {   Louis Leflore
  who are citizens
                              rice rodgers[sic]

Applications for Enrollment of Choctaw Newborn
Act of 1905   Volume X

We hereby certify that we are well acquainted with   Emma Frazier   a   Midwife   and know   her   to be reputable and of good standing in the community.

_____   Louis Leflore

_____   Thomas D Ainsworth

_____

NEW-BORN AFFIDAVIT.

Number............

...Choctaw Enrolling Commission...

_____

IN THE MATTER OF THE APPLICATION FOR ENROLLMENT, as a citizen of the Choctaw   Nation, of   Leola Williams

born on the   11   day of __March__   190 4

Name of father   Jack Williams   a citizen of   Choctaw
Nation final enrollment No.   5528
Name of mother   Mary Jane Williams   a citizen of   non citizen
Nation final enrollment No. ——

Postoffice   Spiro I.T.

AFFIDAVIT OF MOTHER.

UNITED STATES OF AMERICA
INDIAN TERRITORY
   Central   DISTRICT

I   Mary Jane Williams   , on oath state that I am   31   years of age and a citizen by   non   of the   ——   Nation, and as such have been placed upon the final roll of the   — — —Nation, by the Honorable Secretary of the Interior my final enrollment number being   — — ; that I am the lawful wife of   Jack Williams   , who is a citizen of the   Choctaw   Nation, and as such has been placed upon the final roll of said Nation by the Honorable Secretary of the Interior, his final enrollment number being   5528   and that a   female   child was born to me on the   11   day of   March   190 4; that said child has been named   Leola Williams   , and is now living.

Witnesseth.   Mary Jane Williams
  Must be two   Louis Leflore
  Witnesses who
  are Citizens.   Thomas D. Ainsworth

Applications for Enrollment of Choctaw Newborn
Act of 1905   Volume X

Subscribed and sworn to before me this   25   day of   Jan   190 5

James Bower
Notary Public.

My commission expires:
Sept 23 - 1907

BIRTH AFFIDAVIT.

DEPARTMENT OF THE INTERIOR.
COMMISSION TO THE FIVE CIVILIZED TRIBES.

IN RE APPLICATION FOR ENROLLMENT, as a citizen of the   Choctaw   Nation, of Leola Williams   , born on the 11th   day of   March   , 1904

Name of Father: Jack Williams   a citizen of the   Choctaw   Nation.
Name of Mother: Mary Jane Williams   a citizen of the   Choctaw   Nation.

Postoffice   Spiro, Ind Ter

AFFIDAVIT OF MOTHER.

UNITED STATES OF AMERICA, Indian Territory,
Central   DISTRICT.

I,   Mary Jane Williams   , on oath state that I am   31   years of age and a citizen by   marriage   , of the   Choctaw   Nation; that I am the lawful wife of Jack Williams   , who is a citizen, by blood   of the   Choctaw   Nation; that a   female   child was born to me on   11th   day of   March   , 1904; that said child has been named   Leola Williams   , and was living March 4, 1905.

Mary Jane Williams

Witnesses To Mark:

Subscribed and sworn to before me this 30th   day of   March   , 1905

Wirt Franklin
Notary Public.

Applications for Enrollment of Choctaw Newborn
Act of 1905   Volume X

AFFIDAVIT OF ATTENDING PHYSICIAN OR MID-WIFE.

UNITED STATES OF AMERICA, Indian Territory, }
  Central   DISTRICT. }

    I,   Emma Davis   , a   Midwife   , on oath state that I attended on Mrs.   Mary Jane Williams   , wife of   Jack Williams   on the 11th day of March , 1904; that there was born to her on said date a   female   child; that said child was living March 4, 1905, and is said to have been named   Leola Williams

                                                her
                                      Emma x Davis
Witnesses To Mark: mark
    { Chas C Sloan
    { Sam Rose

    Subscribed and sworn to before me this 1st day of   April   , 1905

                                  Chas C Sloan
                                        Notary Public.
My commission expires Aug 17/07

Choc New Born 642
      Mary Kathleen Moore   b. 1-10-05
      Clifford Welsey[sic] Moore   b. 4-22-03

BIRTH AFFIDAVIT.
DEPARTMENT OF THE INTERIOR.
COMMISSION TO THE FIVE CIVILIZED TRIBES.

    IN RE APPLICATION FOR ENROLLMENT, as a citizen of the   Choctaw   Nation, of Mary Kathleen Moore   , born on the 10   day of   January , 1905

Name of Father: David A Moore   a citizen of the   Choctaw   Nation.
                                                  by intermarriage
Name of Mother: Dora M Moore   a citizen of the   Choctaw   Nation.

                              Postoffice   Bokoshe Ind Ter

Applications for Enrollment of Choctaw Newborn
Act of 1905   Volume X

AFFIDAVIT OF MOTHER.

UNITED STATES OF AMERICA, Indian Territory,　}
　　Central　　　　　　DISTRICT.

　　I,　Dora M Moore　, on oath state that I am　25　years of age and a citizen by　intermarriage　, of the　Choctaw　Nation; that I am the lawful wife of David A Moore　, who is a citizen, by　blood　of the　Choctaw　Nation; that a　female　child was born to me on　10　day of　January　, 1905; that said child has been named　Mary Kathleen Moore　, and was living March 4, 1905.

　　　　　　　　　　　　　　　　　Dora M Moore

Witnesses To Mark:
{

　　Subscribed and sworn to before me this　3　day of　April　　, 1905

　　　　　　　　　　　　　　　　　OL Johnson
　　　　　　　　　　　　　　　　　　　Notary Public.

AFFIDAVIT OF ATTENDING PHYSICIAN OR MID-WIFE.

UNITED STATES OF AMERICA, Indian Territory,　}
　　Central　　　　　　DISTRICT.

　　I,　Charles William Ivie　, a　physician　, on oath state that I attended on Mrs.　Dora M Moore　, wife of　David A Moore　on the 10　day of　January　, 1905; that there was born to her on said date a　female　child; that said child was living March 4, 1905, and is said to have been named　Mary Kathleen Moore

　　　　　　　　　　　　　　　　　Charles W Ivie M.D.

Witnesses To Mark:
{

　　Subscribed and sworn to before me this　3　day of　April　　, 1905

　　　　　　　　　　　　　　　　　OL Johnson
　　　　　　　　　　　　　　　　　　　Notary Public.

Applications for Enrollment of Choctaw Newborn
Act of 1905   Volume X

BIRTH AFFIDAVIT.

DEPARTMENT OF THE INTERIOR.
COMMISSION TO THE FIVE CIVILIZED TRIBES.

IN RE APPLICATION FOR ENROLLMENT, as a citizen of the Choctaw Nation, of Clifford Wesley Moore, born on the 22 day of April, 1903

Name of Father: David A Moore   a citizen of the Choctaw Nation.
Name of Mother: Dora M Moore   a citizen *by intermarriage* of the Choctaw Nation.

Postoffice   Bokoshe Ind Ter

AFFIDAVIT OF MOTHER.

UNITED STATES OF AMERICA, Indian Territory,
Central   DISTRICT.

I, Dora M Moore, on oath state that I am 25 years of age and a citizen by intermarriage, of the Choctaw Nation; that I am the lawful wife of David A Moore, who is a citizen, by blood of the Choctaw Nation; that a male child was born to me on 22 day of April, 1903; that said child has been named Clifford Wesley Moore, and was living March 4, 1905.

Dora M Moore

Witnesses To Mark:
{

Subscribed and sworn to before me this 3 day of April, 1905

OL Johnson
Notary Public.

AFFIDAVIT OF ATTENDING PHYSICIAN OR MID-WIFE.

UNITED STATES OF AMERICA, Indian Territory,
Central   DISTRICT.

I, Mary J Rabon, a midwife, on oath state that I attended on Mrs. Dora M Moore, wife of David A Moore on the 22 day of April, 1903; that there was born to her on said date a male child; that said child was living March 4, 1905, and is said to have been named Clifford Wesley Moore

Mary J Rabon

Applications for Enrollment of Choctaw Newborn
Act of 1905   Volume X

Witnesses To Mark:

{

    Subscribed and sworn to before me this 3   day of   April   , 1905

                                           Thomas Rabon
                                                     Notary Public.

Commission Expires December the 3 1906

<u>Choc New Born 643</u>
      Pauline Doshier   b. 9-19-03

                                                                Choctaw N.B. 643.

COPY

                     Muskogee, Indian Territory, April 29, 1905

A. G. Doshier,
    Shadypoint, Indian Territory.

Dear Sir:

    Receipt is hereby acknowledged of the affidavits of Etha M. Doshier (James) and J. J. Hardy to the birth of Pauline Doshier, daughter of A. G. and Etha M. Doshier, September 19, 1903, and the same have been filed with our records in the matter of the enrollment of said child.

                      Respectfully,
                      SIGNED

                                   Tams Bixby
                                   Chairman.

Applications for Enrollment of Choctaw Newborn
Act of 1905   Volume X

COPY

7 N. B. 643

Muskogee, Indian Territory, April 12, 1905.

A. G. Doshier,
    Shadypoint, Indian Territory.

Dear Sir:

    There is inclosed you herewith for execution application for the enrollment of your infant child, Pauline Doshier, born September 19, 1903.

    In having these affidavits executed care should be exercised to see that all names are written in full, as they appear in the body of the affidavit, and in the event that either of the persons signing the affidavit are unable to write, signatures by mark must be attested by two witnesses. Each affidavit must be executed before a Notary Public and the notarial seal and signature of the officer must be attached to each separate affidavit.

                  Respectfully,

                  SIGNED

                  T. B. Needles.
LM 12-1   Commissioner in Charge.

BIRTH AFFIDAVIT.

DEPARTMENT OF THE INTERIOR.
COMMISSION TO THE FIVE CIVILIZED TRIBES.

    IN RE APPLICATION FOR ENROLLMENT, as a citizen of the Choctaw Nation, of Pauline Doshier, born on the 19th day of September, 1903

Name of Father: A. G. Doshier   a citizen of the United States Nation.
Name of Mother: Etha M Doshier (nee James)   a citizen of the Choctaw Nation.

                  Postoffice   Shadypoint I.T.

AFFIDAVIT OF MOTHER.

UNITED STATES OF AMERICA, Indian Territory, }
                           DISTRICT. }

    I, Etha M. Doshier (nee James), on oath state that I am 23 years of age and a citizen by blood, of the Choctaw Nation; that I am the lawful wife of A. G. Doshier, who is a citizen, ~~by~~ ——of the United States Nation; that a

Applications for Enrollment of Choctaw Newborn
Act of 1905 Volume X

female child was born to me on 19th day of September , 1903; that said child has been named Pauline Doshier , and was living March 4, 1905.

Etha M. Doshier (nee) James

Witnesses To Mark:
{

Subscribed and sworn to before me this 15th day of April , 1905

Frank Lewis
Notary Public.

AFFIDAVIT OF ATTENDING PHYSICIAN OR MID-WIFE.

UNITED STATES OF AMERICA, Indian Territory, }
.... DISTRICT.

I,........................., a ...., on oath state that I attended on Mrs. Etha M Doshier (nee James) , wife of A. G. Doshier on the 19th day of September , 190 3; that there was born to her on said date a female child; that said child was living March 4, 190, and is said to have been named Pauline Doshier

J. J. Hardy

Witnesses To Mark:
{

Subscribed and sworn to before me this 15th day of April , 1905

Frank Lewis
Notary Public.

BIRTH AFFIDAVIT.
DEPARTMENT OF THE INTERIOR.
COMMISSION TO THE FIVE CIVILIZED TRIBES.

IN RE APPLICATION FOR ENROLLMENT, as a citizen of the Choctaw Nation, of Pauline Doshier , born on the 19 day of Sept , 1902[sic]

Name of Father: A. G. Doshier   a citizen of the United States Nation.
Name of Mother: Etha M James   a citizen of the Choctaw Nation.

Postoffice Shadypoint I.T.

165

Applications for Enrollment of Choctaw Newborn
Act of 1905 Volume X

AFFIDAVIT OF MOTHER.

UNITED STATES OF AMERICA, Indian Territory, }
Centeral[sic] DISTRICT.

I, Etha M. James , on oath state that I am 22 years of age and a citizen by Blood , of the Choctaw Nation; that I am the lawful wife of A. G. Doshier , who is a citizen, by .... of the United States Nation; that a Female child was born to me on 19th day of September , 1902[sic]; that said child has been named Pauline Doshier , and was living March 4, 1905.

Etha M. Doshier nee James

Witnesses To Mark:
{

Subscribed and sworn to before me this 1st day of April , 1905

Frank Lewis
Notary Public.

AFFIDAVIT OF ATTENDING PHYSICIAN OR MID-WIFE.

UNITED STATES OF AMERICA, Indian Territory, }
Centeral[sic] DISTRICT.

I, J.J. Hardy , a Physician , on oath state that I attended on Mrs. A. G. Doshier , wife of A. G. Doshier on the 19th day of September , 1902; that there was born to her on said date a Female child; that said child was living March 4, 190, and is said to have been named Pauline Doshier

J. J. Hardy M.D.

Witnesses To Mark:
{

Subscribed and sworn to before me this 1st day of April , 1905

Frank Lewis
Notary Public.

Applications for Enrollment of Choctaw Newborn
Act of 1905   Volume X

AFFIDAVIT OF ATTENDING PHYSICIAN OR MIDWIFE

UNITED STATES OF AMERICA
INDIAN TERRITORY
Centeral[sic]   DISTRICT

I,   J.J. Hardy   a   Physician on oath state that I attended on Mrs.   Etha M Doshier   wife of   A.G. Doshier on the   19   day of   September   , 190 3 , that there was born to her on said date a Female   child, that said child is now living, and is said to have been named   Pauline Doshier

J.J. Hardy   𝑚.𝒟.

Subscribed and sworn to before me this, the   28   day of Jan   190 5

WITNESSETH: Frank Lewis   Notary Public.
Must be two witnesses who are citizens
{ Noel Folsom
Daniel Terrill

We hereby certify that we are well acquainted with   J.J. Hardy a   Physician   and know   him   to be reputable and of good standing in the community.

Noel Folsom

Daniel Terrill   Frank Lewis N.P.

NEW-BORN AFFIDAVIT.

Number............

...Choctaw Enrolling Commission...

IN THE MATTER OF THE APPLICATION FOR ENROLLMENT, as a citizen of the Choctaw   Nation, of   Pauline Doshier

born on the   19   day of   September   190 3

Name of father   A.G. Doshier   a citizen of   United States
Nation final enrollment No...............   (Nee Etha M James)
Name of mother   Etha M Doshier   a citizen of   Choctaw
Nation final enrollment No. 8073

Postoffice   Shadypoint, I.T.

Applications for Enrollment of Choctaw Newborn
Act of 1905 Volume X

AFFIDAVIT OF MOTHER.

UNITED STATES OF AMERICA
INDIAN TERRITORY
Centeral   DISTRICT

I   Etha M Doshier   , on oath state that I am 22 years of age and a citizen by Blood of the Choctaw Nation, and as such have been placed upon the final roll of the Choctaw Nation, by the Honorable Secretary of the Interior my final enrollment number being   8073 ; that I am the lawful wife of   A.G. Doshier   , who is a citizen of the   United States   xxxxxxx, and as such has been placed upon the final roll of said Nation by the Honorable Secretary of the Interior, his final enrollment number being .... and that a   Female   child was born to me on the   19th   day of   September   190 3; that said child has been named   Pauline Doshier   , and is now living.

Etha M. Doshier

Witnesseth.

Must be two Witnesses who are Citizens.   } Noel Folsom
Daniel Terrill

Subscribed and sworn to before me this 28 day of Jan 190 5

Frank Lewis
Notary Public.

My commission expires:
Seal

Choc New Born 644
   Fred Leonard Atkinson b. 9-26-04

BIRTH AFFIDAVIT.

DEPARTMENT OF THE INTERIOR.
COMMISSION TO THE FIVE CIVILIZED TRIBES.

IN RE APPLICATION FOR ENROLLMENT, as a citizen of the   Choctaw   Nation, of Fred Leonard Atkinson   , born on the 26 day of Sept , 1904

Name of Father: John H Atkinson   a citizen of the Choctaw Nation.
Name of Mother: Mary Susan Atkinson   a citizen of the Choctaw Nation.

Postoffice   Durant Ind Ter

Applications for Enrollment of Choctaw Newborn
Act of 1905   Volume X

AFFIDAVIT OF MOTHER.

UNITED STATES OF AMERICA, Indian Territory, }
Central   DISTRICT.

I, Mary Susan Atkinson, on oath state that I am 32 years of age and a citizen by blood, of the Choctaw Nation; that I am the lawful wife of John H Atkinson, who is a citizen, by intermarriage of the Choctaw Nation; that a male child was born to me on 26 day of September, 1904; that said child has been named Fred Leonard Atkinson, and was living March 4, 1905.

Mary S Atkinson

Witnesses To Mark:
{

Subscribed and sworn to before me this 1st day of April, 1905

W.L. Bower
My commission expires 14 *day of* May *1*906   Notary Public.

AFFIDAVIT OF ATTENDING PHYSICIAN OR MID-WIFE.

UNITED STATES OF AMERICA, Indian Territory, }
Central   DISTRICT.

I, John J Stephens, a Physician, on oath state that I attended on Mrs. Mary S Atkinson, wife of John H Atkinson on the 26 day of Sept, 1904; that there was born to her on said date a male child; that said child was living March 4, 1905, and is said to have been named Fred Leonard Atkinson

John J Stephens

Witnesses To Mark:
{

Subscribed and sworn to before me this 1st day of April, 1905

W.L. Bower
My commission expires 14 *day of* May *1*906   Notary Public.

Applications for Enrollment of Choctaw Newborn
Act of 1905 Volume X

Choctaw 3536

Muskogee, Indian Territory, April 8, 1905.

John H. Atkinson,
    Durant, Indian Territory.

Dear Sir:

    Receipt is hereby acknowledged of the affidavits of Mary S. Atkinson and John J. Stephens to the birth of Fred Leonard Atkinson, son of John H. Atkinson and Mary S. Atkinson, September 26, 1904, and the same have been filed with our records as an application for the enrollment of said child.

        Respectfully,

            Commissioner in Charge.

<u>Choc New Born 645</u>
    Green Ott b. 3-25-04

Choctaw 3975.

Muskogee, Indian Territory, April 8, 1905.

John Ott,
    Coalgate, Indian Territory.

Dear Sir:

    Receipt is hereby acknowledged of the affidavits of Fannie Ott and Bicy Ott to the birth of Green Ott, son of John and Fannie Ott, March 25, 1904, and the same have been filed with our records as an application for the enrollment of said child.

        Respectfully,

            Commissioner in Charge.

Applications for Enrollment of Choctaw Newborn
Act of 1905 Volume X

NEW-BORN AFFIDAVIT.

Number ....

...Choctaw Enrolling Commission...

IN THE MATTER OF THE APPLICATION FOR ENROLLMENT, as a citizen of the Choctaw Nation, of Green Ott

born on the 25th day of ___March___ 190 4

Name of father   John Ott   a citizen of   Choctaw
Nation final enrollment No.   11128
Name of mother   Fannie Ott   a citizen of   Choctaw
Nation final enrollment No.   11129

Postoffice   Coalgate, I.T.

AFFIDAVIT OF MOTHER.

UNITED STATES OF AMERICA
INDIAN TERRITORY
  Central   DISTRICT

I   Fannie Ott   , on oath state that I am 29 years of age and a citizen by blood of the Choctaw Nation, and as such have been placed upon the final roll of the Choctaw Nation, by the Honorable Secretary of the Interior my final enrollment number being 11129 ; that I am the lawful wife of John Ott , who is a citizen of the Choctaw Nation, and as such has been placed upon the final roll of said Nation by the Honorable Secretary of the Interior, his final enrollment number being 11128 and that a male child was born to me on the 25th day of March 190 4; that said child has been named Green Ott , and is now living.

                                                          her
                                                  Fannie x Ott
Witnesseth.   mark
  Must be two   } Charley Colbert
  Witnesses who
  are Citizens.   Samuel A. Ott

Subscribed and sworn to before me this   11th   day of   Feb   190 5

                                J R Wood
                                        Notary Public.
My commission expires:
  Feb 23, 1907

Applications for Enrollment of Choctaw Newborn
Act of 1905   Volume X

Affidavit of Attending Physician or Midwife

UNITED STATES OF AMERICA,
   INDIAN TERRITORY,
Central   DISTRICT

I, Bicy Ott a midwife on oath state that I attended on Mrs. Fannie Ott wife of John Ott on the 25th day of March, 190 4, that there was born to her on said date a male child, that said child is now living, and is said to have been named Green Ott.

                          her
                       Bicy x Ott   M.D.
                        mark

Subscribed and sworn to before me this the 11th day of February 1905

                J R Wood
                          Notary Public.

WITNESSETH:
Must be two witnesses who are citizens and know the child. { Charley Colbert
Samuel A Ott

We hereby certify that we are well acquainted with Bicy Ott a midwife and know her to be reputable and of good standing in the community.

      Must be two citizen witnesses. { Charley Colbert
Samuel A Ott

BIRTH AFFIDAVIT.

DEPARTMENT OF THE INTERIOR.
COMMISSION TO THE FIVE CIVILIZED TRIBES.

IN RE APPLICATION FOR ENROLLMENT, as a citizen of the Choctaw Nation, of Green Ott, born on the 25th day of March, 1904

Name of Father: John Ott   a citizen of the Choctaw Nation.
Name of Mother: Fannie Ott   a citizen of the Choctaw Nation.

                Postoffice   Coalgate, I.T.

Applications for Enrollment of Choctaw Newborn
Act of 1905   Volume X

AFFIDAVIT OF MOTHER.

UNITED STATES OF AMERICA, Indian Territory, }
    Central   DISTRICT.

    I, Fannie Ott, on oath state that I am thirty years of age and a citizen by blood, of the Choctaw Nation; that I am the lawful wife of John Ott, who is a citizen, by blood of the Choctaw Nation; that a male child was born to me on 25th day of March, 1904; that said child has been named Green Ott, and was living March 4, 1905.

                                      her
                               Fannie x Ott
Witnesses To Mark: mark
  { Frank Williams
    Edward James

    Subscribed and sworn to before me this first day of April, 1905

                              JR Wood
                                  Notary Public.

AFFIDAVIT OF ATTENDING PHYSICIAN OR MID-WIFE.

UNITED STATES OF AMERICA, Indian Territory, }
    Central   DISTRICT.

    I, Bicy Ott, a mid-wife, on oath state that I attended on Mrs. Fannie Ott, wife of John Ott on the 25th day of March, 1904; that there was born to her on said date a male child; that said child was living March 4, 1905, and is said to have been named Green Ott

                                      her
                               Bicy x Ott
Witnesses To Mark: mark
  { Frank Williams
    Edward James

    Subscribed and sworn to before me this first day of April, 1905

                              JR Wood
                                  Notary Public.

Applications for Enrollment of Choctaw Newborn
Act of 1905   Volume X

Choc New Born 646
    Marion Young   b. 6-7-03

Choctaw 3026.

Muskogee, Indian Territory, April 8, 1905.

Jeff Young,
    Russellville, Indian Territory.

Dear Sir:

    Receipt is hereby acknowledged of the affidavits of Catherine Young and J. M. Turner to the birth of Marion Young, son of Jeff and Catherine Young, June 7, 1903, and the same have been filed with our records as an application for the enrollment of said child.

        Respectfully,

        Commissioner in Charge.

BIRTH AFFIDAVIT.
DEPARTMENT OF THE INTERIOR.
COMMISSION TO THE FIVE CIVILIZED TRIBES.

IN RE APPLICATION FOR ENROLLMENT, as a citizen of the   Choctaw   Nation, of Marion Young   , born on the 7th.   day of June   , 1903

Name of Father: Jeff Young   a citizen of the   Choctaw   Nation.
Name of Mother: Catherine Young   a citizen of the   Choctaw   Nation.

        Postoffice   Russellville, I.T.

AFFIDAVIT OF MOTHER.

UNITED STATES OF AMERICA, Indian Territory,
    Western   **DISTRICT.**

    I, Catherine Young   , on oath state that I am   42   years of age and a citizen by   intermarriage   , of the   Choctaw   Nation; that I am the lawful wife of Jeff Young   , who is a citizen, by blood   of the   Choctaw   Nation; that a male   child was born to me on   7th   day of   June   , 1903; that said child has been named   Marion Young   , and was living March 4, 1905.

Applications for Enrollment of Choctaw Newborn
Act of 1905   Volume X

                                            her
                                 Catherine x Young

Witnesses To Mark: mark
{ WB Eatherly
  (Name Illegible)

Subscribed and sworn to before me this 27th. day of March , 1905

                                    Guy A. Curry
                                    Notary Public.

AFFIDAVIT OF ATTENDING PHYSICIAN OR MID-WIFE.

UNITED STATES OF AMERICA, Indian Territory, }
    Western   DISTRICT. }

    I, James M. Turner , a physician , on oath state that I attended on Mrs. Catherine Young , wife of Jeff Young on the 7th day of June , 1903; that there was born to her on said date a male child; that said child was living March 4, 1905, and is said to have been named Marion Young

                                    James M Turner MD

Witnesses To Mark:
{

Subscribed and sworn to before me this 1st day of April , 1905

                                    Guy A. Curry
                                    Notary Public.

<u>Choc New Born 647</u>
    Eliza Lewis   b. 4-3-03

Applications for Enrollment of Choctaw Newborn
Act of 1905   Volume X

7-NB-647

Muskogee, Indian Territory, August 7, 1905.

Johnson Lewis
   Antlers, Indian Territory.

Dear Sir:

   Receipt is hereby acknowledged of the affidavits of Johnson Lewis to the birth of Eliza Lewis, daughter of Johnson and Mary Lewis, April 3, 1903, and the same has been filed with the records of this office in the matter of the enrollment of said child.

   Respectfully,

   Commissioner.

Choctaw 1816.

Muskogee, Indian Territory, April 8, 1905.

Johnson Lewis,
   Antlers, Indian Territory.

Dear Sir:

   Receipt is hereby acknowledged of the affidavits of Emma Gibson and Melissie Gibson to the birth of Eliza Lewis, daughter of Johnson and Mary Lewis, April 3, 1903, and the same have been filed with our records as an application for the enrollment of said child.

   Respectfully,

   Commissioner in Charge.

Applications for Enrollment of Choctaw Newborn
Act of 1905   Volume X

7-NB-647.

Muskogee, Indian Territory, May 27, 1905.

Johnson Lewis,
    Antlers, Indian Territory.

Dear Sir:

    Referring to the application for the enrollment of your infant child, Eliza Lewis, born April 3, 1903, it is noted from the affidavits heretofore filed in this office that Mary Lewis, the applicant's mother, is dead.

    In the event the affidavits of <u>two</u> disinterested persons, who have actual knowledge of the facts that the child was born, the date of her birth; that she was living on March 4, 1905, and that Mary Lewis was her mother, are required.

    The affidavit of Melissie Gibson to these facts has been filed in this office. It will, therefore, be necessary that you secure a similar affidavit from another person.

Respectfully,

VR 27-2.   Chairman.

7-NB-647

Muskogee, Indian Territory, July 29, 1905.

Johnson Lewis,
    Antlers, Indian Territory.

Dear Sir:

    Referring to the application for the enrollment of your infant child, Eliza Lewis, born April 3, 1903.

    It is noted from the affidavits of Emma Gibson and Melissie Gibson, witnesses, heretofore filed in this office, that Mary Lewis, the applicant's mother, is dead.

    In this event it is also necessary for the enrollment of the child that your affidavit to the fact that the child was born, the date of her birth, that she was living March 4, 1905, and that her mother was Mary Lewis, and that her said mother is dead, and the date of her death.

    There is inclosed herewith, affidavit to be executed by you which has been prepared to cover the case. Please have same rpoperly[sic] executed and return to this

Applications for Enrollment of Choctaw Newborn
Act of 1905 Volume X

office immediately, as no further action can be taken relative to the enrollment of your said child until the evidence requested is supplied.

Respectfully,

LM 2/29

Commissioner.

Arnote & Davenport,
.. Lawyers ..

Antlers, J.T.

Central District
Indian Territory,

I, Melisis[sic] Gibson, do solemnly swear that I was present when a female child was born to Johnson Lewis, and his wife Mary Lewis, that said child was born on the 3rd day of April, 1903, and is said to have been named Eliza Lewis, and that said child is now living and that Mary Lewis, the mother of said child died on the _15_ of June 1904, that Johnson Lewis and his wife Mary Lewis are both Indians, Choctaws by Blood, and I was present and know that Mary Lewis is the mother of Eliza Lewis.

Witness to Mark.

Melissie x Gibson
her   mark

Edward Pisachubbee
D.W. Hoover

Subscribed and sworn to before me this the 1st day of April, 1905.

A.J. Arnote
Notary Public.

My commission expires May 16" 1907.

BIRTH AFFIDAVIT.

DEPARTMENT OF THE INTERIOR.
COMMISSION TO THE FIVE CIVILIZED TRIBES.

IN RE APPLICATION FOR ENROLLMENT, as a citizen of the Choctaw Nation, of Eliza Lewis, born on the 3" day of April, 1903.

Name of Father: Johnson Lewis   a citizen of the Choctaw Nation.
Name of Mother: Mary Lewis   a citizen of the Choctaw Nation.

Postoffice   Antlers I.T.

Applications for Enrollment of Choctaw Newborn
Act of 1905 Volume X

AFFIDAVIT OF ATTENDING PHYSICIAN OR MID-WIFE.

UNITED STATES OF AMERICA, Indian Territory,
Central DISTRICT.

I, Emma Gibson , a midwife , on oath state that I attended on Mrs. Mary Lewis , wife of Johnson Lewis on the 3" day of April , 1903; that there was born to her on said date a female child; that said child was living March 4, 1905, and is said to have been named Eliza Lewis

                   her
               Emma x Gibson
Witnesses To Mark: mark
  { Edward Pisachubbee
     D.W. Hoover

Subscribed and sworn to before me this 1st day of April , 1905

         A.J. Arnote
           Notary Public.

---

7 - nB - 647

BIRTH AFFIDAVIT.

DEPARTMENT OF THE INTERIOR.
COMMISSION TO THE FIVE CIVILIZED TRIBES.

IN RE APPLICATION FOR ENROLLMENT, as a citizen of the Choctaw Nation, of Eliza Lewis , born on the 3rd day of April , 1903

Name of Father: Johnson Lewis   a citizen of the Choctaw Nation.
Name of Mother: Mary Lewis   a citizen of the Choctaw Nation.

        Postoffice   Antlers Ind Ter

AFFIDAVIT OF ~~MOTHER.~~ *father*

UNITED STATES OF AMERICA, Indian Territory,
Central DISTRICT.

I, Johnson Lewis , on oath state that I am............years of age and a citizen by blood , of the Choctaw Nation; that I ~~am~~ *was* the lawful *husband* ~~wife~~ of Mary Lewis, deceased , who is ~~was~~ a citizen, by blood of the Choctaw Nation; that a female child was born to ~~me~~ *my said wife* on 3rd day of April ,

Applications for Enrollment of Choctaw Newborn
Act of 1905   Volume X

1903; that said child has been named   Eliza Lewis   , and was living March 4, 1905; that my said wife Mary Lewis died on June 15, 1904.

Johnson Lewis

Witnesses To Mark:
{

Subscribed and sworn to before me this 1st day of   Aug   , 1905

Victor M. Locke JR
Notary Public.

Choc New Born 648
    Birdie Harrison   b. 2-1-03
    Rhoda Harrison   b. 8-11-04

(The affidavit below typed as given.)

United States of America,	Affidavit, in matter of inrole-
Indian Territory,	ment of Rhoda Harrison, infant
Central District,	child of Lyman & Lorena Harrison. ch

    I, Thomas McDaniel   on oath state that I am   37   years of age, that my post-office is Talihina, I. T. That I am a citizen of the Choctaw Nation by blood. That I know Lyman Harrison who is a citizen of the Choctaw Nation by blood. I also know his wife Lorena Harrison, who is a citizen of the Choctaw Nation by Intermarriage. I know that on the 11th day of August 1904 there was born to Lorena Harrison, a female chile, who is said to have been named Rhoda Harrison. That said chile was living on the 4th day of March 1905 and is still living.
    I am no kin to either Lyman Harrison or to any of the parties above mentioned. I am a disinterested party.

Thomas McDaniel

Witnesses.
Alex McIntosh
Jno J Thomas

Subscribed and sworn to before me this the 3rd day of June 1905.

My commission expires Feb. 4, 1908
Commission from U. S. Court, So. McAlester, I.T.
MY OFFICE TALIHINA, I. T.

F.B. Lunsford
Notary Public.

Applications for Enrollment of Choctaw Newborn
Act of 1905   Volume X

(The affidavit below typed as given.)

United States of America,
Indian Territory,
Central District,

Affidavit, in matter of inrole-
ment of Rhoda Harrison, infant
child of Lyman & Lorena Harrison.
ch

    I, Wallace Beans on oath state that I am 36 years of age, that my post-office is Talihina, I. T. That I am a citizen of the Choctaw Nation by blood. That I know Lyman Harrison who is a citizen of the Choctaw Nation by blood. I also know his wife Lorena Harrison, who is a citizen of the Choctaw Nation by Intermarriage. I know that on the 11th day of August 1904 there was born to Lorena Harrison, a female chile, who is said to have been named Rhoda Harrison. That said chile was living on the 4th day of March 1905 and is still living.

    I am no kin to either Lyman Harrison or to any of the parties above mentioned. I am a disinterested party.

                                                     Wallace Beames

Witnesses.
Alex McIntosh
Jno J Thomas

Subscribed and sworn to before me this the 3rd day of June 1905.

My commission expires Feb. 4, 1908
Commission from U. S. Court, So. McAlester, I.T.
MY OFFICE TALIHINA, I. T.

F.B. Lunsford
Notary Public.

BIRTH AFFIDAVIT.

DEPARTMENT OF THE INTERIOR.
COMMISSION TO THE FIVE CIVILIZED TRIBES.

    IN RE APPLICATION FOR ENROLLMENT, as a citizen of the Choctaw Nation, of Rhoda Harrison, born on the 11 day of August, 1904

Name of Father: Lyman Harrison   a citizen of the Choctaw Nation.
Name of Mother: Lorena Harrison   a citizen of the Choctaw Nation.

                            Postoffice   Talihina I.T.

Applications for Enrollment of Choctaw Newborn
Act of 1905   Volume X

AFFIDAVIT OF MOTHER.

UNITED STATES OF AMERICA, Indian Territory, }
Central   DISTRICT.

I, Lorena Harrison, on oath state that I am about 26 years of age and a citizen by Intermarriage, of the Choctaw Nation; that I am the lawful wife of Lyman Harrison, who is a citizen, by Blood of the Choctaw Nation; that a Female child was born to me on 11 day of August, 1904; that said child has been named Rhoda Harrison, and was living March 4, 1905.

                            her
                      Lorena x Harrison

Witnesses To Mark: mark
{ Wallace Beames
{ D. Thomas

Subscribed and sworn to before me this 1 day of April, 1905

                      Sam T. Roberts Jr
                      Notary Public.

AFFIDAVIT OF ATTENDING PHYSICIAN OR MID-WIFE.

UNITED STATES OF AMERICA, Indian Territory, }
Central   DISTRICT.

I, Lyman Harrison, a ———, on oath state that I attended on Mrs. Lorena Harrison, wife of my wife on the 11 day of August, 1905[sic]; that there was born to her on said date a Female child; that said child was living March 4, 1905, and is said to have been named Rhoda Harrison

                    Lyman Harrison

Witnesses To Mark:
{

Subscribed and sworn to before me this 1 day of April, 1905

                    Sam T. Roberts Jr
                    Notary Public.

Applications for Enrollment of Choctaw Newborn
Act of 1905   Volume X

(The affidavit below typed as given.)

United States of America,
Indian Territory,
Central District.

Affidavit, in matter of the in-
rolement of Birdie Harrison &
~~Rhoda Harrison~~, infant children
of Lyman Harrison, and his wife
Lorena Harrison.

I, Thomas McDaniel on oath state that I am 37 years of age, that my post-office is Talihina, Indian Territory, that I am a Choctaw Citizen by blood. That I am acquainted with Lyman Harrison, who is a Choctaw Citizen by blood. That I am also acquainted with his wife Lorena Harrison, who is a citizen of the Choctaw Nation by Intermarriage   I know that on or about February 1st 1903 there was born to Lorena Harrison a female chile, which was said to be named Birdie Harrison, and I know that the said child was living on March 4th 1905. and that she is still living.

I furthe state that I am not kin to any of the parties above ment mentioned, and am a disinterested party.

Thomas McDaniel

Witnesses.
Alex McIntosh
Jno J Thomas

Subscribed and sworn to before me this the 3rd day of June 1905.

My commission expires Feb. 4, 1908
Commission from U. S. Court, So. McAlester, I.T.
MY OFFICE TALIHINA, I. T.

F.B. Lunsford
Notary Public.

BIRTH AFFIDAVIT.

DEPARTMENT OF THE INTERIOR.
COMMISSION TO THE FIVE CIVILIZED TRIBES.

IN RE APPLICATION FOR ENROLLMENT, as a citizen of the   Choctaw   Nation, of Birdie Harrison   , born on the 1 day of Feby , 1903

Name of Father: Lyman Harrison   a citizen of the   Choctaw   Nation.
Name of Mother: Lorena Harrison   a citizen of the   Choctaw   Nation.

Postoffice   Talihina I.T.

Applications for Enrollment of Choctaw Newborn
Act of 1905   Volume X

AFFIDAVIT OF MOTHER.

UNITED STATES OF AMERICA, Indian Territory, }
   Central   DISTRICT. }

    I, Lorena Harrison, on oath state that I am about 26 yrs years of age and a citizen by Intermarriage, of the Choctaw Nation; that I am the lawful wife of Lyman Harrison, who is a citizen, by Blood of the Choctaw Nation; that a Female child was born to me on 1st day of February, 1903; that said child has been named Birdie Harrison, and was living March 4, 1905.

                                        her
                              Lorena x Harrison
Witnesses To Mark: mark
{ Wallace Beames
{ D. Thomas

    Subscribed and sworn to before me this 1 day of April, 1905

                              Sam T. Roberts Jr
                              Notary Public.

AFFIDAVIT OF ATTENDING PHYSICIAN OR MID-WIFE.

UNITED STATES OF AMERICA, Indian Territory, }
   Central   DISTRICT. }

    I, Lyman Harrison, a ———, on oath state that I attended on Mrs. Lorena Harrison, wife of my wife on the 1st day of February, 1903; that there was born to her on said date a Female child; that said child was living March 4, 1905, and is said to have been named Birdie Harrison

                              Lyman Harrison
Witnesses To Mark:
{

    Subscribed and sworn to before me this 1 day of April, 1905

                              Sam T. Roberts Jr
                              Notary Public.

Applications for Enrollment of Choctaw Newborn
Act of 1905   Volume X

(The affidavit below typed as given.)

United States of America,	Affidavit, in matter of the in-
Indian Territory,	rolement of Birdie Harrison &
Central District.	~~Rhoda Harrison~~, infant children of Lyman Harrison, and his wife Lorena Harrison.

I, Wallace Beames on oath state that I am 36 years of age, that my post-office is Talihina, Indian Territory, that I am a Choctaw Citizen by blood. That I am acquainted with Lyman Harrison, who is a Choctaw Citizen by blood. That I am also acquainted with his wife Lorena Harrison, who is a citizen of the Choctaw Nation by Intermarriage I know that on or about February 1st 1903 there was born to Lorena Harrison a female chile, which was said to be named Birdie Harrison, and I know that the said child was living on March 4th 1905. and that she is still living.

I furthe state that I am not kin to any of the parties above ment mentioned, and am a disinterested party.

Wallace Beames

Witnesses.
Alex McIntosh
Jno J Thomas

Subscribed and sworn to before me this the 3rd day of June 1905.

My commission expires Feb. 4, 1908
Commission from U. S. Court, So. McAlester, I.T.
MY OFFICE TALIHINA, I. T.

F.B. Lunsford
Notary Public.

Choctaw 2115.

Muskogee, Indian Territory, April 8, 1905.

Lyman Harrison,
    Talihina, Indian Territory.

Dear Sir:

Receipt is hereby acknowledged of the affidavits of Lorena Harrison and Lyman Harrison to the birth of Birdie Harrison and Rhoda Harrison, children of Lyman and Lorena Harrison, February 1, 1903, and August 11, 1904, respectively, and the same have been filed with our records as applications for the enrollment of the above named children.

Respectfully,

Commissioner in Charge.

Applications for Enrollment of Choctaw Newborn
Act of 1905   Volume X

7 NB 648

Muskogee, Indian Territory, June 8, 1905.

Lymon[sic] Harrison,
    Talihina, Indian Territory.

Dear Sir:

    Receipt is hereby acknowledged of your letter of June 3, 1905, enclosing affidavits of Thomas McDaniel and Wallace Beames to the birth of Birdie Harrison, daughter of Lyman and Lorena Harrison, February 1, 1903, and the same have been filed in the matter of the enrollment of said child.

    Respectfully,

Chairman.

Choc New Born 649
    Maudie Myrtie Beams   b. 11-21-02

NEW-BORN AFFIDAVIT.

    Number..................

Choctaw Enrolling Commission.

    IN THE MATTER OF THE APPLICATION FOR ENROLLMENT, as a citizen of the Choctaw   Nation, of   Maudie Myrtle Beams

born on the 21   day of   November   190 2

Name of father   Joseph Beams   a citizen of   Choctaw Nation
Nation final enrollment No   10891
Name of mother   Minnie Beams   a citizen of   Choctaw
Nation final enrollment No   352

    Postoffice   Bokchito I.T.

Applications for Enrollment of Choctaw Newborn
Act of 1905 Volume X

AFFIDAVIT OF MOTHER.

UNITED STATES OF AMERICA,
INDIAN TERRITORY,
Central   DISTRICT

I   Minnie Beams   on oath state that I am 25 years of age and a citizen by   Marriage   of the Choctaw   Nation, and as such have been placed upon the final roll of the   Choctaw   Nation, by the Honorable Secretary of the Interior my final enrollment number being   352   ; that I am the lawful wife of   Joseph Beams   , who is a citizen of the   Choctaw Nation Nation, and as such has been placed upon the final roll of said Nation by the Honorable Secretary of the Interior, his final enrollment number being   10891   and that a   Female child was born to me on the   21   day of   November   190 2 ; that said child has been named   Maudie Myrtle   , and is now living.

WITNESSETH: Minnie Beams
Must be two   John A.M. Impson
Witnesses who
are Citizens.   Mrs. A. Impson

Subscribed and sworn to before me this   17   day of   January   190 5

(Name Illegible)
Notary Public.

My commission expires   2/19/05

BIRTH AFFIDAVIT.

DEPARTMENT OF THE INTERIOR.
COMMISSION TO THE FIVE CIVILIZED TRIBES.

IN RE APPLICATION FOR ENROLLMENT, as a citizen of the   Choctaw   Nation, of Maudie Myrtie Beames   , born on the 21   day of   November   , 1902

Name of Father: Josiah[sic] Beames   a citizen of the   Choctaw   Nation.
Name of Mother: Minnie Beams   a citizen of the   Choctaw   Nation.

Postoffice   Bokchito I.T.

AFFIDAVIT OF MOTHER.

UNITED STATES OF AMERICA, Indian Territory,
Central   DISTRICT.

I, Minnie Beams   , on oath state that I am   27   years of age and a citizen by   Marriage   , of the   Choctaw   Nation; that I am the lawful wife of   Josiah Beames   , who is a citizen, by Blood   of the   Choctaw   Nation; that a

Applications for Enrollment of Choctaw Newborn
Act of 1905 Volume X

Female child was born to me on 21 day of November , 1902; that said child has been named Maudie Myrtie Beames , and was living March 4, 1905.

                                                Minnie Beames

Witnesses To Mark:
{

Subscribed and sworn to before me this first day of April , 1905

                                        (Name Illegible)
                                                Notary Public.

AFFIDAVIT OF ATTENDING PHYSICIAN OR MID-WIFE.

UNITED STATES OF AMERICA, Indian Territory, }
    Central   DISTRICT.

I, Mary Sauls , a Midwife , on oath state that I attended on Mrs. Minnie Beames , wife of Josiah Beams[sic] on the 21 day of November , 1902; that there was born to her on said date a Female child; that said child was living March 4, 1905, and is said to have been named Maudie Myrtie Beames
                                              her
                                      Mary x Sauls

Witnesses To Mark: mark
{ John A M Impson
  J B Lloyd

Subscribed and sworn to before me this first day of April , 1905

                                        (Name Illegible)
                                              Notary Public.

AFFIDAVIT OF ATTENDING PHYSICIAN OR MIDWIFE

UNITED STATES OF AMERICA }
INDIAN TERRITORY
    Central   DISTRICT

I, L T Jackson a Physician on oath state that I attended on Mrs. Minnie Beams wife of Josiah Beams on the 21 day of November , 190 2 , that there was born to her on said date a Female child, that said child is now living, and is said to have been named Maudie Myrtle Beames[sic]

                                   L T Jackson   M.D.

Applications for Enrollment of Choctaw Newborn
Act of 1905 Volume X

Subscribed and sworn to before me this, the 19 day of   January   190 5

(Name Illegible)
Notary Public.

WITNESSETH:

Must be two witnesses who are citizens and know the child.   { John A M Impson
D J Coelman[sic]

We hereby certify that we are well acquainted with   L T Jackson a Physician   and know   him   to be reputable and of good standing in the community.

{ John A M Impson
D J Coelman[sic]

Choctaw 3862.

Muskogee, Indian Territory, April 8, 1905.

Josiah Beames,
     Bokchito, Indian Territory.

Dear Sir:

Receipt is hereby acknowledged of the affidavits of Minnie Beames and Mary Saul to the birth of Maudie Myrtie Beames, daughter of Josiah and Minnie Beames, November 21, 1902, and the same have been filed with our records as an application for the enrollment of said child.

Respectfully,

Commissioner in Charge.

DR. L. T. JACKSON & ~~CO.~~
~~DRUGGIST~~ S

Bokchito, I. T.   Nov 28th   *190* 2

This is to certify that I   L.T. Jackson   am attending physician in the case of Minnie E. Beames and do hereby certify that she is physically unable to leave her domicile - having given birth to a child Friday Nov. 21st 1902

L.T. Jackson M.D.

Applications for Enrollment of Choctaw Newborn
Act of 1905 Volume X

Sworn to and subscribed before me this 28th day of Nov - 1902

                       R.F. Moore
                             Notary Public
                             Central Cist
                             Indian Ter

<u>Choc New Born 650</u>
       Noa Lewis b. 5-21-04

                                                  Choctaw 3257.

                       Muskogee, Indian Territory, April 8, 1905.

George Lewis,
     Citra, Indian Territory.

Dear Sir:

     Receipt is hereby acknowledged of the affidavits of Nancy Lewis and Susan Frazier to the birth of Noa Lewis, son of George and Nancy Lewis, May 21, 1904, and the same have been filed with our records as an application for the enrollment of said child.

                         Respectfully,

                                       Commissioner in Charge.

BIRTH AFFIDAVIT.

                           DEPARTMENT OF THE INTERIOR.
             COMMISSION TO THE FIVE CIVILIZED TRIBES.

     IN RE APPLICATION FOR ENROLLMENT, as a citizen of the   Choctaw   Nation, of
Noa Lewis   , born on the 21   day of   May   , 1904

Name of Father: George Lewis   a citizen of the   Choctaw   Nation.
Name of Mother: Nancy Lewis   a citizen of the   Choctaw   Nation.

                       Postoffice   Citra I.T.

Applications for Enrollment of Choctaw Newborn
Act of 1905   Volume X

AFFIDAVIT OF MOTHER.

UNITED STATES OF AMERICA, Indian Territory, }
Central   DISTRICT.

I, Nancy Lewis, on oath state that I am 37 years of age and a citizen by Blood, of the Choctaw Nation; that I am the lawful wife of George Lewis, who is a citizen, by Blood of the Choctaw Nation; that a Male child was born to me on 21 day of May, 1904; that said child has been named Noa Lewis, and was living March 4, 1905.

                                        her
                                Nancy x Lewis
Witnesses To Mark: mark
{ Andy Grazier
{ m ross[sic]

Subscribed and sworn to before me this 31 day of March, 1905

                                W.H. Hudlow
                                Notary Public.

AFFIDAVIT OF ATTENDING PHYSICIAN OR MID-WIFE.

UNITED STATES OF AMERICA, Indian Territory, }
                             DISTRICT.

I, Susan Frazier, a ...., on oath state that I attended on Mrs. Nancy Lewis, wife of George Lewis on the 21 day of May, 1904; that there was born to her on said date a Male child; that said child was living March 4, 1905, and is said to have been named Noa Lewis

                                her
                              Susan x Frazier
Witnesses To Mark: mark
{ Andy Frazier
{ m ross

Subscribed and sworn to before me this 31 day of March, 1905

                                W.H. Hudlow
                                Notary Public.

my com exp March 14 1907

Applications for Enrollment of Choctaw Newborn
Act of 1905   Volume X

Choc New Born 651
  Dolly Elizabeth James   b. 4-24-03

BIRTH AFFIDAVIT.

DEPARTMENT OF THE INTERIOR.
COMMISSION TO THE FIVE CIVILIZED TRIBES.

  IN RE APPLICATION FOR ENROLLMENT, as a citizen of the   Choctaw   Nation, of Dolly Elizabeth James , born on the 24th day of April , 1903

Name of Father: William Adolphus James a citizen of the Choctaw   Nation.
Name of Mother: Katie James   a citizen of the Choctaw   Nation.

        Postoffice Calvin, I.T.

AFFIDAVIT OF MOTHER.

UNITED STATES OF AMERICA, Indian Territory,
  Central   **DISTRICT.**

  I, Katie James , on oath state that I am 29 years of age and a citizen by blood , of the Choctaw Nation; that I am the lawful wife of William Adolphus James , who is a citizen, by blood of the Choctaw Nation; that a female child was born to me on 24th day of April , 1903; that said child has been named Dolly Elizabeth James , and was living March 4, 1905.

           Katie James

Witnesses To Mark:
 { N. J. Johnson M.D.

  Subscribed and sworn to before me this 22 day of March , 1905

        Wirt Franklin
         Notary Public.

AFFIDAVIT OF ATTENDING PHYSICIAN OR MID-WIFE.

UNITED STATES OF AMERICA, Indian Territory,
  Central   **DISTRICT.**

  I,..., a physician , on oath state that I attended on Mrs. Katie James , wife of William Adolphus James on the 24th day of

Applications for Enrollment of Choctaw Newborn
Act of 1905   Volume X

April   , 1903; that there was born to her on said date a   female   child; that said child was living March 4, 1905, and is said to have been named Dolly Elizabeth James

N.J. Johnson M.D.

Witnesses To Mark:
{

Subscribed and sworn to before me this   29   day of   march   , 1905

My com March the
11 - 1909

J.H. Ritter
Notary Public.

Choc New Born 652
James H. Choate, Jr. b. 3-15-04

Choctaw 4821.

Muskogee, Indian Territory, April 8, 1905.

James H. Choate,
Paoli, Indian Territory.

Dear Sir:

Receipt is hereby acknowledged of the affidavits of Ida Choate and M. E. Rogers to the birth of James H. Choate, Junior, son of James H. and Ida Choate, March 15, 1904, and the same have been filed with our records as an application for the enrollment of said child.

Respectfully,

Commissioner in Charge.

Applications for Enrollment of Choctaw Newborn
Act of 1905   Volume X

BIRTH AFFIDAVIT.

DEPARTMENT OF THE INTERIOR.
COMMISSION TO THE FIVE CIVILIZED TRIBES.

IN RE APPLICATION FOR ENROLLMENT, as a citizen of the Choctaw Nation, of James H. Choate, Junior, born on the 15th day of March, 1904

Name of Father: John H. Choate   a citizen of the Choctaw Nation.
Name of Mother: Ida Choate   a citizen of the Choctaw Nation.

Postoffice   Paoli, Indian Territory.

AFFIDAVIT OF MOTHER.

UNITED STATES OF AMERICA, Indian Territory,
    Southern   DISTRICT.

I, Ida Choate, on oath state that I am thirty years of age and a citizen by intermarriage, of the Choctaw Nation; that I am the lawful wife of James H. Choate, who is a citizen, by blood of the Choctaw Nation; that a male child was born to me on 15th day of March, 1904; that said child has been named James H. Choate, Junior, and was living March 4, 1905.

                                     Ida Choate

Witnesses To Mark:
    C.R. Crabtree

Subscribed and sworn to before me this 1st day of April, 1905

                                     ?.J. Davenport
                                     Notary Public.

AFFIDAVIT OF ATTENDING PHYSICIAN OR MID-WIFE.

UNITED STATES OF AMERICA, Indian Territory,
    Southern   DISTRICT.

I, M.E. Rodgers, a mid-wife, on oath state that I attended on Mrs. Ida Choate, wife of James H. Choate on the 15th day of March, 1904; that there was born to her on said date a male child; that said child was living March 4, 1905, and is said to have been named James H. Choate, Junior

                                     M E Rodgers

Applications for Enrollment of Choctaw Newborn
Act of 1905   Volume X

Witnesses To Mark:
{ C.R. Crabtree

Subscribed and sworn to before me this 1st day of   April   , 1905

?.J. Davenport
Notary Public.

Choc New Born 653
    Johnece Deal   b. 12-1-04

7-NB-653

Muskogee, Indian Territory, July 12, 1905.

Mrs. Ida I. Deal,
    Wynnewood, Indian Territory.

Dear Madam:

    Receipt is hereby acknowledged of your letter of July 6, 1905, asking if you can file for your child Johnese[sic] Deal.

    In reply to your letter you are advised that the name of your child Johnece Deal has been placed upon a schedule of citizens by blood of the Choctaw Nation prepared for forwarding to the Secretary of the Interior and you will be notified when her enrollment is approved by the Department and pending such approval no selection of allotment can be made in behalf of said child.

                                Respectfully,

                                                  Commissioner.

Applications for Enrollment of Choctaw Newborn
Act of 1905   Volume X

COPY   7 NB 653

Muskogee, Indian Territory, April 27, 1905.

Mrs. Ida I. Deal,
    Wynnewood, Indian Territory.

Dear Madam:

    Receipt is hereby acknowledged of your letter of April 15, 1905, in which you state that you have forwarded an application for the enrollment of your child and you ask if the same has been received.

    In reply to your letter you are informed that the affidavits heretofore forwarded to the birth of your child John East[sic] Deal have been filed with our records as an application for the enrollment of said child.

    That part of your letter referring to appraisments[sic] of land has been made the subject of another communication.

                        Respectfully,
                         SIGNED

                        Tams Bixby
                        Chairman.

BIRTH AFFIDAVIT.

Department of the Interior,
COMMISSION TO THE FIVE CIVILIZED TRIBES.

IN RE APPLICATION FOR ENROLLMENT, as a citizen of the Choctaw Nation, of Johnece Deal, born on the 1st day of Dec., 1904

Name of Father: Frank Deal   a citizen of the   U. S.   Nation.
Name of Mother: Ida Isabell Deal   a citizen of the   Choctaw   Nation.

                Post-Office: Wynnewood, I. T.

AFFIDAVIT OF MOTHER.

UNITED STATES OF AMERICA, ⎫
    INDIAN TERRITORY,   ⎬
  Southern   District. ⎭

    I, Ida Isabell Deal , on oath state that I am 21 years of age and a citizen by Blood , of the Choctaw Nation; that I am the lawful wife of

Applications for Enrollment of Choctaw Newborn
Act of 1905 Volume X

Frank Deal , who is a citizen, by .... of the U. S. Nation; that a female child was born to me on 1st day of Dec. , 190 4, that said child has been named Johnece Deal , and is now living.

Ida Isabell Deal

WITNESSES TO MARK:
{

Subscribed and sworn to before me this 28th day of March,1905. , 190....

(Name Illegible)
Notary Public.

AFFIDAVIT OF ATTENDING PHYSICIAN OR MID-WIFE.

UNITED STATES OF AMERICA, ⎫
    INDIAN TERRITORY,   ⎬
    Southern   District.   ⎭

I, A. J. Hoover , a Physician , on oath state that I attended on Mrs. Ida Isabell Deal , wife of Frank Deal on the 1st day of Dec. , 190 4; that there was born to her on said date a female child; that said child is now living and is said to have been named Johnece Deal

Andrew J. Hoover M.D.

WITNESSES TO MARK:
{

Subscribed and sworn to before me this 28 day of March,1905. , 190....

(Name Illegible)
Notary Public.

Choc New Born 654
    Robbie A. Moore 12-13-04

Applications for Enrollment of Choctaw Newborn
Act of 1905 Volume X

COPY

7 N.B. 654

Muskogee, Indian Territory, April 12, 1905.

Joseph R. Moore,
    Dixie, Indian Territory.

Dear Sir:

    You are hereby advised that before the application for the enrollment of your infant child, Robbie A. Moore, can be finally disposed of, it will be necessary for you to furnish the Commission with either the original or a certified copy of the license and certificate of your marriage to his mother, Lizzie Moore.

    Please give this matter your immediate attention.

                      Respectfully,
                      SIGNED
                      T. B. Needles.
                      Commissioner in Charge.

COPY   Choctaw N.B. 654.

Muskogee, Indian Territory, April 26, 1905.

Joseph R. Moore,
    Dixie, Indian Territory.

Dear Sir:

    Receipt is hereby acknowledged of the marriage license and certificate between J. R. Moore and Lizzie Patrick which you offer in support of the application for the enrollment of your child, Robert A. Moore, and the same have been filed with the records in this case.

                      Respectfully,
                      SIGNED
                      Tams Bixby
                      Chairman.

Applications for Enrollment of Choctaw Newborn
Act of 1905 Volume X

$W^m O.B.$

COMMISSIONERS:
TAMS BIXBY,
THOMAS B. NEEDLES,
C.R. BRECKINBRIDGE.

WM. O. BEALL
Secretary

DEPARTMENT OF THE INTERIOR,
COMMISSIONER TO THE FIVE CIVILIZED TRIBES.

REFER IN REPLY TO THE FOLLOWING:

7-NB-654.

ADDRESS ONLY THE
COMMISSION TO THE FIVE CIVILIZED TRIBES.

Muskogee, Indian Territory, May 27, 1905.

Joseph R. Moore,
    Dixie, Indian Territory.

Dear Sir:

    There is enclosed you herewith for execution application for the enrollment of your infant child, Robbie A. Moore.

    In the physician's affidavit of March 21, 1905, heretofore filed in this office, the date of the applicant's birth is given as March 13, 1904, while the mother, in her affidavit of the same date, gives the date of birth as December 13, 1904. In the enclosed application the date of birth of left blank. Please insert the correct date and, when the affidavits are properly executed, return them to this office.

    In having these affidavits executed care should be exercised to see that all names are written in full, as they appear in the body of the affidavit, and in the event that either of the persons signing the affidavit are unable to write, signatures by mark must be attested by two witnesses. Each affidavit must be executed before a Notary Public and the notarial seal and signature of the officer must be attached to each separate affidavit.

                      Respectfully,

                                    Tams Bixby

VR 27-4.   Chairman.

                                                          7-NB-654.

Muskogee, Indian Territory, June 10, 1905.

Joseph R. Moore,
    Dixie, Indian Territory.

Dear Sir:

    Receipt is hereby acknowledged of the affidavits of Lizzie Moore and Luther J. Cranfill, M. D., to the birth of Robbie A. Moore, child of Joseph R. and Lizzie Moore,

Applications for Enrollment of Choctaw Newborn
Act of 1905   Volume X

December 13, 1904, and the same have been filed with our records in the matter of the enrollment of said child.

Respectfully,

Chairman.

FILED
AT ARDMORE.
Jan 26 1904 8AM
C. M. CAMPBELL, Clerk.
and Exofficio Recorder.
District No 21 Ind. Ter.

Certificate of Record of Marriage

United States of America,
  Indian Territory, } sct.
  Southern District.

I, C. M. CAMPBELL, Clerk of the United States Court, in the Territory and District aforesaid DO HEREBY CERTIFY, that the License for and Certificate of Marriage of

MR   J. R. Moore   and

M   Lizzie Patrick

were filed in my office in said Territory and District the   26   day of   January   A.D., 190 4   and duly recorded in Book   11   of Marriage Record, Page   26

WITNESS my hand and Seal of said Court, at Ardmore, this   26   day of   January   A.D. 190 4

C. M. Campbell
CLERK.

Return this License to the United States Clerk at Ardmore, that it may be recorded, when it will be mailed to the proper address.

Ardmoreite Steam Print.

Applications for Enrollment of Choctaw Newborn
Act of 1905   Volume X

MARRIAGE LICENSE

UNITED STATES OF AMERICA,　　　　To Any Person Authorized by Law to
　　INDIAN TERRITORY,　　ss:　　Solemnize Marriage, Greeting:
　　SOUTHERN DISTRICT.

You are Hereby Commanded, *to solemnize the Rite and publish the Banns of Matrimony between Mr.*   J.R. Moore   *of*   Dixie   *in the Indian Territory, aged*   33   *years, and M*   Lizzie Patrick   *of*   Newport   *in the Indian Territory, aged*   25   *years, according to law; and do you officially sign and return this License to the parties therein named.*

Witness *my hand and official Seal, this*   23   *day of*   January   *A. D. 190* 4

CM Campbell
Clerk of the United States Court.

Certificate of Marriage.

UNITED STATES OF AMERICA,
　　INDIAN TERRITORY,　　ss:
　　SOUTHERN DISTRICT.　　　I,   D N Cinb

An Ordained Minister   *do hereby certify that on the*   24   *day of*   January,
A. D. 190 4 *, I did duly according to law, as commanded in the foregoing License, solemnize the Rite and publish the Banns of Matrimony between the parties therein named.*

Witness *my hand this*   24   *day of*   January   *A. D. 190* 4

My credentials are recorded in the office of the Clerk of the United States Court, Indian Territory, Southern District, at Ardmore, Book   6   *, Page* 198

　　　　　　　　　　　　　D N Cinb
　　　　　　　　　　　　　Pastor Baptist Church
　　　　　　　　　　　　　Lone Grove I.T.

Applications for Enrollment of Choctaw Newborn
Act of 1905   Volume X

BIRTH AFFIDAVIT.

DEPARTMENT OF THE INTERIOR.
COMMISSION TO THE FIVE CIVILIZED TRIBES.

IN RE APPLICATION FOR ENROLLMENT, as a citizen of the   Choctaw   Nation, of Robbie A Moore   , born on the 13" day of Dec , 1904

Name of Father: Joseph R Moore   a citizen of the Choctaw   Nation.
Name of Mother: Lizzie Moore   a citizen of the Choctaw   Nation.

Postoffice   Dixie I.T.

AFFIDAVIT OF MOTHER.

UNITED STATES OF AMERICA, Indian Territory,
   Southern   DISTRICT.

I, Lizzie Moore , on oath state that I am 27 years of age and a citizen by ——, of the United States ~~Nation~~; that I am the lawful wife of   Joseph R Moore , who is a citizen, by Blood of the Choctaw Nation; that a male child was born to me on 13" day of December , 1904; that said child has been named Robbie A Moore , and was living March 4, 1905.

Lizzie Moore

Witnesses To Mark:
{

Subscribed and sworn to before me this 21st day of March , 1905

A M Hightower
Notary Public.

AFFIDAVIT OF ATTENDING PHYSICIAN OR MID-WIFE.

UNITED STATES OF AMERICA, Indian Territory,
   Southern   DISTRICT.

I, L. J. Cranfill , a M.D. , on oath state that I attended on Mrs. Lizzie Moore , wife of Joseph R Moore on the 13" day of March[sic] , 1904; that there was born to her on said date a female child; that said child was living March 4, 1905, and is said to have been named Robbie A Moore

L. J. Cranfill M.D.

Witnesses To Mark:
{

Applications for Enrollment of Choctaw Newborn
Act of 1905   Volume X

Subscribed and sworn to before me this 21st day of March, 1905

A M Hightower
Notary Public.

BIRTH AFFIDAVIT.

DEPARTMENT OF THE INTERIOR.
COMMISSION TO THE FIVE CIVILIZED TRIBES.

IN RE APPLICATION FOR ENROLLMENT, as a citizen of the Choctaw Nation, of Robbie A Moore, born on the 13" day of Dec, 1904

Name of Father: Joseph R Moore   a citizen of the Choctaw Nation.
Name of Mother: Lizzie Moore   a citizen of the U.S. Nation.

Postoffice   Dixie Ind. Ter.

AFFIDAVIT OF MOTHER.

UNITED STATES OF AMERICA, Indian Territory,
Southern   DISTRICT.

I, Lizzie Moore, on oath state that I am 27 years of age and a citizen by ——, of the United States Nation; that I am the lawful wife of Joseph R Moore, who is a citizen, by blood of the Choctaw Nation; that a female child was born to me on 13" day of December, 1904; that said child has been named Robbie A Moore, and was living March 4, 1905.

Lizzie Moore

Witnesses To Mark:

Subscribed and sworn to before me this 5" day of June, 1905

A M Hightower
Notary Public.

AFFIDAVIT OF ATTENDING PHYSICIAN OR MID-WIFE.

UNITED STATES OF AMERICA, Indian Territory,
Southern   DISTRICT.

I, Luther J. Cranfill, a M.D., on oath state that I attended on Mrs. Lizzie Moore, wife of Joseph R Moore on the 13" day of

Applications for Enrollment of Choctaw Newborn
Act of 1905   Volume X

December   , 1904; that there was born to her on said date a   female   child; that said child was living March 4, 1905, and is said to have been named Robbie A Moore

Luther J. Cranfill M.D.

Witnesses To Mark:
{

Subscribed and sworn to before me this 5" day of   June   , 1905

A M Hightower
Notary Public.

Choc New Born 655
    John Edgar Trammell   b. 6-29-03
    Stella May Trammell   b. 8-6-04

The mother of this child is enrolled as Lillie B. Burkes

COPY

Muskogee, Indian Territory April 10, 1905.

J. Ernest Williams,
    Pauls Valley, Indian Territory.

Dear Sir:

    There is returned you herewith application for the enrollment of Stella May Trammell as a citizen of the Choctaw Nation, for the reason that it appears that the affidavit of Margaret L. Trammell was executed before you August 3, 1905, instead of April 3, 1905.

    Please make the necessary correction and return this application immediately.

Respectfully,
SIGNED
T. B. Needles.
Commissioner in Charge.

AB 1-10

Applications for Enrollment of Choctaw Newborn
Act of 1905   Volume X

BIRTH AFFIDAVIT.
DEPARTMENT OF THE INTERIOR.
COMMISSION TO THE FIVE CIVILIZED TRIBES.

IN RE APPLICATION FOR ENROLLMENT, as a citizen of the Choctaw Nation, of John Edgar Trammell, born on the 29th day of June, 1903

Name of Father: Thomas J Trammell   a citizen of the Choctaw Nation.
Name of Mother: Lillie B Trammell   a citizen of the Choctaw Nation.

Postoffice   Bailey, I.T.

AFFIDAVIT OF MOTHER.

UNITED STATES OF AMERICA, Indian Territory,
Southern   DISTRICT.

I, Lillie B Trammell, on oath state that I am 20 years of age and a citizen by blood, of the Choctaw Nation; that I am the lawful wife of Thomas J Trammell, who is a citizen, by blood of the Choctaw Nation; that a male child was born to me on 29th day of June, 1903; that said child has been named John Edgar Trammell, and was living March 4, 1905.

          her
        Lillie B x Trammell
Witnesses To Mark: mark
 J.F. Trammell
 Maud Barnett

Subscribed and sworn to before me this 3rd day of April, 1905

        J E Williams
        Notary Public.

AFFIDAVIT OF ATTENDING PHYSICIAN OR MID-WIFE.

UNITED STATES OF AMERICA, Indian Territory,
Southern   DISTRICT.

I, Margaret L Trammell, a midwife, on oath state that I attended on Mrs. Lillie B Trammell, wife of Thomas J Trammell on the 29th day of June, 1903; that there was born to her on said date a male child; that said child was living March 4, 1905, and is said to have been named John Edgar Trammell

        Margaret L Trammell

Applications for Enrollment of Choctaw Newborn
Act of 1905 Volume X

Witnesses To Mark:
{

    Subscribed and sworn to before me this 3rd day of April , 1905

                                      J E Williams
                                          Notary Public.

BIRTH AFFIDAVIT.

DEPARTMENT OF THE INTERIOR.
COMMISSION TO THE FIVE CIVILIZED TRIBES.

    IN RE APPLICATION FOR ENROLLMENT, as a citizen of the   Choctaw   Nation, of Stella May Trammell , born on the 6th day of August , 1904

Name of Father: Thomas J Trammell   a citizen of the Choctaw Nation.
Name of Mother: Lillie B Trammell   a citizen of the Choctaw Nation.

                        Postoffice   Bailey, I.T.

AFFIDAVIT OF MOTHER.

UNITED STATES OF AMERICA, Indian Territory, }
   Southern   DISTRICT. }

    I, Lillie B Trammell , on oath state that I am 20 years of age and a citizen by blood , of the Choctaw Nation; that I am the lawful wife of Thomas J Trammell , who is a citizen, by blood of the Choctaw Nation; that a female child was born to me on 6th day of August , 1904; that said child has been named Stella May Trammell , and was living March 4, 1905.

                                     her
                             Lillie B x Trammell
Witnesses To Mark: mark
{ J.F. Trammell
  Maud Barnett

    Subscribed and sworn to before me this 3rd day of April , 1905

                                      J E Williams
                                          Notary Public.

Applications for Enrollment of Choctaw Newborn
Act of 1905   Volume X

AFFIDAVIT OF ATTENDING PHYSICIAN OR MID-WIFE.

UNITED STATES OF AMERICA, Indian Territory, }
 Southern   DISTRICT.

I, Margaret L Trammell , a Midwife , on oath state that I attended on Mrs. Lillie B Trammell , wife of Thomas J Trammell on the 6th day of August , 1904; that there was born to her on said date a female child; that said child was living March 4, 1905, and is said to have been named Stella May Trammell

Margaret L Trammell

Witnesses To Mark:
{

Subscribed and sworn to before me this 3rd day of April , 1905

J E Williams
Notary Public.

Choc New Born 656
   Annie Johnson b. 12-22-04

DEPARTMENT OF THE INTERIOR,
COMMISSION TO THE FIVE CIVILIZED TRIBES.
BOKOSHE, INDIAN TERRITORY APRIL 3, 1905.

In the matter of the application for the enrollment of Annie Johnson as a citizen by blood of the Choctaw Nation.

Nelson Morris being first duly sworn testifies as follows:

EXAMINATION BY THE COMMISSION:

Q What is your name: A Nelson Morris.
Q What is your age? A Eighteen.
Q What is your post office address? A Chant.
Q Are you a citizen by blood of the Choctaw Nation? A Yes, sir.
Q Are you acquainted with Arbin Johnson who has made application for the enrollment of his minor child Annie Johnson?
A Yes, sir, I am acquainted with him.
Q Do you know his wife Lula Johnson? A Yes, sir.

Applications for Enrollment of Choctaw Newborn
Act of 1905   Volume X

Q How far do you live from Arbin Johnson? A I live just about about[sic] quarter of a mile.
Q Do you know that this child Annie Johnson is the child of Lula Johnson and was born on December 22, 1904? A Yes, sir.
Q This is the child here (indicating)? A Yes, sir, that is the child.

Witness excused.

Arbin Johnson being duly sworn and examined through an interpreter testifies as follows:

EXAMINATION BY THE COMMISSION:

Q What is your name? A Arbin Johnson.
Q What is your age? A Thirty-eight.
Q What is your post office address? A McCurtain.
Q Is Lula Johnson your wife? A Yes, sir.
Q Lula Johnson has appeared before this Commission and made application for her minor child Annie Johnson; is that your child? A Yes, sir.
Q When was that child born? A December 22, 1904.
Q Was anyone present when that child was born? A No, sir.
Q No one but yourself? A No, sir.

Witness excused.

Chas. T. Difendafer being first duly sworn states that the above and foregoing is a full, true and correct transcript of his stenographic notes as taken in said cause on said date.

Chas. T. Difendafer

Subscribed and sworn to before me this 3rd day of April 1905.

OL Johnson
Notary Public.

(The affidavit below typed as given.)

Chant, Ind. Ter.   June 6   *190* 5

On this day appread before me Floyd Nivins and says that he is personaly acquainted with ~~Osbin~~ *Orlin* Johnson and wife that the have a girly baby that was living March the 4th 1904

Floyd Nivins

And on the same date a bone appeard before me personaly[sic] know to be Elisbeth Baker and she says also that she is personaly[sic] acquainted with Orbin Johnson & wife and that they have a girl baby and that it was liveing on Mch 4th 1905

Applications for Enrollment of Choctaw Newborn
Act of 1905   Volume X

                                                         her
                                        Elisbeth x Baker
                                              mark

witness
        S F Phillips   Jas H Davis
                                            Notary Public
        Floyd Nivins   my com expire 4/5/08

(The affidavit below typed as given.)

J. F. HUDSON
ATTORNEY AT LAW
NOTARY IN OFFICE
McCurtain, Ind. T.

Indian Territory }
Central District }

This 27th day of November 1905 personally appeared before me Frank R. Parke a Notary Public in and for the above named judicial division being duly sworn Loman Thomas to me well known whom says my name is Loman Thomas I am an Indian by blood and a duly enrolled member of the Choctaw tribe my age is 49 my P.O. McCurtain I.T. I am personally acquainted with Arbin Johnson and his wife Lola Johnson both Choctaws by blood and duly enrolled as member of the Choctaw Tribe and know that a female child was born to them on Dec 22 1904 and that said child is now living and is named Annie Johnson.

    Witness my hand this 27th of Nov 1905

                                                    his
                                          Loman x Thomas
               Orvil Hudson   mark
witness
               (Illegible) Parke

Subscribed and sworn to before me at McCurtain I.T. this 27 day of Nov 1905

                                                   Frank E. Parke
My Com Exp   Notary Public
    2/2/08

Applications for Enrollment of Choctaw Newborn
Act of 1905 Volume X

(The affidavit below typed as given.)

Chant. Ind. Ter.   June 6   *190* 5

ul

On this day appeared before me L~~ol~~a Johnson wife of Orbin Johnson and says that on Dec 4th 1904 there was born to her a girl baby that her name is Annie Johnson and that she was liveing on March 4th 1905

Lula Johnson

Witness my hand an seal this 6th day of June 1905

Jas H Davis
Notary Public

my com expires 4/2/08

7- 8481- 8482
BIRTH AFFIDAVIT.

DEPARTMENT OF THE INTERIOR.
COMMISSION TO THE FIVE CIVILIZED TRIBES.

IN RE APPLICATION FOR ENROLLMENT, as a citizen of the Choctaw Nation, of Annie Johnson, born on the 22 day of December, 1904

Name of Father: Arbin Johnson   a citizen of the Choctaw Nation.
Name of Mother: Lula Johnson   a citizen of the Choctaw Nation.

Postoffice   McCurtain Ind Ter

AFFIDAVIT OF MOTHER.

UNITED STATES OF AMERICA, Indian Territory,
Central   DISTRICT.

I, Lula Johnson, on oath state that I am 23 years of age and a citizen by blood, of the Choctaw Nation; that I am the lawful wife of Arbin Johnson, who is a citizen, by blood of the Choctaw Nation; that a female child was born to me on 22 day of December, 1904; that said child has been named Annie Johnson, and was living March 4, 1905.

Lula Johnson

Witnesses To Mark:

Applications for Enrollment of Choctaw Newborn
Act of 1905   Volume X

Subscribed and sworn to before me this 3 day of   April   , 1905

OL Johnson
Notary Public.

AFFIDAVIT OF ATTENDING PHYSICIAN OR MID-WIFE.

UNITED STATES OF AMERICA, Indian Territory,
.... DISTRICT.

I, ... See testimony ...., on oath state that I attended on Mrs. ...., wife of .... on the .... day of ...., 1......; that there was born to her on said date a .... child; that said child was living March 4, 1905, and is said to have been named ....

Witnesses To Mark:
{ ....
   ....

Subscribed and sworn to before me this .... day of ...., 1905.

....
Notary Public.

(The letter below does not belong with the current applicant.)

7- 761

Muskogee, Indian Territory, April 19, 1905.

William Johnson,
    Lukfata, Indian Territory.

Dear Sir:

    Receipt is hereby acknowledged of the affidavits of Sophia Johnson and Jane Butler to the birth of Annie Johnson, daughter of William and Sophia Johnson January 17, 1904, and the same have been filed with our records as an application for the enrollment of said child.

Respectfully,

Chairman.

Applications for Enrollment of Choctaw Newborn
Act of 1905 Volume X

Sub

7-NB-656.

Muskogee, Indian Territory, May 26, 1905.

Arbin Johnson,
    McCurtain, Indian Territory.

Dear Sir:

    Referring to the application for the enrollment of your infant child, Annie Johnson, born December 22, 1904; it is noted from your testimony, taken on the 3rd ultimo, that there was no one present, excepting yourself, at the time of birth of the applicant.

    If this is correct the evidence of two persons, who have actual knowledge of the facts that the child was born, the date of her birth; that she was living on March 4, 1905, and that Lula Johnson is her mother, is required. The testimony of Nelson Morris to these facts has been filed with the Commission, but before this matter can be finally determined it will be necessary that you secure the affidavit of another person to the same facts.

                              Respectfully,

                                                Chairman.

7-NB-656.

Muskogee, Indian Territory, June 12, 1905.

Orbin Johnson,
    McCurtain, Indian Territory.

Dear Sir:

    Receipt is hereby acknowledged of your letter of June 6, transmitting the affidavits of Lula Johnson, Floyd Nevins and Elizabeth Baker to the birth of the infant child of Orbin and Lula Johnson.

    The affidavits of Floyd Nevins and Elizabeth Baker, which were filed in place of the affidavit of the attending physician or midwife, failed to give the name of the child or the date of her birth.

    Before this application can be disposed of, the affidavits of two persons who know that the child was born, the date of her birth, that she was living on March 4, 1905, and that Lula Johnson is her mother, is necessary. As the testimony of Nelson Johnson to

Applications for Enrollment of Choctaw Newborn
Act of 1905 Volume X

these facts has already been filed with the Commission, it will be necessary for you to secure the affidavit of another person in support of the same facts.

This matter should receive your immediate attention as no further action can be taken until this affidavit is furnished the Commission.

Respectfully,

Chairman.

---

7 NB 656

Muskogee, Indian Territory, June 22, 1905.

Orvin[sic] Johnson,
    Chant, Indian Territory.

Dear Sir:

Receipt is hereby acknowledged of your letter of June 17, 1905, transmitting what purports to be affidavits of Peter Fulsom, James Franklin and Elsie Haklochee[sic] to the birth of Annie Johnson and the same are returned herewith for the reason that the affidavits were not signed by the affiants.

Respectfully,

Chairman.

EB 2-21

7-NB-656

Muskogee, Indian Territory, August 18, 1905.

Arbin Johnson,
    McCurtain, Indian Territory.

Dear Sir:

In the matter of the application for the enrollment of your minor daughter Annie Johnson there are on file with this office two affidavits of your wife as to the birth of said child, from one of which it appears that said child was born on December 4, 1904 and from the other that she was born December 22, 1904.

You are requested to immediately inform this office as to which of the above dates, if either of them, is the correct date of the birth of said child.

Applications for Enrollment of Choctaw Newborn
Act of 1905   Volume X

You are also advised that it will be necessary for you to furnish this office the affidavit of an additional disinterested person as to the birth of said child. There is at present on file the testimony of only one disinterested witness, Nelson Morris, as to the birth of said child, affidavits of Floyd Nevins and Elizabeth Baker which now on file fail to set forth said child's name or of her birth.

Respectfully,

Acting Commissioner.

(The letter below typed as given.)

7 N B 656

Mc Curtain, Ind. Ter. Sept. 27th 1905.

Commission to the Five Civilized Tribes
    Muskogee, I. T.

Dear Sir:

Your letter was received and you state that I state before the Notary Public that my child was born on December 22nd 1904 But one my witness state that this child was born on Dec 4th 1904. This is mistake But this child was born on Dec 22nd 1904 was correct. When you received this letter you must write to me and let me know whether this child was approved by the Secretary Interior or not so I can select the land for her.

Yours Respectfully

Auben Johnson.

Choctaw N B 656

Muskogee, Indian Territory, October 12, 1905.

Arbin Johnson,
    McCurtain, Indian Territory.

Dear Sir:

Receipt is hereby acknowledged of your letter of September 27, stating that the correct date of the birth of your child, Annie Johnson, was December 22, 1904, and asking if she has now been approved.

In reply to your letter you are advised that it will be necessary for you to forward the affidavits of another disinterested witness to the birth of your child, Annie Johnson, the date of her birth, the name of her parents, and that she was living on March 4, 1905.

Applications for Enrollment of Choctaw Newborn
Act of 1905   Volume X

This matter should receive your immediate attention as until this evidence is received no further action can be taken looking to the enrollment of this child.

Respectfully,

Commissioner.

7-NB-656

Muskogee, Indian Territory, December 2, 1905.

Arbin Johnson,
    McCurtain, Indian Territory.

Dear Sir:

Receipt is hereby acknowledged of the affidavit of Loman Thomas to the birth of your child Annie Johnson, December 22, 1904, and the same has been filed with the record in the matter of the enrollment of said child.

Respectfully,

Acting Commissioner.

Choc New Born 657
    Mamie Overstreet   b. 11-8-04

COPY

7 N B 657

John T. Overstreet,
    Cowlington, Indian Territory.

Dear Sir:

Receipt is hereby acknowledged of your letter of April 6, 1905, enclosing marriage license and certificate between John F. Overstreet and Clare Barnwell which you offer in the matter of the enrollment of your infant child and the same have been filed with the record in this case.

Respectfully
SIGNED *T. B. Needles.*
Commissioner in Charge.

Applications for Enrollment of Choctaw Newborn
Act of 1905 Volume X

No. 1939

Certificate of Record of Marriages.

DEPARTMENT OF THE INTERIOR,
Commission to the Five Civilized Tribes.
FILED
APR 11 1905
Tams Bixby CHAIRMAN.

UNITED STATES OF AMERICA,
INDIAN TERRITORY,   } SCT:
Central   DISTRICT.

I,   E.J. Fannin   , Clerk of the United States Court in the Indian Territory and District aforesaid, do hereby CERTIFY, that the License for and Certificate of the Marriage of

Mr.   John T. Overstreet   and

Miss Clara Barnwell   was

filed in my office in said Territory and District the   19   day of   November A.D., 190 3   and duly recorded in Book   2   of Marriage Record, Page   352

WITNESS my hand and seal of said Court, at   Poteau   , this   19   day of   November   , A.D. 190 3

E. J. Fannin
Clerk.
By   T.T. Varner   *Deputy.*

Applications for Enrollment of Choctaw Newborn
Act of 1905   Volume X

No. 1939   FORM NO. 598.

MARRIAGE LICENSE.

UNITES STATES OF AMERICA,
  THE INDIAN TERRITORY,   } ss:
  Central   DISTRICT.

To any Person Authorized by Law to Solemnize Marriage—Greeting:

You are hereby commanded to solemnize the Rite and publish the **Banns of Matrimony** *between* Mr. John T Overstreet *of* Cowlington *in the Indian Territory, aged* 21 *years, and* M iss Clara Barnwell *of* Cowlington *in the Indian Territory, aged* 19 *years, according to law, and do you officially sign and return this License to the parties therein named.*

WITNESS my hand and official seal, this 17 day of November A. D. 190 3

                              EJ Fannin
                              Clerk of the United States Court.
By T.T. Varner
          Deputy

CERTIFICATE OF MARRIAGE.

UNITES STATES OF AMERICA,
  THE INDIAN TERRITORY,   } ss: I,   Jesse Uhler
  Central   DISTRICT.   a   Minister of Gospel

do hereby CERTIFY, that on the 18 day of Nov A, D. 190 3; I did duly and according to law, as commanded in the foregoing License, solemnize the Rite and publish the BANNS OF MATRIMONY between the parties therein named.

Witness my hand this 18 day of Nov , A. D. 190 3

My credentials are recorded in the office of the Clerk of the United States Court in the Indian Territory, Central District, Book C Page 17

                                   Jesse Uhler
                              a   Minister of Gospel

Applications for Enrollment of Choctaw Newborn
Act of 1905   Volume X

7- 7819
BIRTH AFFIDAVIT.

DEPARTMENT OF THE INTERIOR.
COMMISSION TO THE FIVE CIVILIZED TRIBES.

IN RE APPLICATION FOR ENROLLMENT, as a citizen of the   Choctaw   Nation, of Mamie Overstreet   , born on the   8   day of   November   , 1904

Name of Father: John T Overstreet   a citizen of the   Choctaw   Nation.
Name of Mother: Clara Overstreet   a citizen of the   United States.

Postoffice   Cowlington Ind Ter

AFFIDAVIT OF MOTHER.

UNITED STATES OF AMERICA, Indian Territory,
Central   DISTRICT.

I,   Clara Overstreet   , on oath state that I am   20   years of age and a citizen by   , of the   United States   Nation; that I am the lawful wife of   John T Overstreet   , who is a citizen, by blood   of the   Choctaw   Nation; that a female   child was born to me on   8   day of   November   , 1904; that said child has been named   Mamie Overstreet   , and was living March 4, 1905.

Clara Overstreet

Witnesses To Mark:

Subscribed and sworn to before me this   3   day of   April   , 1905

OL Johnson
Notary Public.

AFFIDAVIT OF ATTENDING PHYSICIAN OR MID-WIFE.

UNITED STATES OF AMERICA, Indian Territory,
Central   DISTRICT.

I,   F. C. Parrott   , a   physician   , on oath state that I attended on Mrs.   Clara Overstreet   , wife of   John T Overstreet   on the   8   day of November   , 1904; that there was born to her on said date a   female   child; that said child was living March 4, 1905, and is said to have been named   Mamie Overstreet

F. C. Parrott

Applications for Enrollment of Choctaw Newborn
Act of 1905   Volume X

Witnesses To Mark:
{

Subscribed and sworn to before me this 3 day of April , 1905

OL Johnson
Notary Public.

Choc New Born 658
Vera Powell   b. 6-23-04

658
7 NB ~~368~~

Muskogee, Indian Territory, May 12, 1905.

Edgar Louis Powell,
Bokoshe, Indian Territory.

Dear Sir:

Receipt is hereby acknowledged of your letter of May 6, 1905, asking relative to the enrollment of your child Vera Powell and if you will be allowed soon to select an allotment for her.

In reply to your letter you are advised that the affidavits heretofore forwarded to the birth of your child Vera Powell have been filed with our records as an application for the enrollment of said child, but no selection of allotment can be made in her behalf until her enrollment has been approved by the Secretary of the Interior.

Respectfully,

Chairman.

Applications for Enrollment of Choctaw Newborn
Act of 1905 Volume X

7-NB-658

Muskogee, Indian Territory, July 21, 1905.

Edgar L. Powell,
    Bokoshe, Indian Territory.

Dear Sir:

    Receipt is hereby acknowledged of your letter of July 15, 1905, asking if the enrollment of your child has been approved by the Secretary.

    In reply to your letter you are advised that the name of your child, Vera Powell, has been placed upon a schedule of citizens by blood of the Choctaw Nation which has been forwarded to the Secretary of the Interior, and you will be notified when her enrollment has been approved by him.

                           Respectfully,

                                        Commissioner.

7- 7496
BIRTH AFFIDAVIT.

DEPARTMENT OF THE INTERIOR.
COMMISSION TO THE FIVE CIVILIZED TRIBES.

      IN RE APPLICATION FOR ENROLLMENT, as a citizen of the   Choctaw   Nation, of Vera Powell   , born on the 23   day of   June , 1904

Name of Father: Edgar L Powell   a citizen of the   Choctaw   Nation.
Name of Mother: Mary Etta Powell   a citizen of the   United States

                          Postoffice   Bokoshe Ind Ter

AFFIDAVIT OF MOTHER.

UNITED STATES OF AMERICA, Indian Territory,
    Central   **DISTRICT.**

    I,   Mary Etta Powell   , on oath state that I am   years of age and a citizen ~~by~~ ——— , of the   United States   ~~Nation~~; that I am the lawful wife of   Edgar L Powell   , who is a citizen, by blood   of the   Choctaw   Nation; that a female   child was born to me on 23   day of   June   , 1904; that said child has been named   Vera Powell   , and was living March 4, 1905.

Applications for Enrollment of Choctaw Newborn
Act of 1905   Volume X

                                                   her
                                       Mary Etta x Powell

Witnesses To Mark: mark
  { Chas. T. Difendafer
  { *(Name Illegible)*

Subscribed and sworn to before me this 3rd day of   April   , 1905

                                          OL Johnson
                                                  Notary Public.

AFFIDAVIT OF ATTENDING PHYSICIAN OR MID-WIFE.

UNITED STATES OF AMERICA, Indian Territory, }
.... DISTRICT. }

    I,   F C Parrott   , a   physician   , on oath state that I attended on Mrs.   Mary Etta Powell   , wife of   Edgar L Powell   on the 23 day of June , 1904; that there was born to her on said date a   female   child; that said child was living March 4, 1905, and is said to have been named   Vera Powell

                                         F.C. Parrott
Witnesses To Mark:
  {

Subscribed and sworn to before me this 3rd day of   April   , 1905

                                       OL Johnson
                                            Notary Public.

Choc New Born 659
    Louise Garland   b. 8-8-03

Applications for Enrollment of Choctaw Newborn
Act of 1905 Volume X

BIRTH AFFIDAVIT.

DEPARTMENT OF THE INTERIOR.

COMMISSION TO THE FIVE CIVILIZED TRIBES.

IN RE APPLICATION FOR ENROLLMENT, as a citizen of the Choctaw Nation of Louise Garland, born on the 8th day of August, 1903

Name of Father: D. N. Garland a citizen of the Choctaw Nation.
Name of Mother: Inez C. Garland a citizen of the Choctaw Nation.

Postoffice Chickasha Ind Ter

AFFIDAVIT OF MOTHER.

UNITED STATES OF AMERICA, INDIAN TERRITORY,
Southern DISTRICT.

I, Inez C. Garland, on oath state that I am Forty years of age and a citizen by Blood, of the Choctaw Nation; that I am the lawful wife of D.N. Garland, who is a citizen, by Intermarriage of the Choctaw Nation; that a Female child was born to me on 8th day of August, 1903, that said child has been named Louise Garland, and is now living.

WITNESSES TO MARK: Inez C. Garland

Subscribed and sworn to before me this 3rd day of April A D, 1905.

J.D. Carmichael
Notary Public.

AFFIDAVIT OF ATTENDING PHYSICIAN OR MID-WIFE.

UNITED STATES OF AMERICA, INDIAN TERRITORY,
Southern DISTRICT.

I, R.P. Tye, a Physician, on oath state that I attended on Mrs. Inez C. Garland, wife of D. N. Garland on the 8th day of August, 1903; that there was born to her on said date a Female child; that said child is now living and is said to have been named Louise Garland

R.P. Tye

Applications for Enrollment of Choctaw Newborn
Act of 1905 Volume X

WITNESSES TO MARK:

{

Subscribed and sworn to before me this   3rd   day of   April A D   , 1905.

J.D. Carmichael
Notary Public.

Choc New Born 660
Lola Benton   b. 3-7-03

BIRTH AFFIDAVIT.
DEPARTMENT OF THE INTERIOR.
COMMISSION TO THE FIVE CIVILIZED TRIBES.

IN RE APPLICATION FOR ENROLLMENT, as a citizen of the   Choctaw   Nation, of Lola Benton   , born on the 7th   day of   March   , 1903

Name of Father: Rufus F. Benton   a citizen of the   Choctaw   Nation.
Name of Mother: Julia Benton   a citizen of the   Choctaw   Nation.

Postoffice   Ryan Ind. Ter.

AFFIDAVIT OF MOTHER.

UNITED STATES OF AMERICA, Indian Territory, }
Southern   DISTRICT.

I,   Julia Benton   , on oath state that I am   37   years of age and a citizen by Blood   , of the   Choctaw   Nation; that I am the lawful wife of   Rufus F Benton , who is a citizen, by   Marriage   of the   Choctaw   Nation; that a   Girl   child was born to me on   7th   day of   March   , 1903; that said child has been named   Lola Benton   , and was living March 4, 1905.

her
Julia x Benton
mark

Witnesses To Mark:
{ Tom Harper
  Mary Dollar

Applications for Enrollment of Choctaw Newborn
Act of 1905   Volume X

Subscribed and sworn to before me this 31st   day of   March   , 1905

J.H. Harper
Notary Public.

AFFIDAVIT OF ATTENDING PHYSICIAN OR MID-WIFE.

UNITED STATES OF AMERICA, Indian Territory, }
  Southern   DISTRICT.

I,   S E Couch   , a   midwife   , on oath state that I attended on Mrs.   Julia Benton   , wife of   Rufus F Benton   on the 7th   day of   March   , 1903; that there was born to her on said date a   Girl   child; that said child was living March 4, 1905, and is said to have been named   Lola Benton

S E Couch

Witnesses To Mark:
{

Subscribed and sworn to before me this 31st   day of   March   , 1905

J.H. Harper
Notary Public.

Choc New Born 661
    Grady Edwin Lyle b. 10-6-04

IN RE APPLICATION FOR ENROLLMENT, as a citizen of the   Choctaw Nation of   Grady Edwin Lyle   born on the 6 day of October 190 4

Name of Father   Robert Thomas Lyle   citizen of Choctaw Nation
Name of Mother   Lula B. Lyle   citizen of Choctaw Nation

Post Office. Marlow, I.T.

AFFIDAVIT OF MOTHER

United States of America Southern District of the Indian Territory:

I,   Lula B. Lyle   on oath state that I am   35   years of age and a citizen by Blood   of the   Choctaw   Nation that I am the lawful wife of   Robert Thomas Lyle

Applications for Enrollment of Choctaw Newborn
Act of 1905   Volume X

who is a citizen by ~~blood~~ Intermarriage of the Choctaw   Nation that a   Male   Child wa born to me on the   6   day of   October   190 4   that said Child has been named Grady Edwin Lyle   and was living March 4, 1905.

Lula B Lyle

Subscribed and sworn to before me this the   30   day of   March   A.D. 190 5

Geo. T. Putty
Notary Public.

AFFIDAVIT OF ATTENDING PHYSICIAN

United States of America Southern District of the Indian Territory:

    I,   D.M. Montgomery   a   Physician   on oath, state that I attend[sic] on Mrs Lula B Lyle   wife of   Robert Thomas Lyle   on the   6   day of   Oct   190 4   and that there was born to her on that date a   Male   child and that said child was living March 4 1905, and is said to have been named   Grady Edwin Lyle

D.M. Montgomery

Subscribed and sworn to before me this the   30   day of   March   1905

Geo. T. Putty
Notary Public.

Choc New Born 662
    Annie Frances Hampton   *(b.)*   6-8-04

BIRTH AFFIDAVIT.

DEPARTMENT OF THE INTERIOR.
COMMISSION TO THE FIVE CIVILIZED TRIBES.

    IN RE APPLICATION FOR ENROLLMENT, as a citizen of the   Choctaw   Nation, of Annie Frances Hampton   , born on the 8   day of   June   , 1903

Name of Father: Julius C Hampton   a citizen of the   Choctaw   Nation.
Name of Mother: Frances Hampton   a citizen of the   Choctaw   Nation.

Postoffice   Bradley Ind Ter

Applications for Enrollment of Choctaw Newborn
Act of 1905   Volume X

AFFIDAVIT OF MOTHER.

UNITED STATES OF AMERICA, Indian Territory,
Southern Dist   DISTRICT.

    I, Frances Hampton, on oath state that I am 32 years of age and a citizen by Blood, of the Choctaw Nation; that I am the lawful wife of Julius C. Hampton, who is a citizen, by Blood of the Choctaw Nation; that a Female child was born to me on 8th day of June, 1903; that said child has been named Annie Frances Hampton, and was living March 4, 1905.

                                    Frances Hampton

Witnesses To Mark:
{ WP Bradley
{ J H Stanfield

    Subscribed and sworn to before me this 3 day of April, 1905

                                    F. W. Trask
                                           Notary Public.

AFFIDAVIT OF ATTENDING PHYSICIAN OR MID-WIFE.

UNITED STATES OF AMERICA, Indian Territory,
Central   DISTRICT.

    I, W.J. Melton, a Physician, on oath state that I attended on Mrs. Frances Hampton, wife of Julius C Hampton on the 8th day of June, 1903; that there was born to her on said date a Female child; that said child was living March 4, 1905, and is said to have been named Annie Francis[sic] Hampton

                                  W.J. Melton M.D.

Witnesses To Mark:
{

    Subscribed and sworn to before me this 20th day of March, 1905

                                    C.H. Ewing
                                        Notary Public.

Applications for Enrollment of Choctaw Newborn
Act of 1905 Volume X

<u>Choc New Born 663</u>
Lula Perry   b. 7-19-03

DEPARTMENT OF THE INTERIOR,
COMMISSION TO THE FIVE CIVILIZED TRIBES.
BOKOSHE, INDIAN TERRITORY April 3, 1905.

In the matter of the application for the enrollment of Lula Perry as a citizen by blood of the Choctaw Nation.

Lucy Lucas Cooper being first duly sworn through interpreter Joe Folsom testifies as follows:

EXAMINATION BY THE COMMISSION:

Q What is your name? A Lucy Lucas Cooper.
Q What is your age? A Twenty-two.
Q What is your post office address? A Stigler.
Q What was her maiden name? A Lucy Lucas.
Q Who did she marry first? A A. B. Cooper.
Q Is he a citizen of the Choctaw Nation? A Yes, sir.
Q Is she living with Cooper at the present time? A No, sir
Q When was she married to Cooper? A She don't know.
Q How many years ago? A About nine years ago.
Q Was she divorced from Cooper? A Yes, sir.
Q Divorced from Cooper? A Yes, sir.
Q You now wish to make application for your minor child Lula Perry? A Yes, sir.
Q When was this child born? A 19th day of July 1903.
Q Who is the father of this child? A Lewis Perry.
Q When was she married to Perry? A Never was married.
Q So Lula Perry is an illegitimate child? A Yes, sir.
Q Perry wasn't her husband? A No, sir.
Q Is Perry a citizen of the Choctaw Nation by blood? A Yes, sir.
Q Where does Perry live? A Whitefield.

Witness excused.

Chas. T. Difendafer being first duly sworn states that the above and foregoing is a full, true and correct transcript of his stenographic notes taken in said cause on said date.

Chas.T. Difendafer

Subscribed and sworn to before me this 3rd day of April 1905.

OL Johnson
Notary Public.

Applications for Enrollment of Choctaw Newborn
Act of 1905 Volume X

BIRTH AFFIDAVIT.

DEPARTMENT OF THE INTERIOR.
COMMISSION TO THE FIVE CIVILIZED TRIBES.

IN RE APPLICATION FOR ENROLLMENT, as a citizen of the Choctaw Nation, of Lula Perry, born on the 19th day of July, 1903

Name of Father: Lewis Perry   a citizen of the Choctaw Nation.
Name of Mother: Lucy Lucas Cooper   a citizen of the Choctaw Nation.

Postoffice   Stigler, Ind. Ter.

AFFIDAVIT OF MOTHER.

UNITED STATES OF AMERICA, Indian Territory, } Central DISTRICT.

I, Lucy Lucas Cooper, on oath state that I am 22 years of age and a citizen by blood, of the Choctaw Nation; that I am the ~~lawful~~ wife of Lewis Perry, who is a citizen, by blood of the Choctaw Nation; that a female child was born to me on 19th day of July, 1903; that said child has been named Lula Perry, and was living March 4, 1905.

                 her
             Lucy Lucas x Cooper
Witnesses To Mark: mark
   { Chas. T. Difendafer
   { Joseph Folsom

Subscribed and sworn to before me this 3rd day of April, 1905

             OL Johnson
                Notary Public.

AFFIDAVIT OF ATTENDING PHYSICIAN OR MID-WIFE.

UNITED STATES OF AMERICA, Indian Territory, } Central DISTRICT.

I, Jincy Folsom, a midwife, on oath state that I attended on Mrs. Lucy Lucas Cooper, wife of Lewis Perry on the 19th day of July, 1903; that there was born to her on said date a female child; that said child was living March 4, 1905, and is said to have been named Lula Perry

Applications for Enrollment of Choctaw Newborn
Act of 1905 Volume X

her
Jincy x Folsom
mark

Witnesses To Mark:
  { Chas. T. Difendafer
    Joseph Folsom

Subscribed and sworn to before me this 3rd day of April , 1905

                              OL Johnson
                                  Notary Public.

<u>Choc New Born 664</u>
    Harland H. Whitner[sic] b. 2-13-05

                                           Choctaw 247.

                     Muskogee, Indian Territory, April 8, 1905.

A. J. Whitener,
    Orr, Indian Territory.

Dear Sir:

    Receipt is hereby acknowledged of the affidavits of Lizzie Whitener and Jerry Ashley to the birth of Harland H. Whitener, son of A. J. and Lizzie Whitener, February 13, 1905, and the same have been filed with our records as an application for the enrollment of said child.

                        Respectfully,

                                       Commissioner in Charge.

Applications for Enrollment of Choctaw Newborn
Act of 1905   Volume X

7-NB-664

Muskogee, Indian Territory, July 21, 1905.

A. J. Whitener,
    Orr, Indian Territory.

Dear Sir:

    Receipt is hereby acknowledged of your letter of July 10, 1904, asking if the enrollment of Harland H. Whitener has been approved.

    In reply to your letter you are advised that the name of Harland H. Whitner[sic] has been placed upon a schedule of citizens of the Choctaw Nation prepared for forwarding to the Secretary of the Interior, and you will be notified when his enrollment is approved by the Department.

                      Respectfully,

                                        Commissioner.

BIRTH AFFIDAVIT.

DEPARTMENT OF THE INTERIOR.
COMMISSION TO THE FIVE CIVILIZED TRIBES.

IN RE APPLICATION FOR ENROLLMENT, as a citizen of the   Choctaw   Nation, of Harland H. Whitener   , born on the 13th day of   February , 1905

Name of Father: A. J. Whitener   a citizen of the United States ~~Nation~~.
Name of Mother: Lizzie Whitener   a citizen of the   Choctaw   Nation.

                      Postoffice   Orr Ind Terr

AFFIDAVIT OF MOTHER.

UNITED STATES OF AMERICA, Indian Territory,
    Southern   DISTRICT.

    I, Lizzie Whitener   , on oath state that I am 26   years of age and a citizen by   blood   , of the   Choctaw   Nation; that I am the lawful wife of   A. J. Whitener , who is a citizen, ~~by~~ _____ of the   United States ~~Nation~~; that a male   child was born to me on   13th day of   February   , 1905; that said child has been named   Harland H Whitener   , and was living March 4, 1905.

                                   Lizzie Whitener

Applications for Enrollment of Choctaw Newborn
Act of 1905   Volume X

Witnesses To Mark:
  { E A Downing
  { J L Harper

    Subscribed and sworn to before me this 31st day of March , 1905

                       Walter Hodges
                       Notary Public.

AFFIDAVIT OF ATTENDING PHYSICIAN OR MID-WIFE.

UNITED STATES OF AMERICA, Indian Territory, }
   Southern   DISTRICT. }

    I, Jerry Ashley , a physician , on oath state that I attended on Mrs. Lizzie Whitener , wife of A. J. Whitener on the 13th day of February , 1905; that there was born to her on said date a male child; that said child was living March 4, 1905, and is said to have been named Harland H Whitener

                       Jerry Ashley

Witnesses To Mark:
  {   C.A. King
  {

    Subscribed and sworn to before me this 31st day of March , 1905

                       Walter Hodges
                       Notary Public.

Choc New Born 665
    George Lafayett Harkins b. 1-25-05

Applications for Enrollment of Choctaw Newborn
Act of 1905   Volume X

Choctaw 4011.

Muskogee, Indian Territory, April 8, 1905.

C. M. Threadgill,
    Attorney at Law,
        Coalgate, Indian Territory.

Dear Sir:

    Receipt is hereby acknowledged of your letter of April 3, transmitting the affidavits of Mollie Harkins and Giles W. Harkins to the birth of George Lafayett Harkins, son of Giles W. and Mollie Harkins, January 25, 1905, and the same have been filed with our records as an application for the enrollment of said child.

        Respectfully,

                Commissioner in Charge.

BIRTH AFFIDAVIT.

DEPARTMENT OF THE INTERIOR.
COMMISSION TO THE FIVE CIVILIZED TRIBES.

IN RE APPLICATION FOR ENROLLMENT, as a citizen of the   Choctaw   Nation, of George Lafayett Harkins   , born on the 25th day of   January   , 1905

Name of Father: Giles W. Harkins   a citizen of the   Choctaw   Nation.
Name of Mother: Mollie Harkins   a citizen of the   Choctaw   Nation.

        Postoffice   Coalgate, I.T.

AFFIDAVIT OF MOTHER.

UNITED STATES OF AMERICA, Indian Territory, ⎱
    Central   DISTRICT. ⎰

    I,   Mollie Harkins   , on oath state that I am   33   years of age and a citizen by   Marriage   , of the   Choctaw   Nation; that I am the lawful wife of   Giles W Harkins   , who is a citizen, by Blood   of the   Choctaw   Nation; that a male   child was born to me on 25th day of   January   , 1905; that said child has been named   George Lafayett Harkins   , and was living March 4, 1905.

                Mollie Harkins

Applications for Enrollment of Choctaw Newborn
Act of 1905 Volume X

Witnesses To Mark:
   { Maud Olsan[sic]
    M A * Rider

Witness to mark
C.M. Threadgill
Maud Olsan

Subscribed and sworn to before me this 3rd day of April , 1905

                            C.M. Threadgill
                            Notary Public.

AFFIDAVIT OF ATTENDING PHYSICIAN OR MID-WIFE.

UNITED STATES OF AMERICA, Indian Territory,
    Central   DISTRICT.

    I, Giles W Harkins , a Physician , on oath state that I attended on Mrs. Mollie Harkins , wife of Giles W Harkins on the 25th day of January , 1905; that there was born to her on said date a male child; that said child was living March 4, 1905, and is said to have been named George Lafayett Harkins

                            Giles W Harkins

Witnesses To Mark:
   { Maud Olsan[sic]
    M A Rider

Witness to mark
C.M. Threadgill
Maud Olsan

Subscribed and sworn to before me this 3rd day of April , 1905

                            C.M. Threadgill
                            Notary Public.

Choc New Born 666
    Cassie Lewis b. 1-25-05

Applications for Enrollment of Choctaw Newborn
Act of 1905   Volume X

BIRTH AFFIDAVIT.

DEPARTMENT OF THE INTERIOR.
COMMISSION TO THE FIVE CIVILIZED TRIBES.

IN RE APPLICATION FOR ENROLLMENT, as a citizen of the Choctaw Nation, of Cassie Lewis, born on the 25 day of January, 1905

Name of Father: Benjaman Lewis   a citizen of the Freedman Nation.
Name of Mother: Cora Sexton   a citizen of the Choctaw Nation.

Postoffice   Kinta I.T

AFFIDAVIT OF MOTHER.

UNITED STATES OF AMERICA, Indian Territory,
Western   DISTRICT.

I, Cora Sexton, on oath state that I am 15 years of age and a citizen by Blood, of the Choctaw Nation; ~~that I am the lawful wife of~~   ~~, who is a citizen~~, by ~~25~~ of the ~~January~~ Nation; that a female child was born to me on 25 day of January, 1905; that said child has been named Cassie Lewis, and was living March 4, 1905.

Cora Sexton

Witnesses To Mark:
{

Subscribed and sworn to before me this Third day of April, 1905

L D Allen
Notary Public.

AFFIDAVIT OF ATTENDING PHYSICIAN OR MID-WIFE.

UNITED STATES OF AMERICA, Indian Territory,
Western   DISTRICT.

I, Elsie Moore, a Midwife, on oath state that I attended on Mrs. Cora Sexton, ~~wife of~~   on the 25 day of January, 1905; that there was born to her on said date a female child; that said child was living March 4, 1905, and is said to have been named Cassie Lewis

her
Elsie x Moore
mark

Witnesses To Mark:
{ Calvin Lewis
  (Name Illegible)

Applications for Enrollment of Choctaw Newborn
Act of 1905   Volume X

Subscribed and sworn to before me this 3rd day of   April   , 1905

L D Allen
Notary Public.

Choctaw 2830.

Muskogee, Indian Territory, April 8, 1905.

Cora Sexton,
    Kinta, Indian Territory.

Dear Madam:

Receipt is hereby acknowledged of the affidavits of Cora Sexton and Elsie Moore to the birth of Cassie Lewis, daughter of Cora Sexton and Benjaman Lewis, January 25, 1905, and the same have been filed with our records as an application for the enrollment of said child.

Respectfully,

Commissioner in Charge.

7-NB-666

Muskogee, Indian Territory, September 12, 1906.

Guy A. Curry,
    Quinton, Indian Territory.

Dear Sir:

Receipt is hereby acknowledged of your letter of September 4, 1906, asking the status of the enrollment of Cassie Lewis.

In reply you are advised that the name of Cassie Lewis appears upon the final roll of citizens by blood of the Choctaw Nation, enrolled under the Act of Congress approved March 3, 1905.

Respectfully,

Commissioner.

Applications for Enrollment of Choctaw Newborn
Act of 1905 Volume X

Choc New Born 667
 Ridgely Bond   b. 1-27-03

Choctaw 4606.

Muskogee, Indian Territory, April 8, 1905.

Ridgely Bond,
 Sans Bois, Indian Territory.

Dear Sir:

Receipt is hereby acknowledged of the affidavits of Sina Bond and E. Johnson to the birth of Ridgely Bond, son of Sina and Ridgely Bond, January 27, 1903, and the same have been filed with our records as an application for the enrollment of said child.

Respectfully,

Commissioner in Charge.

BIRTH AFFIDAVIT.

DEPARTMENT OF THE INTERIOR.
COMMISSION TO THE FIVE CIVILIZED TRIBES.

IN RE APPLICATION FOR ENROLLMENT, as a citizen of the   Choctaw   Nation, of Ridgely Bond   , born on the   27   day of   January, 1903. , 1.........

Name of Father: Ridgely Bond   a citizen of the   Choctaw   Nation.
Name of Mother: Sina Bond   a citizen of the   Choctaw   Nation.

Postoffice   Sans Bois, I.T.

AFFIDAVIT OF MOTHER.

UNITED STATES OF AMERICA, Indian Territory, }
        Western   DISTRICT.

I,   Sina Bond   , on oath state that I am   39   years of age and a citizen by blood   , of the   Choctaw   Nation; that I am the lawful wife of   Ridgely Bond   , who is a citizen, by   Intermarriage   of the   Choctaw   Nation; that a   Male   child was born to me on   27   day of   January, 1903   , 1.........; that said child has been named   Ridgely Bond   , and was living March 4, 1905.

236

Applications for Enrollment of Choctaw Newborn
Act of 1905   Volume X

                                her
                              Sina x Bond

Witnesses To Mark: mark
  { Green McCurtain
    CC Wellshear

      Subscribed and sworn to before me this   3rd day of   April   , 1905

                                    PF Hester
                                          Notary Public
My Commission expires March 4th 1907

AFFIDAVIT OF ATTENDING PHYSICIAN OR MID-WIFE.

UNITED STATES OF AMERICA, Indian Territory, }
    Western   DISTRICT. }

      I,   E Johnson   , a   Physician   , on oath state that I attended on Mrs.   Sina Bond   , wife of   Ridgely Bond   on the 27 day of   January, 1903, 1........; that there was born to her on said date a   male   child; that said child was living March 4, 1905, and is said to have been named   Ridgely Bond

                                E Johnson MD

Witnesses To Mark:
  {

      Subscribed and sworn to before me this   day of   , 1905
      Subscribed and sworn to before me this   3rd day of   April   , 1905

                                   PF Hester
                                       Notary Public
My Commission expires March 4th 1907

NEW-BORN AFFIDAVIT.

             Number................

...Choctaw Enrolling Commission...

      IN THE MATTER OF THE APPLICATION FOR ENROLLMENT, as a citizen of the Choctaw   Nation, of   Ridgely E Bond Jr

born on the 27   day of ___January___ 190 3

Applications for Enrollment of Choctaw Newborn
Act of 1905   Volume X

Name of father   Ridgely Bond   a citizen of   Choctaw
Nation final enrollment No. 462
Name of mother   Sina Bond   a citizen of   Choctaw
Nation final enrollment No. 12740

                                             Postoffice   San Bois I.T.

AFFIDAVIT OF MOTHER.

UNITED STATES OF AMERICA
INDIAN TERRITORY
   Western   DISTRICT

        I   Sina B ond   , on oath state that I am   40   years of age and a citizen by   blood   of the   Choctaw   Nation, and as such have been placed upon the final roll of the   Choctaw   Nation, by the Honorable Secretary of the Interior my final enrollment number being   12740 ; that I am the lawful wife of   Ridgely Bond   , who is a citizen of the   Choctaw   Nation, and as such has been placed upon the final roll of said Nation by the Honorable Secretary of the Interior, his final enrollment number being   462   and that a   male   child was born to me on the   27th day of   January   190 3; that said child has been named   Ridgely E Bond Jr   , and is now living.

                                      Sina Bond

Witnesseth.
  Must be two } J W Rabon
  Witnesses who
  are Citizens.   James H Beckle

    Subscribed and sworn to before me this   6"   day of   Jan   190 5

                                    L.C. Tuey
                                                 Notary Public.

My commission expires: Jan 17 - 1907

AFFIDAVIT OF ATTENDING PHYSICIAN OR MIDWIFE

UNITED STATES OF AMERICA
INDIAN TERRITORY
   Western   DISTRICT

    I,   E Johnson   a   Practicing Physician
on oath state that I attended on Mrs.   Sina Bond   wife of   Ridgely Bond
on the   27th day of   January   , 190 3 , that there was born to her on said date a   male
child, that said child is now living, and is said to have been named   Ridgely E Bond Jr

                                          E Johnson   *M.D.*

    Subscribed and sworn to before me this, the   6   day of
    Jan   190 5

Applications for Enrollment of Choctaw Newborn
Act of 1905   Volume X

WITNESSETH: L C Tuey   Notary Public.

Must be two witnesses who are citizens { J W Rabon

James H Beckle

We hereby certify that we are well acquainted with   E Johnson   a practicing physician   and know   him   to be reputable and of good standing in the community.

J W Rabon

James H Beckle

Choc New Born 668
         Rena Pauline Ervin b. 6-10-04

Affidavit of Attending Physician or Midwife

UNITED STATES OF AMERICA,
     INDIAN TERRITORY,
   Central   DISTRICT

I,   J E Cofer   a   Physician   on oath state that I attended on Mrs. Lizzie H Ervin   wife of Columbus C Ervin on the 10th day of   June , 190 4, that there was born to her on said date a   female child, that said child is now living, and is said to have been named Rena Pauline Ervin

                           J E Cofer   M. D.

Subscribed and sworn to before me this the   19   day of   Jan   1905

                         (Name Illegible)
                             Notary Public.

WITNESSETH:

Must be two witnesses who are citizens and know the child. { J H Everidge

B A Nelson

We hereby certify that we are well acquainted with   J E Cofer   a   Physician   and know   him   to be reputable and of good standing in the community.

Applications for Enrollment of Choctaw Newborn
Act of 1905   Volume X

Must be two citizen witnesses. { J H Everidge
B A Nelson

NEW-BORN AFFIDAVIT.

Number............

Choctaw Enrolling Commission.

IN THE MATTER OF THE APPLICATION FOR ENROLLMENT, as a citizen of the Choctaw   Nation, of   Rena Pauline Ervin

born on the   10th   day of   June   1904

Name of father   Columbus C Ervin   a citizen of   Choctaw Nation final enrollment No   3974
Name of mother   Lizzie H Ervin   a citizen of   Choctaw Nation final enrollment No   3975

Postoffice   Soper, IT

AFFIDAVIT OF MOTHER.

UNITED STATES OF AMERICA,
INDIAN TERRITORY,
Central   DISTRICT

I   Lizzie H Ervin   on oath state that I am 39 years of age and a citizen by   blood   of the   Choctaw   Nation, and as such have been placed upon the final roll of the   Choctaw   Nation, by the Honorable Secretary of the Interior my final enrollment number being ....; that I am the lawful wife of   Columbus C Ervin   , who is a citizen of the   Choctaw   Nation, and as such has been placed upon the final roll of said Nation by the Honorable Secretary of the Interior, his final enrollment number being .... and that a   female   child was born to me on the   10th   day of   June   1904 ; that said child has been named   Rena Pauline Ervin   , and is now living.

Lizzie H Ervin

WITNESSETH:
Must be two Witnesses who are Citizens. { J H Everidge
B A Nelson

Subscribed and sworn to before me this   19   day of   Jan   1905

(Name Illegible)
Notary Public.

My commission expires   July 9 - 1908

Applications for Enrollment of Choctaw Newborn
Act of 1905 Volume X

BIRTH AFFIDAVIT.

DEPARTMENT OF THE INTERIOR.
COMMISSION TO THE FIVE CIVILIZED TRIBES.

IN RE APPLICATION FOR ENROLLMENT, as a citizen of the Choctaw Nation, of Rena Pauline Ervin , born on the 10 day of June , 1904

Name of Father: Columbus C Ervin   a citizen of the Choctaw Nation.
Name of Mother: Lizzie H Ervin   a citizen of the Choctaw Nation.

Postoffice   Soper I.T.

AFFIDAVIT OF MOTHER.

UNITED STATES OF AMERICA, Indian Territory, }
Central   DISTRICT.

I, Lizzie H Ervin , on oath state that I am 39 years of age and a citizen by Blood , of the Choctaw Nation; that I am the lawful wife of Columbus C Ervin , who is a citizen, by Blood of the Choctaw Nation; that a Female child was born to me on 10 day of June , 1904; that said child has been named Rena Pauline Ervin , and was living March 4, 1905.

Lizzie H Ervin

Witnesses To Mark:
{

Subscribed and sworn to before me this 3 day of Apr , 1905

(Name Illegible)
My com expires July 9 - 1908   Notary Public.

AFFIDAVIT OF ATTENDING PHYSICIAN OR MID-WIFE.

UNITED STATES OF AMERICA, Indian Territory, }
Central   DISTRICT.

I, J.E. Cofer , a Physician , on oath state that I attended on Mrs. Lizzie H Ervin , wife of Columbus C Ervin on the 10 day of June , 1904; that there was born to her on said date a Female child; that said child was living March 4, 1905, and is said to have been named Rena Pauline Ervin

J E Cofer MD

Witnesses To Mark:
{

Applications for Enrollment of Choctaw Newborn
Act of 1905   Volume X

Subscribed and sworn to before me this 3   day of   Apr   , 1905

(Name Illegible)
Notary Public.

<u>Choc New Born 669</u>
    Corine Cooper   b. 9-6-03

Choctaw 3197.

Muskogee, Indian Territory, April 8, 1905.

Stephen Cooper,
    Hartshorne, Indian Territory.

Dear Sir:

    Receipt is hereby acknowledged of the affidavits of Ada Cooper and Elizzie Beth Lance to the birth of Corine Cooper, daughter of Ada and Stephen Cooper, September 6, 1903, and the same have been filed with our records as an application for the enrollment of said child.

    Respectfully,

Commissioner in Charge.

COPY   7 N.B. 669

Muskogee, Indian Territory, April 12, 1905.

Stephen Cooper,
    Hartshorne, Indian Territory.

Dear Sir:

    You are hereby advised that before the application for the enrollment of your infant child, Corine Cooper, can be finally disposed of, it will be necessary for you to furnish the Commission either the original or a certified copy of the license and certificate of your marriage to her mother, Ada Cooper.

    Please attend to this matter as once.

Applications for Enrollment of Choctaw Newborn
Act of 1905   Volume X

Respectfully,
SIGNED
T. B. Needles.
Commissioner in Charge.

---

7 NB 669

COPY

Muskogee, Indian Territory, April 20, 1905.

Hulsey & Patterson,
    Attorneys at Law,
        Hartshorne, Indian Territory.

Gentlemen:

    Receipt is hereby acknowledged of your letter of April 15, 1905, enclosing marriage license and certificate between Stephen Cooper and Ada Hunter which you offer in support of the application for the enrollment of Corrine[sic] Cooper as a citizen by blood of the Choctaw Nation and the same have been filed with the record in this case.

Respectfully,

SIGNED *Tams Bixby*
Chairman.

Applications for Enrollment of Choctaw Newborn
Act of 1905   Volume X

DEPARTMENT OF THE INTERIOR,
Commission to the Five Civilized Tribes.
FILED
APR 20 1905
Tams Bixby
CHAIRMAN.

No. 3398

Certificate of Record of Marriages.

UNITED STATES OF AMERICA,
INDIAN TERRITORY,   } SCT:
.................................DISTRICT.

I, *E.J. Fannin*, Clerk of the United States Court in the Indian Territory and District aforesaid, do hereby CERTIFY, that the License for and Certificate of the Marriage of

Mr.   Stephen Cooper   and

Miss Ada Hunter   was

filed in my office in said Territory and District the day of   **FEB 18 1903**   A.D., 190 and duly recorded in Book   10   of Marriage Record, Page   406

WITNESS my hand and seal of said Court, at   South McAlester.   , this .... day of   **FEB 18 1903**   , A.D. 190

E.J. Fannin
Clerk.

By   WC Donnelly   Deputy.

No.   3398   FORM NO. 598.

MARRIAGE LICENSE.

UNITES STATES OF AMERICA,
THE INDIAN TERRITORY,   } ss:
Cent   DISTRICT.

To any Person Authorized by Law to Solemnize Marriage—Greeting:

You are hereby commanded to solemnize the Rite and publish the Banns of Matrimony between
Mr.   Stephen Cooper   of   Hartshorne   in

Applications for Enrollment of Choctaw Newborn
Act of 1905   Volume X

the *Indian Territory, aged*   29   *years, and M*   iss Ada Hunter
of   Hartshorne   *in the Indian Territory, aged*   24   *years, according to law, and do you officially sign and return this License to the parties therein named.*

WITNESS *my hand and official seal, this*   12   *day of*   Feby   A. D. 190 3

E.J. Fannin
Clerk of the United States Court.

WC Donnelly   *Deputy*

CERTIFICATE OF MARRIAGE.

UNITES STATES OF AMERICA, ⎫
THE INDIAN TERRITORY, ⎬ ss: I,   IC Mathers
DISTRICT.   ⎭   *a*   Minister

do hereby CERTIFY, *that on the*   14   *day of*   feb[sic]   A, D. 190 3 ; *I did duly and according to law, as commanded in the foregoing License, solemnize the Rite and publish the* BANNS OF MATRIMONY *between the parties therein named.*

Witness my hand this   14   *day of*   feb   , A. D. 190 3

My credentials are recorded in the office of the Clerk of the United States Court in the Indian Territory, Central District, Book   B   *Page*   145

I C Mathers
a   Minister

NEW-BORN AFFIDAVIT.

Number................

...Choctaw Enrolling Commission...

IN THE MATTER OF THE APPLICATION FOR ENROLLMENT, as a citizen of the Choctaw   Nation, of   Corine Cooper

born on the   6th   day of   September   190 3

Applications for Enrollment of Choctaw Newborn
Act of 1905 Volume X

Name of father   S.C. Cooper   a citizen of   Choctaw
Nation final enrollment No.   9253
Name of mother   Adah[sic] Cooper   a citizen of   Choctaw
Nation final enrollment No.   ——

                                          Postoffice   Hartshorne I.T.

AFFIDAVIT OF MOTHER.

UNITED STATES OF AMERICA
INDIAN TERRITORY
   Central   DISTRICT

   I   Adah Cooper   , on oath state that I am 27 years of age and a citizen   of the United States   Nation, and as such have been placed upon the final roll of the   ——   Nation, by the Honorable Secretary of the Interior my final enrollment number being   ——   ; that I am the lawful wife of   S. C. Cooper   , who is a citizen of the   Choctaw   Nation, and as such has been placed upon the final roll of said Nation by the Honorable Secretary of the Interior, his final enrollment number being   9253   and that a   Female   child was born to me on the   6th day of September   190 3; that said child has been named   Corean Cooper   , and is now living.

                                          Adah Cooper

Witnesseth.
   Must be two   }   J D Chastain
   Witnesses who
   are Citizens.   D.N. Jackson

   Subscribed and sworn to before me this   5th day of   Jan   190 5

                                          W^m J Hulsey
                                                     Notary Public.
My commission expires:

AFFIDAVIT OF ATTENDING PHYSICIAN OR MIDWIFE

UNITED STATES OF AMERICA
INDIAN TERRITORY
   Central   DISTRICT

   I,   C C Savage   a   physician   on oath state that I attended on Mrs.   S.C. Cooper   wife of   S.C. Cooper   on the   9   day of September   , 190 3 , that there was born to her ~~on said date~~ *a few days prior* a   Female   child, that said child is now living, and is said to have been named Corine Cooper

                                          C C Savage   *M.D.*

Applications for Enrollment of Choctaw Newborn
Act of 1905 Volume X

Subscribed and sworn to before me this, the 6th day of Jan 1905

WITNESSETH:
Must be two witnesses who are citizens
{ Robert Gardner
William L Ervin

Wm J Hulsey   Notary Public.

We hereby certify that we are well acquainted with C C Savage a Physician and know him to be reputable and of good standing in the community.

Eastman Nelson
County Clerk Gaines Co
J.D. Chastain   *Hartshorne IT*

Wm J Hulsey
Hartshorne, I.T.
Will Anderson
Hartshorne, I.T.

BIRTH AFFIDAVIT.

DEPARTMENT OF THE INTERIOR.
COMMISSION TO THE FIVE CIVILIZED TRIBES.

IN RE APPLICATION FOR ENROLLMENT, as a citizen of the Choctaw Nation, of Corine Cooper, born on the 6 day of September, 1903

Name of Father: Stephen Cooper   a citizen of the Choctaw Nation.
                                           United States
Name of Mother: Ada Cooper   a citizen of the intermarriage Nation.

Postoffice   Hartshorne I T

AFFIDAVIT OF MOTHER.

UNITED STATES OF AMERICA, Indian Territory,
Central   DISTRICT.

I, Ada Cooper, on oath state that I am 24 years of age and a citizen by Marriage, of the Choctaw Nation; that I am the lawful wife of Stephen Cooper, who is a citizen, by Blood of the Choctaw Nation; that a Female child was born to me on 6 day of September, 1903; that said child has been named Corine, and was living March 4, 1905.

                                           Ada Cooper

Witnesses To Mark:

Applications for Enrollment of Choctaw Newborn
Act of 1905 Volume X

Subscribed and sworn to before me this 3 day of   April   , 1905

My COmmission Expires
MAY 20 1908

Samuel A Maysey
Notary Public.

AFFIDAVIT OF ATTENDING PHYSICIAN OR MID-WIFE.

UNITED STATES OF AMERICA, Indian Territory,
Central   DISTRICT.

I, Elizabeth Lance , a mid wife , on oath state that I attended on Mrs. Ada Cooper , wife of Stephen Cooper on the 6 day of September , 1903; that there was born to her on said date a Female child; that said child was living March 4, 1905, and is said to have been named Corine

Elizzie Beth Lance

Witnesses To Mark:

Subscribed and sworn to before me this 3 day of   April   , 1905

My COmmission Expires
MAY 20 1908

Samuel A Maysey
Notary Public.

Choc New Born 670
     Lorena Le Flore   b. 10-6-04

7-NB-670.

Muskogee, Indian Territory, May 27, 1905.

Noel LeFlore,
     Ironbridge, Indian Territory.

Dear Sir:

Referring to the application for the enrollment of your infant child, Lorena LeFlore, born October 6, 1904, it is noted from the testimony taken in this case on the 4th ultimo, that you were the only one in attendance upon your wife at the time of Birth of the applicant.

Applications for Enrollment of Choctaw Newborn
Act of 1905 Volume X

If this is correct it will be necessary that you file in this office the affidavits of two persons, who are disinterested and not related the[sic] the applicant, who have actual knowledge of the facts that the child was born, the date of her birth; that she was living on March 4, 1905, and that Mary LeFlore is her mother.

Respectfully,

Chairman.

7-NB-670

Muskogee, Indian Territory, July 18, 1905.

Noel LeFlore,
    Ironbridge, Indian Territory.

Dear Sir:

Receipt is hereby acknowledged of the affidavits of Adam E. Watson and Joe L. McCann to the birth of Lorena Leflore, daughter of Noel and Mary Leflore, October 6, 1904, and the same have been filed with the records of this office in the matter of the enrollment of said child.

Respectfully,

Commissioner.

United State of America }   Personally appeared before me a
Ind Tery Central Dist   Notary Public in and for the Central dist of the U S Court for the Ind Tey Adam E. Watson who being duly sworn says on his oath that he is personally acquainted with Noel E Leflore and his wife Mary Leflore who are citizens of the Choctaw Nation by blood, that said Noel E Leflore and wife Mary Leflore have a Female child born to them on or about the 6th day of Oct 1904, that said child is named Lorena Leflore and was liveing[sic] on the 4th day of March 1905 and is now liveing[sic].

Adam E Watson

Sworn to and subscribed before me this the 8th day of July 1905

M W Newman

Applications for Enrollment of Choctaw Newborn
Act of 1905   Volume X

United States of America   Personally appeared before me a Notary Public
Ind Tery Central Dist   in and for the Central Dist of the U.S. Court for the Ind Tery Joe L McCann who after being sworn says on his oath that he is personally acquainted with Noel E Leflore and his wife Mary Leflore who are citizens of the Choctaw Nation by blood, that said Leflore Noel E. and his wife Mary Leflore have a Female child born to them on or about the 6th day of Oct 1904 that said child is named Lorena Leflore and was liveing[sic] on the 4" day of March 1905 and is liveing[sic] at this time.

Joe L McCann

Sworn to and subscribed this the 8th day if July 1905

M W Newman
Notary Public.

7-7671
7-7141

DEPARTMENT OF THE INTERIOR,
COMMISSION TO THE FIVE CIVILIZED TRIBES.
BOKOSHE, INDIAN TERRITORY APRIL 4, 1905.

In the matter of the application for the enrollment of Lorena LeFlore as a citizen by blood of the Choctaw Nation.

Lorena LeFlore being first duly sworn testifies as follows:

EXAMINATION BY THE COMMISSION:

Q What is your name? A Lorena LeFlore.
Q What is your age? A About forth-six[sic].
Q What is your post office? A Ironbridge.
Q Are you acquainted with Mary LeFlore who has this day made application for the enrollment of her infant daughter Lorena LeFlore? A Yes, sir.
Q Are you a citizen by blood of the Choctaw Nation? A Yes, sir.
Q Were you present when Lorena LeFlore was born? A I was there the next day but wasn't there at the time.
Q When was this child born? A 1904.
Q This child is now living? A Yes, sir.
Q What is the name of the father of this child? A Noel LeFlore.

Witness excused.

Applications for Enrollment of Choctaw Newborn
Act of 1905   Volume X

Noel LeFlore being first duly sworn testifies as follows:

EXAMINATION BY THE COMMISSION:

Q What is your name? A Noel LeFlore.
Q What is your age? A About twenty-three.
Q What is your post office address? A Ironbridge.
Q Are you a citizen by blood of the Choctaw Nation? A Yes, sir.
Q Is Mary Leflore who has this day made application for the enrollment of her minor child Lorena LeFlore your wife? A Yes, sir.
Q When was this child born? A October 6, 1904.
Q Was any one present besides yourself when that child was born? A No, except my wife.
Q What is your wife's name? A Mary.
Q Is she a citizen by blood of the Choctaw Nation? A Yes, sir.
Q Is this child Lorena LeFlore living? A Yes, sir.

Witness excused.

Chas. T. Difendafer being first duly sworn states that the above and foregoing is a full, true and correct transcript of his stenographic notes taken in said cause on said date.

Chas T Difendafer

Subscribed to and sworn to before me this 4th day of April 1905.

OL Johnson
Notary Public.

7- 7671 = 7- 7141

BIRTH AFFIDAVIT.

DEPARTMENT OF THE INTERIOR.
COMMISSION TO THE FIVE CIVILIZED TRIBES.

IN RE APPLICATION FOR ENROLLMENT, as a citizen of the   Choctaw   Nation, of Lorena Le Flore   , born on the 6 day of October , 1904

Name of Father: Noel Le Flore   a citizen of the Choctaw Nation.
Name of Mother: Mary Le Flore   a citizen of the Choctaw Nation.

Postoffice   Ironbridge I.T.

Applications for Enrollment of Choctaw Newborn
Act of 1905 Volume X

AFFIDAVIT OF MOTHER.

UNITED STATES OF AMERICA, Indian Territory,
   Central   DISTRICT.

I, Mary Le Flore, on oath state that I am 26 years of age and a citizen by blood, of the Choctaw Nation; that I am the lawful wife of Noel Le Flore, who is a citizen, by blood of the Choctaw Nation; that a female child was born to me on 6th day of October, 1904; that said child has been named Lorena Le Flore, and was living March 4, 1905.

                                        Mary Leflore

Witnesses To Mark:
{

   Subscribed and sworn to before me this 4th day of April, 1905

                                        OL Johnson
                                        Notary Public.

Choc New Born 671
   Sinie Cobb b. 12-13-04

                                        7-NB-671.

                    Muskogee, Indian Territory, May 27, 1905.

Loren Cobb,
   Shady Point, Indian Territory.

Dear Sir:

   There is enclosed you herewith for execution application for the enrollment of your infant child, Sinie Cobb.

   In the affidavits of February 6, 1905, heretofore filed in this office, the date of the applicant's birth is given as December 13, 1904, while the affidavits of the 4th ultimo, give the date of birth as September 13, 1904. In the enclosed application the date of birth is left blank. Please insert the correct date and, when the affidavits are properly executed, return them to this office.

   In having these affidavits executed care should be exercised to see that all names are written in full, as they appear in the body of the affidavit, and in the event that either

Applications for Enrollment of Choctaw Newborn
Act of 1905   Volume X

of the persons signing the affidavit are unable to write, signatures by mark must be attested by two witnesses. Each affidavit must be executed before a Notary Public and the notarial seal and signature of the officer must be attached to each separate affidavit.

Respectfully,

VR 27-3.   Chairman.

---

7 NB 671

Muskogee, Indian Territory, June 17, 1905.

Loren Cobb,
    Shadypoint, Indian Territory.

Dear Sir:

    Receipt is hereby acknowledged of the affidavits of Sarah E. Cobb and Emmaline[sic] Terrell to the birth of Sinie Cobb, daughter of Loren Cobb and Sarah E. Cobb (James), December 13, 1904, and the same have been filed with our records in the matter of the enrollment of said child.

Respectfully,

Chairman.

7-NB-671

Muskogee, Indian Territory, July 11, 1905.

Loren Cobb,
    Shadypoint, Indian Territory.

Dear Sir:

    Receipt is hereby acknowledged of your letter of July 7, 1905, asking when you can file on land for Sinie Cobb.

    In reply to your letter you are advised that the name of Sinie Cobb daughter of Loren and Sarah E. Cobb, has not yet been placed upon a schedule of citizens by blood of the Choctaw Nation prepared for forwarding to the Secretary of the Interior, and pending her enrollment and approval thereof by the Department no selection of allotment could be made in her behalf.

Respectfully,

Commissioner.

Applications for Enrollment of Choctaw Newborn
Act of 1905 Volume X

7- 7890
BIRTH AFFIDAVIT.

DEPARTMENT OF THE INTERIOR.
COMMISSION TO THE FIVE CIVILIZED TRIBES.

IN RE APPLICATION FOR ENROLLMENT, as a citizen of the Choctaw Nation, of Sinie Cobb, born on the 13 day of September[sic], 1904

Name of Father: Loren Cobb — a citizen of the Choctaw Nation.
Name of Mother: Sarah E Cobb, nee James — a citizen of the Choctaw Nation.

Postoffice Shady Point

AFFIDAVIT OF MOTHER.

UNITED STATES OF AMERICA, Indian Territory,
Central DISTRICT.

I, Sarah E Cobb nee James, on oath state that I am 26 years of age and a citizen by blood, of the Choctaw Nation; that I am the lawful wife of Loren Cobb, who is a citizen, by blood of the Choctaw Nation; that a female child was born to me on 13 day of September[sic], 1904; that said child has been named Sinie Cobb, and was living March 4, 1905.

Sarah E Cobb

Witnesses To Mark:

Subscribed and sworn to before me this 4th day of April, 1905

OL Johnson
Notary Public.

AFFIDAVIT OF ATTENDING PHYSICIAN OR MID-WIFE.

UNITED STATES OF AMERICA, Indian Territory,
Central DISTRICT.

I, Emaline Terrell, a midwife, on oath state that I attended on Mrs. Sarah E Cobb nee James, wife of Loren Cobb on the 13 day of September[sic], 1904; that there was born to her on said date a female child; that said child was living March 4, 1905, and is said to have been named Sinie Cobb

Applications for Enrollment of Choctaw Newborn
Act of 1905   Volume X

                                  her
                             Emaline x Terrell

Witnesses To Mark: mark
{ Chas. T. Difendafer
{ OL Johnson

Subscribed and sworn to before me this 4th day of April , 1905

                        OL Johnson
                             Notary Public.

Affidavit of Attending Physician or Midwife

UNITED STATES OF AMERICA,
INDIAN TERRITORY,
Central   DISTRICT

    I, Emiline[sic] Terrell a midwife on oath state that I attended on Mrs. Sarah E Cobb wife of Loring[sic] Cobb on the 13 day of December , 190 4, that there was born to her on said date a female child, that said child is now living, and is said to have been named Sina[sic] Cobb

                         her
                  Emiline Terrell x   M. D.
                         mark

Subscribed and sworn to before me this the 6 day of February 1905

                     James Bower
                          Notary Public.

WITNESSETH:
Must be two witnesses { Martin Whistler
who are citizens and
know the child.   { John Johnice

    We hereby certify that we are well acquainted with Emiline Terrell a midwife and know her to be reputable and of good standing in the community.

                     Must be two citizen { Martin Whistler
                     witnesses.   { John Johnice

Applications for Enrollment of Choctaw Newborn
Act of 1905 Volume X

NEW BORN AFFIDAVIT

No ....

CHOCTAW ENROLLING COMMISSION

IN THE MATTER OF THE APPLICATION FOR ENROLLMENT as a citizen of the Choctaw Nation, of Sina Cobb born on the 13 day of December 190 4

Name of father Loring Cobb a citizen of Choctaw Nation, final enrollment No............ Daws (sic) Com Sarah E James

Name of mother Sarah E Cobb a citizen of Choctaw Nation, final enrollment No. 7890

Shady Point I.T. Postoffice.

AFFIDAVIT OF MOTHER

UNITED STATES OF AMERICA
INDIAN TERRITORY
DISTRICT Central

I Sarah E Cobb , on oath state that I am 26 years of age and a citizen by blood of the Choctaw Nation, and as such have been placed upon the final roll of the Choctaw Nation, by the Honorable Secretary of the Interior my final enrollment number being 7890 ; that I am the lawful wife of Loring Cobb , who is a citizen of the Choctaw Nation, and as such has been placed upon the final roll of said Nation by the Honorable Secretary of the Interior, his final enrollment number being .... and that a female child was born to me on the 13 day of December 190 4; that said child has been named Sina Cobb , and is now living.

WITNESSETH: Sarah E Cobb

Must be two witnesses { Martin Whistler
who are citizens { John Johnice

Subscribed and sworn to before me this, the 6 day of February , 190 5

James Bower
Notary Public.

My Commission Expires:
Sept 23 - 1907

Applications for Enrollment of Choctaw Newborn
Act of 1905   Volume X

BIRTH AFFIDAVIT.
DEPARTMENT OF THE INTERIOR.
COMMISSION TO THE FIVE CIVILIZED TRIBES.

IN RE APPLICATION FOR ENROLLMENT, as a citizen of the Choctaw Nation, of Sinie Cobb, born on the 13 day of December, 1904

Name of Father: Loren Cobb   a citizen of the Choctaw Nation.
Name of Mother: Sarah E Cobb (James)   a citizen of the Choctaw Nation.

Postoffice   Shady Point Ind Ter

AFFIDAVIT OF MOTHER.

UNITED STATES OF AMERICA, Indian Territory, }
       Central   DISTRICT.

I, Sarah E Cobb (James), on oath state that I am 26 years of age and a citizen by blood, of the Choctaw Nation; that I am the lawful wife of Loren Cobb, who is a citizen, by blood of the Choctaw Nation; that a female child was born to me on 13 day of December, 1904; that said child has been named Sinie Cobb, and was living March 4, 1905.

Sarah E Cobb

Witnesses To Mark:

Subscribed and sworn to before me this 3 day of June, 1905

WH Phillips
Notary Public.

AFFIDAVIT OF ATTENDING PHYSICIAN OR MID-WIFE.

UNITED STATES OF AMERICA, Indian Territory, }
       Central   DISTRICT.

I, Emmaline Terrell, a Midwife, on oath state that I attended on Mrs. Sarah E Cobb, wife of Loren Cobb on the 13 day of December, 1904; that there was born to her on said date a female child; that said child was living March 4, 1905, and is said to have been named Sinie Cobb

her
Emmaline x Terrell
mark

Applications for Enrollment of Choctaw Newborn
Act of 1905 Volume X

Witnesses To Mark:
{ Solomon James
{ W J Lewis

Subscribed and sworn to before me this 3 day of June , 1905

W H Philips
Notary Public.

Choc New Born 672
    Isom Wallen b. 11-21-03

7- 8008

BIRTH AFFIDAVIT.
DEPARTMENT OF THE INTERIOR,
COMMISSION TO THE FIVE CIVILIZED TRIBES.

IN RE Application for Enrollment, as a citizen of the Choctaw Nation, of Isom Wallen , born on the 21 day of Nov , 1903

Name of Father: Sim Wallen   a citizen of the Choctaw Nation.
Name of Mother: Siney Wallen nee Thomas   a citizen of the Choctaw Nation.

Post-Office: Milton, I.T.

AFFIDAVIT OF MOTHER.

UNITED STATES OF AMERICA, }
    INDIAN TERRITORY.
    Central   District.

    I, Siney Wallen , on oath state that I am 17 years of age and a citizen by blood , of the Choctaw Nation; that I am the lawful wife of Sim Wallen , who is a citizen, by blood of the Choctaw Nation; that a boy child was born to me on 21 day of Nov , 1903 , that said child has been named Isom Wallen , and is now living.

                              her
                          Siney x Wallen
WITNESSES TO MARK: mark
{ Marth[sic] Thomas
{ Isaac Thomas

Applications for Enrollment of Choctaw Newborn
Act of 1905   Volume X

Subscribed and sworn to before me this 25 *day of* March , 1905.

J. L. Lewis
NOTARY PUBLIC.

AFFIDAVIT OF ATTENDING PHYSICIAN OR MID-WIFE.

UNITED STATES OF AMERICA,
INDIAN TERRITORY.
Central   District.

I, Sickey Thomas , a midwife , on oath state that I attended on Mrs. Siney Wallen , wife of Sim Wallen on the 21 day of Nov , 1903 ; that there was born to her on said date a boy child; that said child is now living and is said to have been named Isom Wallen her

Sickey x Thomas
mark

WITNESSES TO MARK:
  Isaac Thomas
  Ed Atkinson

Subscribed and sworn to before me this 25 *day of* March , 1905.

My commission expires Mar. 16, 1906   J. L. Lewis
NOTARY PUBLIC.

7-NB-673[sic]

Muskogee, Indian Territory, July 18, 1905.

Sim Wallen,
  Milton, Indian Territory.

Dear Sir:

Receipt is hereby acknowledged of your letter of July 11, 1905, asking relative to the enrollment of your child Isam[sic] Wallen.

In reply to your letter you are advised that the name of your child Isam Wallen has been placed upon a schedule of citizens by blood of the Choctaw Nation and you will be notified when his enrollment is approved by the Secretary of the Interior.

Respectfully,

Commissioner.

Applications for Enrollment of Choctaw Newborn
Act of 1905 Volume X

Choc New Born 673
Georgie Lee Smith b. 1-21-05

NEW BORN AFFIDAVIT

No _____

CHOCTAW ENROLLING COMMISSION

IN THE MATTER OF THE APPLICATION FOR ENROLLMENT as a citizen of the Choctaw Nation, of Georgia[sic] Lee Smith born on the 21ˢᵗ day of January 190 5

Name of father George L Smith a citizen of Choctaw Nation, final enrollment No. 7786
Name of mother Mary E Smith a citizen of Choctaw Nation, final enrollment No. 263

Cowlington I.T. Postoffice.

AFFIDAVIT OF MOTHER

UNITED STATES OF AMERICA
INDIAN TERRITORY
DISTRICT Central

I Mary E Smith , on oath state that I am 30 years of age and a citizen by Inter M of the Choctaw Nation, and as such have been placed upon the final roll of the Choctaw Nation, by the Honorable Secretary of the Interior my final enrollment number being 263 ; that I am the lawful wife of George L Smith , who is a citizen of the Choctaw Nation, and as such has been placed upon the final roll of said Nation by the Honorable Secretary of the Interior, his final enrollment number being 7786 and that a Female child was born to me on the 21ˢᵗ day of January 1905 ; that said child has been named Georgia Lee Smith , and is now living.

WITNESSETH: Mary E Smith
Must be two witnesses { Elmore Smith
who are citizens { George S. Cowan

Subscribed and sworn to before me this, the 7 day of March , 190 5

A.H. Crouthamel
Notary Public.

My Commission Expires: Feb 3 - 1907

Applications for Enrollment of Choctaw Newborn
Act of 1905 Volume X

BIRTH AFFIDAVIT.

DEPARTMENT OF THE INTERIOR.
COMMISSION TO THE FIVE CIVILIZED TRIBES.

IN RE APPLICATION FOR ENROLLMENT, as a citizen of the Choctaw Nation, of Georgie Lee Smith, born on the 21st day of January, 1905

Name of Father: George L. Smith a citizen of the Choctaw Nation.
Name of Mother: Mary E. Smith a citizen of the Choctaw Nation.

Postoffice Cowlington, Ind. Ter.

AFFIDAVIT OF MOTHER.

UNITED STATES OF AMERICA, Indian Territory, }
Central DISTRICT. }

I, Mary E. Smith, on oath state that I am 30 years of age and a citizen by intermarriage, of the Choctaw Nation; that I am the lawful wife of George L. Smith, who is a citizen, by blood of the Choctaw Nation; that a female child was born to me on 21st day of January, 1905; that said child has been named Georgie Lee Smith, and was living March 4, 1905.

Mary E Smith

Witnesses To Mark:
{

Subscribed and sworn to before me this 4th day of April, 1905

OL Johnson
Notary Public.

AFFIDAVIT OF ATTENDING PHYSICIAN OR MID-WIFE.

UNITED STATES OF AMERICA, Indian Territory, }
Central DISTRICT. }

I, J. B. Beckett, a Physician, on oath state that I attended on Mrs. Mary E Smith, wife of George L Smith on the 21 day of January, 1905; that there was born to her on said date a female child; that said child was living March 4, 1905, and is said to have been named Georgie Lee Smith

J. B. Beckett M.D.

Applications for Enrollment of Choctaw Newborn
Act of 1905   Volume X

Witnesses To Mark:

{

   Subscribed and sworn to before me this   31   day of   March   , 1905

My Com ex 2-3-1907

A. H. Crouthamel
Notary Public.

Choc New Born 674
   Pauline Smith   b. 7-8-03

NEW-BORN AFFIDAVIT.

Number............

...Choctaw Enrolling Commission...

   IN THE MATTER OF THE APPLICATION FOR ENROLLMENT, as a citizen of the Choctaw   Nation, of   Pauline Smith

born on the   18   day of ___July___ 190 3

Name of father   Elmore Smith   a citizen of   Choctaw
Nation final enrollment No.   13195
Name of mother   Essie Smith   a citizen of   Choctaw
Nation final enrollment No.   933

                              Postoffice   Cowlington

AFFIDAVIT OF MOTHER.

UNITED STATES OF AMERICA
INDIAN TERRITORY
   Central   DISTRICT

         I   Essie Smith   , on oath state that I am
   23   years of age and a citizen by   intermarriage   of the   Choctaw
Nation, and as such have been placed upon the final roll of the   Choctaw   Nation, by the
Honorable Secretary of the Interior my final enrollment number being   933 ; that I am the
lawful wife of   Elmore Smith   , who is a citizen of the   Choctaw   Nation, and as
such has been placed upon the final roll of said Nation by the Honorable Secretary of the
Interior, his final enrollment number being   13195   and that a   Female   child was

Applications for Enrollment of Choctaw Newborn
Act of 1905   Volume X

born to me on the   18   day of   July   190 3; that said child has been named   Pauline Smith   , and is now living.

Essie Smith

Witnesseth.

Must be two Witnesses who are Citizens. } George S Cowan
Nathan W. Folsom

Subscribed and sworn to before me this   23   day of   Feb   190 5

A. H. Crouthamel
Notary Public.

My commission expires: Feb 3 - 1907

AFFIDAVIT OF ATTENDING PHYSICIAN OR MIDWIFE

UNITED STATES OF AMERICA
INDIAN TERRITORY
   Western   DISTRICT

I,   Geo. W. West   a   Physician on oath state that I attended on Mrs.   Essie Smith   wife of   Elmore Smith on the   18th day of   July   , 190 3 , that there was born to her on said date a   Female child, that said child is now living, and is said to have been named   Pauline Smith

Geo W. West   M.D.

Subscribed and sworn to before me this, the   24th day of   January   190 5

WITNESSETH: *(Name Illegible)*   Notary Public.

Must be two witnesses who are citizens { K R Smith
Hill T Smith

We hereby certify that we are well acquainted with   Geo W West a   Physician   and know   him   to be reputable and of good standing in the community.

K R Smith

Hill T. Smith

Applications for Enrollment of Choctaw Newborn
Act of 1905   Volume X

7- 933 7.W. 7- 13195

BIRTH AFFIDAVIT.

DEPARTMENT OF THE INTERIOR.
COMMISSION TO THE FIVE CIVILIZED TRIBES.

IN RE APPLICATION FOR ENROLLMENT, as a citizen of the   Choctaw   Nation, of Pauline Smith   , born on the 18   day of   July   , 1903

Name of Father: Elmore Smith   a citizen of the   Choctaw   Nation.
Name of Mother: Essie Smith   a citizen of the   Choctaw   Nation.

Postoffice   Cowlington Ind Ter

AFFIDAVIT OF MOTHER.

UNITED STATES OF AMERICA, Indian Territory,
Central   DISTRICT.

I,   Essie Smith   , on oath state that I am   23   years of age and a citizen by intermarriage   , of the   Choctaw   Nation; that I am the lawful wife of   Elmore Smith   , who is a citizen, by blood   of the   Choctaw   Nation; that a female   child was born to me on   18   day of   July   , 1903; that said child has been named   Pauline Smith   , and was living March 4, 1905.

Essie Smith

Witnesses To Mark:

Subscribed and sworn to before me this   4th   day of   April   , 1905

OL Johnson
Notary Public.

AFFIDAVIT OF ATTENDING PHYSICIAN OR MID-WIFE.

UNITED STATES OF AMERICA, Indian Territory,
Western   DISTRICT.

I,   Geo W. West   , a   Physician   , on oath state that I attended on Mrs.   Essie Smith   , wife of   Elmore Smith   on the 18   day of   July   , 1903; that there was born to her on said date a   Female   child; that said child was living March 4, 1905, and is said to have been named   Pauline Smith

Geo. W. West M.D.

Applications for Enrollment of Choctaw Newborn
Act of 1905   Volume X

Witnesses To Mark:
{

    Subscribed and sworn to before me this 28th day of March , 1905

                              B.A. Jennings
                                 Notary Public.

Choc New Born 675
    Lena Whistler   b. 10-21-03

7-8020   7-8021
BIRTH AFFIDAVIT.
DEPARTMENT OF THE INTERIOR.
COMMISSION TO THE FIVE CIVILIZED TRIBES.

IN RE APPLICATION FOR ENROLLMENT, as a citizen of the Choctaw Nation, of Lena Whistler , born on the 21st day of October , 1903

Name of Father: Martin Whistler   a citizen of the Choctaw Nation.
Name of Mother: Nancy Whistler   a citizen of the Choctaw Nation.

                Postoffice   Sutter, Ind. Ter.

AFFIDAVIT OF MOTHER.

UNITED STATES OF AMERICA, Indian Territory, }
    Central   DISTRICT.

    I, Nancy Whistler , on oath state that I am 27 years of age and a citizen by blood , of the Choctaw Nation; that I am the lawful wife of Martin Whistler , who is a citizen, by blood of the Choctaw Nation; that a female child was born to me on 21st day of October , 1903; that said child has been named Lena Whistler , and was living March 4, 1905.

                              Nancy Whistler

Witnesses To Mark:
{

Applications for Enrollment of Choctaw Newborn
Act of 1905 Volume X

Subscribed and sworn to before me this 4th day of April, 1905

OL Johnson
Notary Public.

AFFIDAVIT OF ATTENDING PHYSICIAN OR MID-WIFE.

UNITED STATES OF AMERICA, Indian Territory,
Central DISTRICT.

I, Mollie McCurtain, a midwife, on oath state that I attended on Mrs. Nancy Whistler, wife of Martin Whistler on the 21st day of October, 1903; that there was born to her on said date a female child; that said child was living March 4, 1905, and is said to have been named Lena Whistler

                                  her
                          Mollie x McCurtain

Witnesses To Mark: mark
    Chas T. Difendafer
    OL Johnson

Subscribed and sworn to before me this 4th day of April, 1905

OL Johnson
Notary Public.

NEW BORN AFFIDAVIT

No ....

CHOCTAW ENROLLING COMMISSION

IN THE MATTER OF THE APPLICATION FOR ENROLLMENT as a citizen of the Choctaw Nation, of Lena Whistler born on the 21 day of October 190 3

Name of father Martin Whistler   a citizen of Choctaw Nation, final enrollment No. 8020
Name of mother Nancy Whistler   a citizen of Choctaw Nation, final enrollment No. 8021

Sutter, I.T.   Postoffice.

Applications for Enrollment of Choctaw Newborn
Act of 1905   Volume X

AFFIDAVIT OF MOTHER

UNITED STATES OF AMERICA
INDIAN TERRITORY
DISTRICT   Central

I   Nancy Whistler   , on oath state that I am   27   years of age and a citizen by   blood   of the   Choctaw   Nation, and as such have been placed upon the final roll of the   Choctaw   Nation, by the Honorable Secretary of the Interior my final enrollment number being   8021   ; that I am the lawful wife of   Martin Whistler   , who is a citizen of the   Choctaw   Nation, and as such has been placed upon the final roll of said Nation by the Honorable Secretary of the Interior, his final enrollment number being   8020   and that a   Female   child was born to me on the   21   day of   October   190 3; that said child has been named   Lena Whistler   , and is now living.

WITNESSETH: Nancy Whistler
Must be two witnesses { John Johnice
who are citizens   { Loren Cobb

Subscribed and sworn to before me this, the   6   day of   February   , 190 5

James Bower
Notary Public.

My Commission Expires:
      Sept - 23 - 1907

Affidavit of Attending Physician or Midwife

UNITED STATES OF AMERICA,
INDIAN TERRITORY,
Central   DISTRICT

I,   Mollie McCurtain   a   midwife on oath state that I attended on Mrs.   Nancy Whistler   wife of   Martin Whistler   on the   21   day of   October   , 190 3, that there was born to her on said date a   Female   child, that said child is now living, and is said to have been named   Lena Whistler

                                                       her   *midwife*
                                       Mollie x McCurtain   ~~M. D.~~
                                                       mark
Subscribed and sworn to before me this the   9th   day of   Feb   1905

WN Estes
Notary Public.

WITNESSETH:
Must be two witnesses { John Johnice
who are citizens and {
know the child.   { Loren Cobb

Applications for Enrollment of Choctaw Newborn
Act of 1905   Volume X

We hereby certify that we are well acquainted with   Mollie McCurtain
a   midwife   and know   her   to be reputable and of good standing in the community.

Must be two citizen ⎰ John Johnice
witnesses.   ⎱ Loren Cobb

Choc New Born 676
    Vernon Pate   b. 11-26-04

Choctaw 5741.

Muskogee, Indian Territory, April 7, 1905.

J. L. Rappolee,
    Attorney at law,
        Caddo, Indian Territory.

Dear Sir:

    Receipt is hereby acknowledged of your letter of April 3, enclosing the affidavits of Vercy Pate and H. E. Rappolee to the birth of Vernon Pate, son of B. K. and Vercy Pate, November 26, 1904, and the same have been filed with our records as an application for the enrollment of said child.

    Receipt is also acknowledged of the marriage certificate between B. K. Pate and Versie[sic] Hamilton, which has been filed with the records in the matter of the enrollment of the above named child.

Respectfully,

Commissioner in Charge.

Applications for Enrollment of Choctaw Newborn
Act of 1905 Volume X

No. 488

Certificate of Record of Marriages.

United States of America,
The Indian Territory, } sct.
Central District.

I, *E. J. Fannin* Clerk of the United States Court, in the Indian Territory and District aforesaid, do hereby CERTIFY, that the License for and Certificate of the Marriage of

Mr. B.K. Pate and

M iss Versie Hamilton was

filed in my office in said Territory and District the 29 day of Dec A.D., 190___, and duly recorded in Book 1 of Marriage Record, Page 244

WITNESS my hand and Seal of said Court, at Durant this 29 day of Dec A.D. 190 3

E J Fannie
Clerk.
By W^mB Stone Deputy.

P. O. Durant, I. T.

DEPARTMENT OF THE INTERIOR,
COMMISSION TO THE FIVE CIVILIZED TRIBES.
FILED
APR 7 1905
TanBely CHAIRMAN.

Applications for Enrollment of Choctaw Newborn
Act of 1905 Volume X

No. 488

MARRIAGE LICENSE

United States of America,   The Indian Territory,
   Central DISTRICT, SS.

To any Person Authorized by Law to Solemnize Marriage, Greeting:

You are hereby commanded to Solemnize the Rite and publish the Banns of Matrimony between Mr.   B.K. Pate
of   Caddo   in the Indian Territory, aged   26   years,
and M iss Versie Hamilton   of   Caddo
in the Indian Territory., aged   21   years, according to law, and do you officially sign and return this License to the parties therein named.

WITNESS my hand and official seal, this   29th day of   December   A. D. 190 3

E.J. Fannin
Clerk of the United States Court.

W^{m}B Stone   *Deputy*

Certificate of Marriage.

United States of America, ⎫
  The Indian Territory,   ⎬ ss.
  Cent   District.   ⎭   I,   Chas G Parker

a   N. S. Comr   , do hereby certify, that on the   29   day of   Dec   A. D. 190 3 , I did, duly and according to law, as commanded in the foregoing License, solemnize the Rite and publish the Banns of Matrimony between the parties therein named.

Witness my hand, this   29   day of   Dec   A. D. 190 3

My credentials are recorded in the office of the Clerk of ⎫   Chas G Parker
 the United States Court in the Indian Territory,   ⎬
 Central District, Book .... , Page ....   ⎭   a   NS Comr

Note—This License and Certificate of Marriage must be returned to the Office of the Clerk of the United States Court of the Indian Territory, from whence it was issued, within sixty days from the date thereof, or the party to whom the License was issued will be liable in the amount of the One Hundred Dollars ($100.00)

Applications for Enrollment of Choctaw Newborn
Act of 1905 Volume X

BIRTH AFFIDAVIT.

DEPARTMENT OF THE INTERIOR.
COMMISSION TO THE FIVE CIVILIZED TRIBES.

IN RE APPLICATION FOR ENROLLMENT, as a citizen of the Choctaw Nation, of Vernon Pate , born on the 26th day of November , 1904

Name of Father: B. K. Pate a citizen of the Choctaw Nation.
Name of Mother: Vercy Pate (nee Vercy Hamilton) a citizen of the Choctaw Nation.

Postoffice Caddo Ind. Ter

AFFIDAVIT OF MOTHER.

UNITED STATES OF AMERICA, Indian Territory,
Central DISTRICT.

I, Vercy Pate (nee Vercy Hamilton) , on oath state that I am 22 years of age and a citizen by Blood , of the Choctaw Nation; that I am the lawful wife of B. K. Pate , who is a citizen, by marriage of the Choctaw Nation; that a Male child was born to me on 26th day of November , 1904; that said child has been named Vernon Pate , and was living March 4, 1905.

Vercy Pate

Witnesses To Mark:
{

Subscribed and sworn to before me this 1st day of April , 1905

JL Rappolee
Notary Public.

AFFIDAVIT OF ATTENDING PHYSICIAN OR MID-WIFE.

UNITED STATES OF AMERICA, Indian Territory,
Central DISTRICT.

I, H. E. Rappolee , a Physician , on oath state that I attended on Mrs. Vercy Pate , wife of B. K. Pate on the 26th day of November , 1904; that there was born to her on said date a Male child; that said child was living March 4, 1905, and is said to have been named Vernon Pate

H E Rappolee

Witnesses To Mark:
{

Applications for Enrollment of Choctaw Newborn
Act of 1905   Volume X

Subscribed and sworn to before me this 3rd day of   April   , 1905

                              JL Rappolee
                              Notary Public.

Choc New Born 677
    Mary I. Choate   b. 2-22-05
    James Luke Choate   b. 2-27-03

Choctaw 3474.

Muskogee, Indian Territory, April 7, 1905.

David Choate,
    Celestine, Indian Territory.

Dear Sir:

    Receipt is hereby acknowledged of the affidavits of Belle D. Choate Mellie[sic] Parsons to the birth of Mary I. Choate, daughter of David and Belle D. Choate, February 22, 1905, and the same have been filed with our records as an application for the enrollment of said child.

                   Respectfully,

                                 Commissioner in Charge.

$W^m O.B.$

COMMISSIONERS: TAMS BIXBY, THOMAS B. NEEDLES, C.R. BRECKINBRIDGE. WM. O. BEALL Secretary	**DEPARTMENT OF THE INTERIOR,** **COMMISSIONER TO THE FIVE CIVILIZED TRIBES.**	REFER IN REPLY TO THE FOLLOWING: 7-3274

ADDRESS ONLY THE
COMMISSION TO THE FIVE CIVILIZED TRIBES.

Muskogee, Indian Territory, April 19, 1905.

David Choate,
    Celeste[sic], Indian Territory.

Dear Sir:

    Receipt is hereby acknowledged of the affidavits of Belle D. Choate and Nancy C. Pate to the birth of James Luke Choate, son of David and Belle D. Choate, February

Applications for Enrollment of Choctaw Newborn
Act of 1905   Volume X

27, 1903, and the same have been filed with our records as an application for the enrollment of said child.

Respectfully,

Tams Bixby
Chairman.

BIRTH AFFIDAVIT.

DEPARTMENT OF THE INTERIOR.
COMMISSION TO THE FIVE CIVILIZED TRIBES.

IN RE APPLICATION FOR ENROLLMENT, as a citizen of the   Choctaw   Nation, of Mary I. Choate   , born on the 22nd day of Feb , 1905

Name of Father: David Choate   a citizen of the   Choctaw   Nation.
Name of Mother: Belle D Choate   a citizen of the   Choctaw   Nation.

Postoffice   Celestine I.T.

AFFIDAVIT OF MOTHER.

UNITED STATES OF AMERICA, Indian Territory, }
Central   DISTRICT.

I,   Belle D. Choate   , on oath state that I am 31   years of age and a citizen by   entermarriage[sic] , of the   Choctaw   Nation; that I am the lawful wife of David Choate   , who is a citizen, by blood   of the   Choctaw   Nation; that a   Female   child was born to me on 22nd day of Feb. , 1905; that said child has been named   Mary I Choate   , and was living March 4, 1905.

Belle D. Choate

Witnesses To Mark:
{

Subscribed and sworn to before me this 3rd day of April   , 1905

My commission expires   Andrew J Turner
   Mar-17-1909   Notary Public.

Applications for Enrollment of Choctaw Newborn
Act of 1905 Volume X

AFFIDAVIT OF ATTENDING PHYSICIAN OR MID-WIFE.

UNITED STATES OF AMERICA, Indian Territory,
    Central   DISTRICT.

    I, Millie Parsons , a Mid-wife , on oath state that I attended on Mrs. Belle D Choate , wife of David Choate on the 22nd day of Feb , 1905; that there was born to her on said date a Female child; that said child was living March 4, 1905, and is said to have been named Mary I. Choate

                              Millie Parsons

Witnesses To Mark:

{

    Subscribed and sworn to before me this   3rd day of   April   , 1905

                              Andrew J Turner
                              Notary Public.

Affidavit of Attending Physician or Midwife

UNITED STATES OF AMERICA,
    INDIAN TERRITORY,
    Suthern[sic] DISTRICT

    I, Nancy C Pate a mid wife on oath state that I attended on Mrs. Belle D Choate wife of David Choate on the 27 day of Feb , 190 3, that there was born to her on said date a male child, that said child is now living, and is said to have been named James Luke Choate

                                    midwife
                        Nancy C Pate   ~~M.D~~.

    Subscribed and sworn to before me this the   28 day of Mch   1905

                            (Name Illegible)
                                Notary Public.

WITNESSETH:

Must be two witnesses { WR Underwood
who are citizens and
know the child.   Mary Underwood

    We hereby certify that we are well acquainted with Nancy C Pate a Mid wife and know her to be reputable and of good standing in the community.

                      Must be two citizen   W.R. Underwood
                      witnesses.   Mary Underwood

Applications for Enrollment of Choctaw Newborn
Act of 1905   Volume X

BIRTH AFFIDAVIT.

DEPARTMENT OF THE INTERIOR.
COMMISSION TO THE FIVE CIVILIZED TRIBES.

IN RE APPLICATION FOR ENROLLMENT, as a citizen of the Choctaw Nation, of James Luke Choate, born on the 27th day of Feb, 1903

Name of Father: David Choate   a citizen of the Choctaw Nation.
Name of Mother: Belle D Choate   a citizen of the Choctaw Nation.

Postoffice   Celestine Ind Ter

AFFIDAVIT OF MOTHER.

UNITED STATES OF AMERICA, Indian Territory,
Centrial[sic]   DISTRICT.

I, Belle D Choate, on oath state that I am 31 years of age and a citizen by intermarriage, of the Choctaw Nation; that I am the lawful wife of David Choate, who is a citizen, by Blood of the Choctaw Nation; that a male child was born to me on 27th day of Feb., 1903; that said child has been named James Luke Choate, and was living March 4, 1905.

                                         Belle D Choate

Witnesses To Mark:
{

Subscribed and sworn to before me this 3rd day of April, 1905

My com expires   Andrew J Turner
Mar-17-1909   Notary Public.

AFFIDAVIT OF ATTENDING PHYSICIAN OR MID-WIFE.

UNITED STATES OF AMERICA, Indian Territory,
Southern   DISTRICT.

I, Nancy C Pate, a Mid-wife, on oath state that I attended on Mrs. Belle D Choate, wife of David Choate on the 27 day of Feb, 1903; that there was born to her on said date a male child; that said child was living March 4, 1905, and is said to have been named James Luke Choate

                                         Nancy C Pate

Applications for Enrollment of Choctaw Newborn
Act of 1905   Volume X

Witnesses To Mark:
{ W.G. Currie
  (Name Illegible)

Subscribed and sworn to before me this 8th day of   April   , 1905

W.G. Currie
Notary Public.

NEW BORN AFFIDAVIT

No ....

CHOCTAW ENROLLING COMMISSION

IN THE MATTER OF THE APPLICATION FOR ENROLLMENT as a citizen of the Choctaw Nation, of   James Luke Choate   born on the 27 day of Feb   190 3

Name of father David Choate   a citizen of Choctaw Nation, final enrollment No. 9443
Name of mother Belle D Choate   a citizen of Choctaw Nation, final enrollment No. 308

Celestine I.T.   Postoffice.

AFFIDAVIT OF MOTHER

UNITED STATES OF AMERICA
   INDIAN TERRITORY
DISTRICT   Centrial[sic]

I   Belle D Choate   , on oath state that I am 31 years of age and a citizen by intermarriage of the   Choctaw   Nation, and as such have been placed upon the final roll of the Choctaw   Nation, by the Honorable Secretary of the Interior my final enrollment number being 308 ; that I am the lawful wife of David Choate , who is a citizen of the Choctaw   Nation, and as such has been placed upon the final roll of said Nation by the Honorable Secretary of the Interior, his final enrollment number being 9443   and that a male child was born to me on the 27th day of Feb 190 3; that said child has been named James Luke Choate , and is now living.

Belle D Choate

Applications for Enrollment of Choctaw Newborn
Act of 1905 Volume X

WITNESSETH:

Must be two witnesses who are citizens { Ida F Turner
June H Bond

Subscribed and sworn to before me this, the 3rd day of April , 190 5

Andrew J Turner
Notary Public.

My Commission Expires: Mar-17-1909

Choc New Born 678
    Mary Francis Baker b. 2-28-03

BIRTH AFFIDAVIT.

DEPARTMENT OF THE INTERIOR.
COMMISSION TO THE FIVE CIVILIZED TRIBES.

IN RE APPLICATION FOR ENROLLMENT, as a citizen of the Chocktaw[sic] Nation, of Mary Francis Baker , born on the 28th day of Feb , 1903

Name of Father: Jackson Baker   a citizen of the Chocktaw Nation.
Name of Mother: Agustia[sic] Baker   a citizen of the Chocktaw Nation.

Postoffice   Valliant I T

AFFIDAVIT OF MOTHER.

UNITED STATES OF AMERICA, Indian Territory,
Central   DISTRICT.

I, Augustia Baker , on oath state that I am 40 years of age and a citizen by Marriage , of the Chocktaw Nation; that I am the lawful wife of Jackson Baker , who is a citizen, by blood of the Chocktaw Nation; that a female child was born to me on 28th day of Feb , 1903; that said child has been named Mary Francis Baker , and was living March 4, 1905.

Augustia Baker

Witnesses To Mark:
{

Applications for Enrollment of Choctaw Newborn
Act of 1905 Volume X

Subscribed and sworn to before me this 31st day of March , 1905

John Brewer
Notary Public.

AFFIDAVIT OF ATTENDING PHYSICIAN OR MID-WIFE.

UNITED STATES OF AMERICA, Indian Territory, }
  Central   DISTRICT. }

I, Mary C Burnes , a Midwife , on oath state that I attended on Mrs. Augustia Baker , wife of Jackson Baker on the 28th day of Feb , 1903; that there was born to her on said date a female child; that said child was living March 4, 1905, and is said to have been named Mary Francis Baker

Mary C Burnes

Witnesses To Mark:
{

Subscribed and sworn to before me this 31st day of March , 1905

John Brewer
Notary Public.

Choctaw 1849.

Muskogee, Indian Territory, April 7, 1905.

Jackson Baker,
  Valliant, Indian Territory.

Dear Sir:

Receipt is hereby acknowledged of the affidavits of Augustia Baker and Mary C. Burnes to the birth of Mary Francis Baker, daughter of Jackson and Agustia[sic] Baker, February 28, 1903, and the same have been filed with our records as an application for the enrollment of said child.

Respectfully,

Commissioner in Charge.

Applications for Enrollment of Choctaw Newborn
Act of 1905   Volume X

NEW-BORN AFFIDAVIT.

Number..............

Choctaw Enrolling Commission.

IN THE MATTER OF THE APPLICATION FOR ENROLLMENT, as a citizen of the Choctaw   Nation, of   Mary Frances[sic] Baker

born on the   28   day of   February   190 3

Name of father   Jackson Baker   a citizen of   Choctaw
Nation final enrollment No   5273
Name of mother   Augustia Baker   a citizen of   _____
Nation final enrollment No   816

Postoffice   Valliant I.T.

AFFIDAVIT OF MOTHER.

UNITED STATES OF AMERICA,
   INDIAN TERRITORY,
   Central   DISTRICT

I   Augustia Baker   on oath state that I am   40   years of age and a citizen by   Ind Mar   of the   Choctaw   Nation, and as such have been placed upon the final roll of the   Choctaw   Nation, by the Honorable Secretary of the Interior my final enrollment number being   816   ; that I am the lawful wife of   Jackson Baker   , who is a citizen of the   Choctaw   Nation, and as such has been placed upon the final roll of said Nation by the Honorable Secretary of the Interior, his final enrollment number being   5273   and that a   Female   child was born to me on the   28   day of   Ferby[sic]   190 3 ; that said child has been named   Mary Frances Baker   , and is now living.

   Augustia Baker

WITNESSETH:
   Must be two
   Witnesses who   } H J Bohanan
   are Citizens.   John McIntosh

Subscribed and sworn to before me this   20   day of   Jany   190 5

   W T Glenn
   Notary Public.

My commission expires   1907

Applications for Enrollment of Choctaw Newborn
Act of 1905   Volume X

Affidavit of Attending Physician or Midwife

UNITED STATES OF AMERICA,
  INDIAN TERRITORY,
  Central   DISTRICT

I, Mary Burns[sic]   a   Midwife on oath state that I attended on Mrs. Augustia Baker   wife of Jackson Baker on the 28 day of Febry, 190 3, that there was born to her on said date a Female child, that said child is now living, and is said to have been named Mary Frances Baker

                              Mary Burnes   M. D.

Subscribed and sworn to before me this the 20 day of Jany 1905

                              W.T. Glenn
                                  Notary Public.

WITNESSETH:
Must be two witnesses who are citizens and know the child. { H J Bohanan
John McIntosh }

We hereby certify that we are well acquainted with   Mary Burns[sic] a   Midwife   and know   her   to be reputable and of good standing in the community.

                Must be two citizen witnesses. { H J Bohanan
John McIntosh }

<u>Choc New Born 679</u>
    Bessie May Secor   b. 12-15-02

Applications for Enrollment of Choctaw Newborn
Act of 1905 Volume X

Choctaw 3339.

Muskogee, Indian Territory, April 7, 1905.

William H. Secor,
    Scipio, Indian Territory.

Dear Sir:

    Receipt is hereby acknowledged of the affidavits of Lucy Secor and N. F. Coleman to the birth of Bessie May Secor, daughter of William H. and Lucy Secor, December 15, 1902, and the same have been filed with our records as an application for the enrollment of said child.

                  Respectfully,

                                  Commissioner in Charge.

BIRTH AFFIDAVIT.

DEPARTMENT OF THE INTERIOR.
COMMISSION TO THE FIVE CIVILIZED TRIBES.

    IN RE APPLICATION FOR ENROLLMENT, as a citizen of the   Choctaw   Nation, of Bessie May Secor   , born on the 15th   day of Dec   , 1902

Name of Father: William H Secor   a citizen of the   Choctaw   Nation.
Name of Mother: Lucy Secor   a citizen of the   Choctaw   Nation.

                    Postoffice   Scipio, I.T.

AFFIDAVIT OF MOTHER.

UNITED STATES OF AMERICA, Indian Territory, }
    Central   DISTRICT. }

    I, Lucy Secor   , on oath state that I am 30 years of age and a citizen by Ind Marriage   , of the   Choctaw   Nation; that I am the lawful wife of William H Secor   , who is a citizen, by Blood   of the   Choctaw   Nation; that a Female   child was born to me on 15 day of Dec , 1902; that said child has been named   Bessie May Secor   , and was living March 4, 1905.

                                  Lucy Secor

Witnesses To Mark:

Applications for Enrollment of Choctaw Newborn
Act of 1905   Volume X

Subscribed and sworn to before me this 1st day of   April   , 1905

J.G. Givens
Notary Public.

AFFIDAVIT OF ATTENDING PHYSICIAN OR MID-WIFE.

UNITED STATES OF AMERICA, Indian Territory, ⎫
15th Recording   DISTRICT. ⎭

I,   N. F. Coleman   , a   Midwife   , on oath state that I attended on Mrs.   Lucy Secor   , wife of Wm H. Secor   on the   15th day of Dec   , 1902; that there was born to her on said date a   Female   child; that said child was living March 4, 1905, and is said to have been named Bessie May Secor

N. F. Coleman

Witnesses To Mark:
{ I N Vanzandt
{ S.W. Coleman

Subscribed and sworn to before me this 27th day of   March   , 1905

R.S. Coleman
Notary Public.

Choc New Born 680
  Joseph Jeflow   b. 12-11-02

  Cancelled and transferred to Chick #NB 511

  empty

Choc New Born 681
  Thelma Lee Thompson   b. 12-26-03
  Cancelled
  record transferred to Choc NB 812
           8-8-06

  empty

Applications for Enrollment of Choctaw Newborn
Act of 1905 Volume X

Choc New Born 682
    Abel H. Johnson b. 12-3-03

Choctaw 3138.

Muskogee, Indian Territory, April 10, 1905.

Hulsey & Patterson,
    Attorneys at Law,
        Hartshorne, Indian Territory.

Gentlemen:

    Receipt is hereby acknowledged of your letter of March 30, transmitting the affidavits of Emeline Johnson and E. L. Evins to the birth of Abel H. Johnson, son of Ben F. and Emeline Johnson, December 3, 1903, and the same have been filed with our records as an application for the enrollment of said child.

        Respectfully,

        Commissioner in Charge.

BIRTH AFFIDAVIT.

DEPARTMENT OF THE INTERIOR.
COMMISSION TO THE FIVE CIVILIZED TRIBES.

IN RE APPLICATION FOR ENROLLMENT, as a citizen of the Choctaw Nation, of Abel H Johnson, born on the 3rd day of December, 1903

Name of Father: Ben F. Johnson   a citizen of the Choctaw Nation.
Name of Mother: Emeline Johnson   a citizen of the Choctaw Nation.

Postoffice   Damon, I.T.

AFFIDAVIT OF MOTHER.

UNITED STATES OF AMERICA, Indian Territory,
    Central   DISTRICT.

    I, Emeline Johnson, on oath state that I am 29 years of age and a citizen by blood, of the Choctaw Nation; that I am the lawful wife of Ben F Johnson, who is a citizen, by intermarriage of the Choctaw Nation; that a male child was born to me on 3rd day of December, 1903; that said child has been named Abel H Johnson, and was living March 4, 1905.

Applications for Enrollment of Choctaw Newborn
Act of 1905   Volume X

Emeline Johnson

Witnesses To Mark:
{

Subscribed and sworn to before me this 28th day of   March   , 1905

Wm J Hulsey
Notary Public.

AFFIDAVIT OF ATTENDING PHYSICIAN OR MID-WIFE.

UNITED STATES OF AMERICA, Indian Territory,
Central   DISTRICT.

I,   E.L. Evins   , a physician   , on oath state that I attended on Mrs.   Emeline Johnson   , wife of   Ben F Johnson   on the 3rd day of December   , 1903; that there was born to her on said date a   male   child; that said child was living March 4, 1905, and is said to have been named Abel H Johnson

E. L. Evins M.D.

Witnesses To Mark:
{

Subscribed and sworn to before me this 28th day of   March   , 1905

Wm J Hulsey
Notary Public.

Choc New Born 683
   Laura Tohkubbi   b. 8-28-03

NEW BORN AFFIDAVIT

No ....

CHOCTAW ENROLLING COMMISSION

IN THE MATTER OF THE APPLICATION FOR ENROLLMENT as a citizen of the Choctaw Nation, of   Laura Tohkubbi   born on the 28th day of   August   190 3

Applications for Enrollment of Choctaw Newborn
Act of 1905   Volume X

Name of father   Cephus Tohkubbi   a citizen of   Choctaw   Nation, final enrollment No.   1703

Name of mother   Seon Tohkubbi   a citizen of   Choctaw   Nation, final enrollment No.   1704

Kullituklo I.T.   Postoffice.

AFFIDAVIT OF MOTHER

UNITED STATES OF AMERICA
INDIAN TERRITORY
DISTRICT   Central

I   Seon Tohkubbi   , on oath state that I am   28   years of age and a citizen by   blood   of the   Choctaw   Nation, and as such have been placed upon the final roll of the   Choctaw   Nation, by the Honorable Secretary of the Interior my final enrollment number being   1704   ; that I am the lawful wife of   Cephus Tohkubbi   , who is a citizen of the   Choctaw   Nation, and as such has been placed upon the final roll of said Nation by the Honorable Secretary of the Interior, his final enrollment number being   1703   and that a   female   child was born to me on the   28th   day of August 190 3; that said child has been named   Laura Tohkubbi   , and is now living.

WITNESSETH:
Must be two witnesses { Wilson E Frazier
who are citizens   { Moody Byington

Seon x Tohkubbi
      her   mark

Subscribed and sworn to before me this, the   14   day of   March   , 190 5

W.A. Shoney
Notary Public.

My Commission Expires: Jan 10, 1909.

Affidavit of Attending Physician or Midwife

UNITED STATES OF AMERICA,
INDIAN TERRITORY,
Central   DISTRICT

I,   Silvia Thomas   a   midwife on oath state that I attended on Mrs. Seon Tohkubbi   wife of   Cephus Tohkubbi on the   28th   day of   August   , 190 3, that there was born to her on said date a   female child, that said child is now living, and is said to have been named   Laura Tohkubbi

Silvia Thomas   ~~M.D.~~

285

Applications for Enrollment of Choctaw Newborn
Act of 1905 Volume X

Subscribed and sworn to before me this the 14 day of March 1905

W.A. Shoney
Notary Public.

WITNESSETH:

Must be two witnesses who are citizens and know the child.
{ Wilson E. Frazier
  Moody Byington

We hereby certify that we are well acquainted with Silvia Thomas a midwife and know her to be reputable and of good standing in the community.

Must be two citizen witnesses.
{ Wilson E Frazier
  Moody Byington

BIRTH AFFIDAVIT.

DEPARTMENT OF THE INTERIOR.
COMMISSION TO THE FIVE CIVILIZED TRIBES.

IN RE APPLICATION FOR ENROLLMENT, as a citizen of the Choctaw Nation, of Laura Tohkubbi , born on the 28th day of August , 1903

Name of Father: Cephus Tohkubbi   a citizen of the Choctaw Nation.
Name of Mother: Seon Tohkubbi   a citizen of the Choctaw Nation.

Postoffice Kullituklo, Ind. Ter.

AFFIDAVIT OF MOTHER.

UNITED STATES OF AMERICA, Indian Territory,
    Central   DISTRICT.

I, Seon Tohkubbi , on oath state that I am 28 years of age and a citizen by blood , of the Choctaw Nation; that I am the lawful wife of Cephus Tohkubbi , who is a citizen, by blood of the Choctaw Nation; that a female child was born to me on 28th day of August , 1903; that said child has been named Laura Tohkubbi , and was living March 4, 1905.

her
Seon x Tohkubbi
mark

Witnesses To Mark:
{ Robert Anderson
  Vester W Rose

Applications for Enrollment of Choctaw Newborn
Act of 1905   Volume X

Subscribed and sworn to before me this 10th day of April , 1905

                      Wirt Franklin
                      Notary Public.

AFFIDAVIT OF ATTENDING PHYSICIAN OR MID-WIFE.

UNITED STATES OF AMERICA, Indian Territory,
    Central   DISTRICT.

I, Silvia Thomas , a mid-wife , on oath state that I attended on Mrs. Seon Tohkubbi , wife of Cephus Tohkubbi on the 28th day of August , 1903; that there was born to her on said date a female child; that said child was living March 4, 1905, and is said to have been named Laura Tohkubbi

                    her
                  Silvia x Thomas
Witnesses To Mark: mark
   { Robert Anderson
   { Vester W Rose

Subscribed and sworn to before me this 10th day of April , 1905

                    Wirt Franklin
                    Notary Public.

Choc New Born 684
    Nannie Lucile Taliaferro b. 5-7-04

BIRTH AFFIDAVIT.
DEPARTMENT OF THE INTERIOR.
COMMISSION TO THE FIVE CIVILIZED TRIBES.

IN RE APPLICATION FOR ENROLLMENT, as a citizen of the Choctaw Nation, of Nannie Lucile Taliaferro , born on the 7th day of May , 1904

Name of Father: John D Taliaferro   a citizen of the Choctaw Nation.
Name of Mother: Nora Taliaferro   a citizen of the Choctaw Nation.

            Postoffice Wapanucka, I.T.

Applications for Enrollment of Choctaw Newborn
Act of 1905   Volume X

AFFIDAVIT OF MOTHER.

UNITED STATES OF AMERICA, Indian Territory, }
Central   DISTRICT.

I, Nora Taliferro , on oath state that I am 22 years of age and a citizen by Blood , of the Choctaw Nation; that I am the lawful wife of John D. Taliaferro , who is a citizen, by intermarriage of the Choctaw Nation; that a female child was born to me on 7th day of May , 1904; that said child has been named Nannie Lucile Taliaferro , and was living March 4, 1905.

                                              Nora Taliaferro

Witnesses To Mark:
{ Mrs L M Bright
{ Mrs L L Arnold

Subscribed and sworn to before me this 5th day of   April   , 1905

                                              W.H. Angell
                                                Notary Public.

AFFIDAVIT OF ATTENDING PHYSICIAN OR MID-WIFE.

UNITED STATES OF AMERICA, Indian Territory, }
Central   DISTRICT.

I, Thomas M. Morgan , a Physician , on oath state that I attended on Mrs. Nora Taliaferro , wife of John D. Taliaferro on the 7th day of May , 1904; that there was born to her on said date a female child; that said child was living March 4, 1905, and is said to have been named Nannie Lucile Taliaferro

                                     Thos. M. Morgan M.D.

Witnesses To Mark:
{ C.A. Snider
{ J.N Jones

Subscribed and sworn to before me this 4th day of   April   , 1905

                                             J.T. Hoover
                                            Notary Public.

Applications for Enrollment of Choctaw Newborn
Act of 1905 Volume X

Choc New Born 685
  Willie Jones   b. 1-8-03

Choc N.B. 1335

BIRTH AFFIDAVIT.

DEPARTMENT OF THE INTERIOR.
COMMISSION TO THE FIVE CIVILIZED TRIBES.

IN RE APPLICATION FOR ENROLLMENT, as a citizen of the   Choctaw   Nation, of Willie Jones   , born on the 18 day of January , 1903

Name of Father: Mike Jones   a citizen of the Choctaw   Nation.
Name of Mother: Emma Jones   a citizen of the Choctaw   Nation.

Postoffice   McCurtain Ind. Ter.

AFFIDAVIT OF MOTHER.

UNITED STATES OF AMERICA, Indian Territory, ⎱
  Central   DISTRICT.   ⎰

I, Emma Jones , on oath state that I am 25 years of age and a citizen by blood , of the Choctaw Nation; that I am the lawful wife of Mike Jones , who is a citizen, by blood of the Choctaw Nation; that a male child was born to me on 18 day of January , 1903; that said child has been named Willie Jones , and was living March 4, 1905.

                          her
                 Emma x Jones
Witnesses To Mark: mark
  ⎰ John Bascom
  ⎱ Joe McCann

Subscribed and sworn to before me this 5th day of June , 1905

                    M.W. Newman
                       Notary Public.

Applications for Enrollment of Choctaw Newborn
Act of 1905 Volume X

AFFIDAVIT OF ATTENDING PHYSICIAN OR MID-WIFE.

UNITED STATES OF AMERICA, Indian Territory, }
Central DISTRICT. }

I, Betsey McCann, a Midwife, on oath state that I attended on Mrs. Emma Jones, wife of Mike Jones on the 18 day of January, 1903; that there was born to her on said date a male child; that said child was living March 4, 1905, and is said to have been named Willie Jones

                                            her
                                Betsey x McCann

Witnesses To Mark: mark
{ John Bascom
{ Joe McCann

Subscribed and sworn to before me this 5th day of June, 1905

                                M.W. Newman
                                Notary Public.

My com expires Jan 17th 1907

                                                  7-NB-685.

                      Muskogee, Indian Territory, May 27, 1905.

Mike Jones,
      McCurtain, Indian Territory.

Dear Sir:

      Referring to your letter of the 12th instant, in which you inquire about the application for the enrollment of your infant child, Willie Jones, born January 8[sic], 1903, there is enclosed herewith an application for the enrollment of this child.

      It is noted from the testimony taken in this case on the 5th ultimo, that Betsey McCann, the midwife that attended upon your wife at the time of birth of the applicant, was sich[sic] and unable to be present on that date and give her testimony. Before this matter can be finally determined, it will be necessary for you to secure her affidavit, for which the above mentioned application is enclosed.

      In the event that you are unable to secure her affidavit the affidavits of two disinterested parties, who have actual knowledge of the facts that the child was born, the date of his birth; that he was living on March 4, 1905, and that Emma Jones is his mother, are required. The testimony of Joe McCann in support of thes[sic] these facts is on file in this office. It will, therefore, be necessary that you secure the affidavit of another person to the same fact.

Applications for Enrollment of Choctaw Newborn
Act of 1905 Volume X

In having these affidavits executed care should be exercised to see that all names are written in full, as they appear in the body of the affidavit, and in the event that either of the persons signing the affidavit are unable to write, signatures by mark must be attested by two witnesses. Each affidavit must be executed before a Notary Public and the notarial seal and signature of the officer must be attached to each separate affidavit.

Respectfully,

Chairman.

VR 27-2.

7-NB-685,

Muskogee, Indian Territory, June 10, 1905.

Mike Jones,
    McCurtain, Indian Territory.

Dear Sir:

Receipt is hereby acknowledged of the affidavits of Emma Jones and Betsey McCann to the birth of Willie Jones, son of Mike and Emma Jones, January 18, 1903, and the same have been filed with our records in the matter of the enrollment of said child.

Respectfully,

Commissioner in Charge.

7-NB-685

Muskogee, Indian Territory, September 9, 1905.

M. W. Jones,
    McCurtain, Indian Territory.

Dear Sir:

Replying to your letter of August 8th you are advised that on August 22, 1905, the Secretary of the Interior approved the enrollment of Willie Jones as a citizen by blood of the Choctaw Nation and the name of said child appears upon the final roll of the newborn citizens by blood of the Choctaw Nation opposite number 1335.

The child is now entitled to an allotment, and selection thereof should be made without delay at the land office for the nation in which the prospective allotment is located.

Applications for Enrollment of Choctaw Newborn
Act of 1905   Volume X

Respectfully,

Acting Commissioner.

NEW-BORN AFFIDAVIT.

Number............

...Choctaw Enrolling Commission...

IN THE MATTER OF THE APPLICATION FOR ENROLLMENT, as a citizen of the Choctaw   Nation, of   Willie Jones

born on the 18   day of ___Jan_____ 190 3

Name of father   Mike Jones   a citizen of   Choctaw
Nation final enrollment No. 7961
Name of mother Emma Jones   a citizen of   Choctaw
Nation final enrollment No. 2338

Postoffice   Iron Bridge I.T.

AFFIDAVIT OF MOTHER.

UNITED STATES OF AMERICA
INDIAN TERRITORY
   Central   DISTRICT

I   Emma Jones   , on oath state that I am   25   years of age and a citizen by Blood   of the   Choctaw   Nation, and as such have been placed upon the final roll of the   Choctaw   Nation, by the Honorable Secretary of the Interior my final enrollment number being   2328 ; that I am the lawful wife of   Mike Jones   , who is a citizen of the   Choctaw   Nation, and as such has been placed upon the final roll of said Nation by the Honorable Secretary of the Interior, his final enrollment number being   7961   and that a   Male   child was born to me on the 18th   day of   Jan   190 3; that said child has been named   Willie Jones   , and is now living.

                                                 her
                                  Emma x Jones
Witnesseth.   mark
   Must be two   ⎱ J L McCann
   Witnesses who   ⎰
   are Citizens.   Noel Leflore

Applications for Enrollment of Choctaw Newborn
Act of 1905   Volume X

Subscribed and sworn to before me this   14   day of   Jan   190 5

M W Newman
Notary Public.

My commission expires:
(Illegible)

AFFIDAVIT OF ATTENDING PHYSICIAN OR MIDWIFE

UNITED STATES OF AMERICA
INDIAN TERRITORY
Central   DISTRICT

I,   Betsey McCann   a   midwife
on oath state that I attended on Mrs.   Emma Jones   wife of   Mike Jones
on the   18   day of   Jan , 190 3 , that there was born to her on said date a   Male   child, that said child is now living, and is said to have been named   Willie Jones
                                                                           her
                                                Betsey x McCann
                                                           mark

Subscribed and sworn to before me this, the   14th   day of   Jan   190 5

WITNESSETH: M W Newman   Notary Public.
Must be two witnesses
who are citizens
J L McCann
Noel Leflore

We hereby certify that we are well acquainted with   Betsey McCann
a   Midwife   and know   her   to be reputable and of good standing in the community.

_____   Noel Leflore

_____   Osborne McGilberry

DEPARTMENT OF THE INTERIOR,
COMMISSION TO THE FIVE CIVILIZED TRIBES.
BOKOSHE, INDIAN TERRITORY APRIL 5, 1905.

In the matter of the application for the enrollment [sic] Willie Jones as a citizen by blood of the Choctaw Nation.

Emma Jones being first duly sworn testifies as follows:

Applications for Enrollment of Choctaw Newborn
Act of 1905   Volume X

EXAMINATION BY THE COMMISSION:

Q What is your name? A Emma Jones.
Q What is your age? A Twenty-five
Q What is your post office address? A McCurtain.
Q You have this day made application for your minor child Willie Jones? A Yes, sir.
Q Who attended you in the capacity of midwife or physician when this child was born?
A My mother was there.
Q What is her name? A Betsey McCann.
Q Why isn't she able to be here today? A She is sick.
Q She is sick abed? A Yes, sir.
Q That is the reason she isn't here today? A Yes, sir.

Witness excused.

Mike Jones being first duly sworn testifies as follows:

EXAMINATION BY THE COMMISSION:

Q What is your name? A Mike Jones.
Q What is your age? A Twenty-eight.
Q What is your post office address? A McCurtain.
Q Are you a citizen by blood of the Choctaw Nation? A Yes sir.
Q What is the name of your wife? A Emma Jones.
Q She has this day made application for the enrollment of her minor child Willie Jones?
A Yes, sir.
Q The midwife who attended your wife through sickness is unable to be here today?
A Yes, sir.
Q Sick abed? A Yes, sir.

Witness excused.

Joe McCann being first duly sworn testifies as follows:

EXAMINATION BY THE COMMISSION:

Q What is your name? A Joe McCann.
Q What is your age? A Thirty-eight.
Q What is your post office address? A Ironbridge.
Q Are you a citizen by blood of the Choctaw Nation? A Yes, sir.
Q Are you acquainted with Emma Jones who has this day made application for the enrollment of her minor child Willie Jones? A Yes, sir.
Q When was Willie Jones born? A January 18, 1903.
Q Were you present when he was born? A Yes, sir.
Q Is that child living today? A Yes, sir.
Q Who attended Mrs. Jones when this child was born? A My wife.
Q What is her name? A Betsey McCann.
Q Why is she unable to be here today? A Sick.
Q Sick abed? A Yes, sir.

Witness excused.

Applications for Enrollment of Choctaw Newborn
Act of 1905 Volume X

Chas. T. Difendafer being first duly sworn states that the above and foregoing is a full, true and correct transcript of his stenographic notes taken in said cause on said date.

                          Chas T Difendafer

Subscribed and sworn to before me this 5th day of April, 1905.

                          OL Johnson
                          Notary Public.

7- 8328   7- 7961
BIRTH AFFIDAVIT.

DEPARTMENT OF THE INTERIOR.
COMMISSION TO THE FIVE CIVILIZED TRIBES.

IN RE APPLICATION FOR ENROLLMENT, as a citizen of the   Choctaw   Nation, of Willie Jones   , born on the 18 day of January , 1903

Name of Father: Mike Jones   a citizen of the Choctaw Nation.
Name of Mother: Emma Jones   a citizen of the Choctaw Nation.

                Postoffice   McCurtain I.T.

AFFIDAVIT OF MOTHER.

UNITED STATES OF AMERICA, Indian Territory, }
    Central   DISTRICT. }

I, Emma Jones , on oath state that I am 25 years of age and a citizen by blood , of the Choctaw Nation; that I am the lawful wife of Mike Jones , who is a citizen, by blood of the Choctaw Nation; that a male child was born to me on 18 day of January , 1903; that said child has been named Willie Jones , and was living March 4, 1905.

                                    her
                          Emma x Jones
Witnesses To Mark: mark
  { Chas T Difendafer
  { OL Johnson

    Subscribed and sworn to before me this 5 day of April , 1905

                          OL Johnson
                          Notary Public.

Applications for Enrollment of Choctaw Newborn
Act of 1905   Volume X

Choc New Born 686
    John William Tubby   b. 2-4-04

7-14331
BIRTH AFFIDAVIT.

DEPARTMENT OF THE INTERIOR.
COMMISSION TO THE FIVE CIVILIZED TRIBES.

IN RE APPLICATION FOR ENROLLMENT, as a citizen of the Choctaw Nation, of John William Tubby, born on the 4th day of February, 1904

Name of Father: William Tubby   a citizen of the Choctaw Nation.
Name of Mother: Cora Tubby   a citizen of the Choctaw Nation.

    Postoffice   Tucker, Ind. Ter.

AFFIDAVIT OF MOTHER.

UNITED STATES OF AMERICA, Indian Territory, }
    Central   DISTRICT.

    I, Cora Tubby, on oath state that I am 21 years of age and a citizen by intermarriage, of the Choctaw Nation; that I am the lawful wife of William Tubby, who is a citizen, by blood of the Choctaw Nation; that a male child was born to me on 4th day of February, 1904; that said child has been named John William Tubby, and was living March 4, 1905.

                    Cora Tubby

Witnesses To Mark:
{

    Subscribed and sworn to before me this 5th day of April, 1905

                  OL Johnson
                      Notary Public.

AFFIDAVIT OF ATTENDING PHYSICIAN OR MID-WIFE.

UNITED STATES OF AMERICA, Indian Territory, }
    Central   DISTRICT.

    I, A. D. Hill, a midwife, on oath state that I attended on Mrs. Cora Tubby, wife of William Tubby on the 4th day of February,

Applications for Enrollment of Choctaw Newborn
Act of 1905   Volume X

1903; that there was born to her on said date a   male   child; that said child was living March 4, 1905, and is said to have been named John William Tubby

her
A. D. x Hill
mark

Witnesses To Mark:
   { Chas T Difendafer
    William Tubby

Subscribed and sworn to before me this 5th day of April   , 1905

OL Johnson
Notary Public.

Choc New Born 687
    Ira Lee Riley Cowan   b. 5-2-04

Choctaw 2658.

Muskogee, Indian Territory, April 11, 1905.

George S. Cowan,
    Cowlington, Indian Territory.

Dear Sir:

    Receipt is hereby acknowledged of the affidavits of Sarah Cowan and J. B. Beckette to the birth of Ira Lee Riley Cowan, son of George S. and Sarah Cowan, May 2, 1904, and the same have been filed with our records as an application for the enrollment of said child.

Respectfully,

Commissioner in Charge.

Applications for Enrollment of Choctaw Newborn
Act of 1905   Volume X

7- 7714   No. 118
BIRTH AFFIDAVIT.

DEPARTMENT OF THE INTERIOR.
COMMISSION TO THE FIVE CIVILIZED TRIBES.

IN RE APPLICATION FOR ENROLLMENT, as a citizen of the   Choctaw   Nation, of Ira Lee Riley Cowan   , born on the 2   day of   May , 1904

Name of Father: George S Cowan   a citizen *by intermarriage* of the   Choctaw   Nation.
Name of Mother: Sarah Cowan   a citizen of the   Choctaw   Nation.

Postoffice   Cowlington Ind Ter

AFFIDAVIT OF MOTHER.

UNITED STATES OF AMERICA, Indian Territory,
Central   DISTRICT.

I,   Sarah Cowan   , on oath state that I am   31   years of age and a citizen by blood , of the   Choctaw   Nation; that I am the lawful wife of   George S Cowan, who is a citizen, by intermarriage   of the   Choctaw   Nation; that a   male   child was born to me on   2   day of   May   , 1904; that said child has been named Ira Lee Riley Cowan   , and was living March 4, 1905.

Sarah Cowan

Witnesses To Mark:

Subscribed and sworn to before me this   3   day of   April   , 1905

A. H. Crouthamel
My Com ex 2-3-1907   Notary Public.

AFFIDAVIT OF ATTENDING PHYSICIAN OR MID-WIFE.

UNITED STATES OF AMERICA, Indian Territory,
Central   DISTRICT.

I,   J. B. Beckette   , a   physician   , on oath state that I attended on Mrs.   Sarah Cowan   , wife of   George S Cowan   on the   2 day of May   , 1904; that there was born to her on said date a   male   child; that said child was living March 4, 1905, and is said to have been named Ira Lee Riley Cowan

J. B. Beckette M.D.

Applications for Enrollment of Choctaw Newborn
Act of 1905   Volume X

Witnesses To Mark:
{

Subscribed and sworn to before me this 3 day of April , 1905

My Com ex 2-3-1907

A. H. Crouthamel
Notary Public.

Choc New Born 688
    James Ellis Wiltsey b. 12-5-04

BIRTH AFFIDAVIT.

DEPARTMENT OF THE INTERIOR.
COMMISSION TO THE FIVE CIVILIZED TRIBES.

IN RE APPLICATION FOR ENROLLMENT, as a citizen of the   Choctaw   Nation, of James Ellis Wiltsey   , born on the   5   day of   Dec   , 1904

Name of Father: John M Wiltsey   a citizen of the   Choctaw   Nation.
Name of Mother: Annie Wiltsey   a citizen of the   Choctaw   Nation.

Postoffice   Coalgate I.T.

AFFIDAVIT OF MOTHER.

UNITED STATES OF AMERICA, Indian Territory, }
    Central   DISTRICT.

I,   Annie Wiltsey   , on oath state that I am   28   years of age and a citizen by   blood   , of the   Choctaw   Nation; that I am the lawful wife of   John M Wiltsey   , who is a citizen, by Marriage   of the   Choctaw   Nation; that a   Male   child was born to me on   5th   day of   Dec   , 1904; that said child has been named   James Ellis Wiltsey   , and was living March 4, 1905.

                                  her
                            Annie x Wiltsey
Witnesses To Mark: mark
{ *(Name Illegible)*
  (Name Illegible)

Applications for Enrollment of Choctaw Newborn
Act of 1905   Volume X

Subscribed and sworn to before me this   30   day of   Mch   , 1905

P E Wilkerson
Notary Public.

AFFIDAVIT OF ATTENDING PHYSICIAN OR MID-WIFE.

UNITED STATES OF AMERICA, Indian Territory, }
Central   DISTRICT. }

I,   J B Clark   , a   physician   , on oath state that I attended on Mrs.   Annie Wiltsey   , wife of   John M Wiltsey   on the   5   day of   Dec   , 1904; that there was born to her on said date a   male   child; that said child was living March 4, 1905, and is said to have been named James Ellis Wiltsey

J.B. Clark M.D.

Witnesses To Mark:
{ Emmeron A Allen

Subscribed and sworn to before me this 1st   day of   April   , 1905

P E Wilkerson
Notary Public.

Choc New Born 689
   Wilbert M. Brians   b. 2-22-04

Choctaw 3325.

Muskogee, Indian Territory, April 11, 1905.

R. H. Brians,
   Non, Indian Territory.

Dear Sir:

Receipt is hereby acknowledged of the affidavits of Mrs. Mary M. Brians and A. E. Brians to the birth of Wilbert M. Brians, son of R. H. and Mary M. Brians, February 22, 1904, and the same have been filed with our records as an application for the enrollment of said child.

Applications for Enrollment of Choctaw Newborn
Act of 1905 Volume X

Respectfully,

Commissioner in Charge.

BIRTH AFFIDAVIT.

DEPARTMENT OF THE INTERIOR.
COMMISSION TO THE FIVE CIVILIZED TRIBES.

IN RE APPLICATION FOR ENROLLMENT, as a citizen of the   Choctaw   Nation, of Wilbert M. Brians   , born on the 22   day of Feb   , 1904

Name of Father: R. H. Brians   a citizen of the U. S.   Nation.
Name of Mother: Mary M Brians   a citizen of the Choctaw   Nation.

Postoffice   Non I.T.

AFFIDAVIT OF MOTHER.

UNITED STATES OF AMERICA, Indian Territory, }
    Central   DISTRICT.   }

I, Mary M. Brians   , on oath state that I am 22   years of age and a citizen by Blood , of the   Choctaw   Nation; that I am the lawful wife of R. H. Brians   , who is a citizen, ~~by~~ .... of the   U. S.   ~~Nation~~; that a   male   child was born to me on   22   day of   Feb   , 1904; that said child has been named   Wilbert M Brians   , and was living March 4, 1905.

                                                her
                                      Mrs Mary M x Brians

Witnesses To Mark: mark
   { *(Name Illegible)*
   { Mrs C E McCain

Subscribed and sworn to before me this 1   day of   April   , 1905

                                      C.E. McCain
                                           Notary Public.

Applications for Enrollment of Choctaw Newborn
Act of 1905   Volume X

AFFIDAVIT OF ATTENDING PHYSICIAN OR MID-WIFE.

UNITED STATES OF AMERICA, Indian Territory, }
.... DISTRICT. }

I,   Mrs A. E. Brians   , a midwife   , on oath state that I attended on Mrs.   Mary M Brians   , wife of   R. H. Brians   on the   22   day of   Feb   , 1904; that there was born to her on said date a   male   child; that said child was living March 4, 1905, and is said to have been named   Wilbert M Brians

A. E. Brians

Witnesses To Mark:
{

Subscribed and sworn to before me this 1 day of   April   , 1905

C.E. McCain
Notary Public.

Choc New Born 690
    Harrol Van Turner b. 9-30-02

Choctaw 4773.

Muskogee, Indian Territory, April 11, 1905.

Robert S. Turner,
    Indianola, Indian Territory.

Dear Sir:

Receipt is hereby acknowledged of the affidavits of Lena Turner and P. S. Johnston to the birth of Harrol Van Turner, son of Robert S. and Lena Turner, September 30, 1902, and the same have been filed with our records as an application for the enrollment of said child.

Respectfully,

Commissioner in Charge.

Applications for Enrollment of Choctaw Newborn
Act of 1905   Volume X

7 NB 690

Muskogee, Indian Territory, June 26, 1905.

R. S. Turner,
    Indianola, Indian Territory.

Dear Sir:

    Receipt is hereby acknowledged of your letter of June 23, 1905, asking to be notified of the approval of your son Harrol V. Turner.

    In reply to your letter you are advised that the name of Harrol Van Turner has been placed upon a schedule of citizens by blood of the Choctaw Nation and you will be notified when his enrollment is approved by the Secretary of the Interior.

                      Respectfully,

                                          Chairman.

9-NB-690.

Muskogee, Indian Territory, June 29, 1905.

R. S. Turner,
    Indianola, Indian Territory.

Dear Sir:

    Receipt is hereby acknowledged of your letter of June 23, 1905, asking to be notified of the approval of your son Harrol V. Turner.

    In reply to your letter you are advised that the name of Harrol Van Turner has been placed upon a schedule of citizens by blood of the Choctaw Nation prepared for forwarding to the Secretary of the Interior, and you will be notified when his enrollment is approved by the Department.

                      Respectfully,

                                          Chairman.

Applications for Enrollment of Choctaw Newborn
Act of 1905   Volume X

BIRTH AFFIDAVIT.

DEPARTMENT OF THE INTERIOR.
COMMISSION TO THE FIVE CIVILIZED TRIBES.

IN RE APPLICATION FOR ENROLLMENT, as a citizen of the   Choctaw   Nation, of Harrol Van Turner   , born on the 30   day of September   , 1902

Name of Father: Robert S Turner   a citizen of the   Choctaw   Nation.
Name of Mother: Lena Turner   a citizen of the   Choctaw   Nation.

Postoffice   Indianola, Indian Territory

AFFIDAVIT OF MOTHER.

UNITED STATES OF AMERICA, Indian Territory,
   Western   DISTRICT.

I,   Lena Turner   , on oath state that I am   25   years of age and a citizen by Inter M   , of the   Choctaw   Nation; that I am the lawful wife of   Robert S Turner, who is a citizen, by Blood   of the   Choctaw   Nation; that a   male   child was born to me on 30   day of   September   , 1902; that said child has been named Harrol Van Turner, and was living March 4, 1905.

Lena Turner

Witnesses To Mark:

Subscribed and sworn to before me this 3rd day of   April   , 1905

T. J. Rice
Notary Public.

AFFIDAVIT OF ATTENDING PHYSICIAN OR MID-WIFE.

UNITED STATES OF AMERICA, Indian Territory,
   Western   DISTRICT.

I,   P S Johnston   , a   Physician   , on oath state that I attended on Mrs.   Lena Turner   , wife of   Robert S Turner   on the 30 day of   September, 1902; that there was born to her on said date a   male   child; that said child was living March 4, 1905, and is said to have been named Harrol Van Turner

P.S. Johnston M.D.

Witnesses To Mark:

Applications for Enrollment of Choctaw Newborn
Act of 1905   Volume X

Subscribed and sworn to before me this 3rd day of   April   , 1905

T. J. Rice
Notary Public.

Choc New Born 691
    Clarence Martin   b. 6-30-03

Choctaw 2628.

Muskogee, Indian Territory, April 11, 1905.

Foster & Dalton,
    Attorneys at Law,
        Stigler, Indian Territory.

Gentlemen:

Receipt is hereby acknowledged of your letter of March 4, transmitting the affidavits of Maggie Martin and Kizzie Martin to the birth of Clarence Martin, son of James and Maggie Martin, June 30, 1903, and the same have been filed with our records as an application for the enrollment of said child.

Respectfully,

Commissioner in Charge.

7-NB-616
7-NB-691

Muskogee, Indian Territory, July 24, 1905.

G. A. Holley,
    Attorney at law,
        Stigler, Indian Territory.

Dear Sir:

Receipt is hereby acknowledged of your letter of July 18, 1905, asking if Clarence Martin, son of James and Maggie Martin has been enrolled; also the two year old son of Alex and Elizabeth Johnson.

Applications for Enrollment of Choctaw Newborn
Act of 1905   Volume X

In reply to your letter you are advised that the name of Simon Johnson, son of Alexander and Elizabeth Johnson and Clarence Martin, son of James and Maggie Martin, have been placed upon a schedule of citizens by blood of the Choctaw Nation which has been forwarded the Secretary of the Interior but this office has not yet been notified of Departmental action thereon.

Respectfully,

Commissioner.

BIRTH AFFIDAVIT.

DEPARTMENT OF THE INTERIOR.
COMMISSION TO THE FIVE CIVILIZED TRIBES.

IN RE APPLICATION FOR ENROLLMENT, as a citizen of the Choctaw Nation, of Clarence Martin, born on the 30 day of June, 1903

Name of Father: James Martin   a citizen of the Choctaw Nation.
Name of Mother: Maggie Martin   a citizen of the white race ~~Nation~~.

Postoffice   Stigler, Ind Ter

AFFIDAVIT OF MOTHER.

UNITED STATES OF AMERICA, Indian Territory,
Central   DISTRICT.

I, Maggie Martin, on oath state that I am 22 years of age and a citizen by white race, of the White race ~~Nation~~; that I am the lawful wife of James Martin, who is a citizen, by blood of the Choctaw Nation; that a male child was born to me on 30 day of June, 1903; that said child has been named Clarence Martin, and was living March 4, 1905.

Maggie Martin

Witnesses To Mark:

Subscribed and sworn to before me this 4 day of April, 1905.

E.M. Dalton
Notary Public.
My commission expires Oct 20, 1908

Applications for Enrollment of Choctaw Newborn
Act of 1905 Volume X

AFFIDAVIT OF ATTENDING PHYSICIAN OR MID-WIFE.

UNITED STATES OF AMERICA, Indian Territory, }
Central DISTRICT.

I, Kizzie Martin , a mid-wife , on oath state that I attended on Mrs. Maggie Martin , wife of James Martin on the 30 day of June , 1903; that there was born to her on said date a male child; that said child was living March 4, 1905, and is said to have been named Clarence Martin

her
Kizzie x Martin
mark

Witnesses To Mark:
{ E M Dalton
  William Martin

Subscribed and sworn to before me this 4 day of April , 1905

E.M. Dalton
Notary Public.
My commission expires Oct 20, 1908

Choc New Born 692
  Ellistan Cephus b. 11-2-04

Choctaw 557.

Muskogee, Indian Territory, April 10, 1905.

H. L. Fowler,
  Valliant, Indian Territory.

Dear Sir:

Receipt is hereby acknowledged of your letter of April 4, transmitting the affidavits of Bessie Cephus (Wallace) and Celia Wallace to the birth of Ellistan Cephus, son of Bessie and T. J. Cephus, March 2[sic], 1904, and the same have been filed with our records as an application for the enrollment of said child.

Respectfully,

Commissioner in Charge.

Applications for Enrollment of Choctaw Newborn
Act of 1905 Volume X

COPY

7 N. B. 692

Muskogee, Indian Territory, April 12, 1905.

T. J. Cephus,
   Rufe, Indian Territory.

Dear Sir:

There is inclosed you herewith for execution application for the enrollment of your infant child, Ellistan Cephus, born November 2, 1904.

In having these affidavits executed care should be exercised to see that all names are written in full, as they appear in the body of the affidavit, and in the event that either of the persons signing the affidavit are unable to write, signatures by mark must be attested by two witnesses. Each affidavit must be executed before a Notary Public and the notarial seal and signature of the officer must be attached to each separate affidavit.

Respectfully,

SIGNED *T. B. Needles.*
LM 12-4.   Commissioner in Charge.

COPY   7 NB *692*

Muskogee, Indian Territory, April 26, 1905.

T. J. Cephus,
   Rufe, Indian Territory.

Dear Sir:

Receipt is hereby acknowledged of the affidavits of Bessie Cephus (Wallace) and Celia Wallace to the birth of Ellistan Cephus, son of T. J. and Bessie Cephus (Wallace), November 2, 1904, and the same have been filed with our records in the matter of the enrollment of said child.

Respectfully,

SIGNED

Tams Bixby
Chairman.

Applications for Enrollment of Choctaw Newborn
Act of 1905 Volume X

NEW-BORN AFFIDAVIT.

Number

Choctaw Enrolling Commission.

IN THE MATTER OF THE APPLICATION FOR ENROLLMENT, as a citizen of the Choctaw Nation, of Elliston[sic] Cephas[sic]

born on the 2 day of November 1904

Name of father Timothy J Cephas a citizen of Choctaw
Nation final enrollment No 1862
Name of mother Bessie Wallace now Cephas a citizen of Choctaw
Nation final enrollment No 1233

Postoffice Rufe I.T.

AFFIDAVIT OF MOTHER.

UNITED STATES OF AMERICA,
INDIAN TERRITORY,
Central DISTRICT

I Bessie Wallace now Cephus on oath state that I am 34 years of age and a citizen by ——— of the Choctaw Nation, and as such have been placed upon the final roll of the Choctaw Nation, by the Honorable Secretary of the Interior my final enrollment number being 1233 ; that I am the lawful wife of Timothy J Cephas , who is a citizen of the Choctaw Nation, and as such has been placed upon the final roll of said Nation by the Honorable Secretary of the Interior, his final enrollment number being 1862 and that a male child was born to me on the 2 day of November 190 4; that said child has been named Elliston Cephas , and is now living.

 her
Bessie Wallace now Cephas x
 mark

WITNESSETH:
Must be two Witnesses who are Citizens. Montford Harley
Enos Tantubbee

Subscribed and sworn to before me this 18 day of Jany 190 5

W.T. Glenn
Notary Public.

My commission expires 1907

Applications for Enrollment of Choctaw Newborn
Act of 1905   Volume X

AFFIDAVIT OF ATTENDING PHYSICIAN OR MIDWIFE

UNITED STATES OF AMERICA
INDIAN TERRITORY
Central   DISTRICT

I,   Celia Wallace   a   mid wife
on oath state that I attended on Mrs. Bessie Wallace now Cephas   wife of   Timothy J Cephas   on the   2   day of   November   , 190 4 , that there was born to her on said date a   Male   child, that said child is now living, and is said to have been named   Elliston Cephas

Celia Wallace   M.D.

Subscribed and sworn to before me this, the 18   day of   Jany   190 5

W.T. Glenn
Notary Public.

WITNESSETH:
Must be two witnesses who are citizens and know the child.
{ Montford Harley
  Enos Tantubbee

We hereby certify that we are well acquainted with   Celia Wallace
a   mid wife   and know   her   to be reputable and of good standing in the community.

{ Montford Harley
  Enos Tantubbee

BIRTH AFFIDAVIT.

DEPARTMENT OF THE INTERIOR.
COMMISSION TO THE FIVE CIVILIZED TRIBES.

IN RE APPLICATION FOR ENROLLMENT, as a citizen of the   Choctaw   Nation, of Ellistan Cephus   , born on the   2   day of   Nov   , 1904

Name of Father: Bessie Wallice[sic]   a citizen of the   Choctaw   Nation.
Name of Mother: T J Cephus[sic]   a citizen of the   Choctaw   Nation.

Postoffice   Rufe I T

Applications for Enrollment of Choctaw Newborn
Act of 1905   Volume X

AFFIDAVIT OF MOTHER.

UNITED STATES OF AMERICA, Indian Territory,
    Central   DISTRICT.

I, Bessie Wallice[sic], on oath state that I am 36 years of age and a citizen by Blood, of the Choctaw Nation; that I am the lawful wife of T J Cephus, who is a citizen, by Blood of the Choctaw Nation; that a male child was born to me on 2 day of Nov, 1904; that said child has been named Ellistan Cephus, and was living March 4, 1905.

                                      Bessie Cephus or Wallace

Witnesses To Mark:
{ John Fowler
{ T.J. Cephus

Subscribed and sworn to before me this 3 day of Aprile[sic], 1905

                                      H L Fowler
                                            Notary Public.

AFFIDAVIT OF ATTENDING PHYSICIAN OR MID-WIFE.

UNITED STATES OF AMERICA, Indian Territory,
    Central   DISTRICT.

I, Cealis[sic] Wallice[sic], a................, on oath state that I attended on Mrs. Bessie Wallice, wife of T J Cephus on the 2 day of Nov, 1904; that there was born to her on said date a male child; that said child was living March 4, 1905, and is said to have been named Ellistan Cephus

                                      Celia Wallace

Witnesses To Mark:
{ John Fowler
{ T.J. Cephus

Subscribed and sworn to before me this 3 day of Aprile[sic], 1905

                                      H L Fowler
                                            Notary Public.

Applications for Enrollment of Choctaw Newborn
Act of 1905   Volume X

BIRTH AFFIDAVIT.

DEPARTMENT OF THE INTERIOR.
COMMISSION TO THE FIVE CIVILIZED TRIBES.

IN RE APPLICATION FOR ENROLLMENT, as a citizen of the   Choctaw   Nation, of Ellistan Cephus   , born on the 2nd day of   November   , 1904

Name of Father: T. J. Cephus   a citizen of the   Choctaw   Nation.
Name of Mother: Bessie Cephus (Wallace) a citizen of the   Choctaw   Nation.

Postoffice   Rufe I T

AFFIDAVIT OF MOTHER.

UNITED STATES OF AMERICA, Indian Territory,
Central   DISTRICT.

I,   Bessie Cephus (Wallace)   , on oath state that I am   36   years of age and a citizen by   blood   , of the   Choctaw   Nation; that I am the lawful wife of   T J Cephus, who is a citizen, by   blood   of the   Choctaw   Nation; that a   male child was born to me on 2nd day of   November   , 1904; that said child has been named   Ellistan Cephus   , and was living March 4, 1905.

Bessie Cephus (Wallace)

Witnesses To Mark:
{ (Name Illegible)
{ (Name Illegible)

Subscribed and sworn to before me this 21   day of Aprile[sic]   , 1905

H L Fowler
Notary Public.

AFFIDAVIT OF ATTENDING PHYSICIAN OR MID-WIFE.

UNITED STATES OF AMERICA, Indian Territory,
Central   DISTRICT.

I,   Celia Wallace midwife   , a................, on oath state that I attended on Mrs.   Bessie Cephus (Wallace)   , wife of   T J Cephus   on the 2nd day of   November   , 1904; that there was born to her on said date a   Male   child; that said child was living March 4, 1905, and is said to have been named   Ellistan Cephus

Celia Wallace

Applications for Enrollment of Choctaw Newborn
Act of 1905 Volume X

Witnesses To Mark:
{ *(Name Illegible)*
{ *(Name Illegible)*

Subscribed and sworn to before me this 21 day of Aprile[sic] , 1905

H L Fowler
Notary Public.

Choc New Born 693
Clifford Barnett b. 7-7-04

NEW-BORN AFFIDAVIT.

Number

...Choctaw Enrolling Commission...

IN THE MATTER OF THE APPLICATION FOR ENROLLMENT, as a citizen of the Choctaw   Nation, of   Clifford Barnett

born on the   7   day of ___July___ 190 4

Name of father   James W Barnett   a citizen of   Choctaw
Nation *intermarried* final enrollment No. 7690
Name of mother   Ella Barnett   a citizen of   Choctaw
Nation final enrollment No. 7690

Postoffice   Bokoshe I.T.

AFFIDAVIT OF MOTHER.

UNITED STATES OF AMERICA
INDIAN TERRITORY
  Central   DISTRICT

I   Ella Barnett   , on oath state that I am 39   years of age and a citizen by   blood   of the   Choctaw   Nation, and as such have been placed upon the final roll of the   Choctaw   Nation, by the Honorable Secretary of the Interior my final enrollment number being   7690 ; that I am the lawful wife of   James W Barnett   , who is a citizen of the — — —Nation, and as such has been placed upon the final roll of said Nation by the Honorable Secretary of the Interior, his final

Applications for Enrollment of Choctaw Newborn
Act of 1905   Volume X

enrollment number being   7690   and that a   Male   child was born to me on the 7th day of   July   190 4; that said child has been named   Clifford Barnett   , and is now living.

Ella Barnett

Witnesseth.

Must be two Witnesses who are Citizens. } James Taylor
C.B. Ward

Subscribed and sworn to before me this   16   day of   Jan   190 5

John R Smoot
Notary Public.

My commission expires:
July 21-1906

AFFIDAVIT OF ATTENDING PHYSICIAN OR MIDWIFE

UNITED STATES OF AMERICA
INDIAN TERRITORY
Central   DISTRICT

I,   E.F. Hodges   a   physician on oath state that I attended on Mrs.   Ella Barnett   wife of   James W. Barnett   on the   7th   day of   July   , 190 4 , that there was born to her on said date a   male   child, that said child is now living, and is said to have been named   Clifford Barnett

E. F. Hodges   M.D.

Subscribed and sworn to before me this, the   16th   day of   Jan   190 5

WITNESSETH:
Must be two witnesses who are citizens { James Taylor
C B Ward

Jno R Smoot   Notary Public.
Com Ex July 21st 1906

We hereby certify that we are well acquainted with ~~James W Barnett~~ E.F. Hodges a ~~n intermarried citizen~~ physician   and know   him   to be reputable and of good standing in the community.

James Taylor   James Taylor

C B Ward   C B Ward

Applications for Enrollment of Choctaw Newborn
Act of 1905   Volume X

7-7690
BIRTH AFFIDAVIT.

DEPARTMENT OF THE INTERIOR.
COMMISSION TO THE FIVE CIVILIZED TRIBES.

IN RE APPLICATION FOR ENROLLMENT, as a citizen of the Choctaw Nation, of Clifford Barnett, born on the 7th day of July, 1904

Name of Father: James W. Barnett   a citizen of the Choctaw Nation.
Name of Mother: Ella Barnett   a citizen of the Choctaw Nation.

Postoffice   Bokoshe, Ind. Ter.

AFFIDAVIT OF MOTHER.

UNITED STATES OF AMERICA, Indian Territory,
Central   DISTRICT.

I, Ella Barnett, on oath state that I am 39 years of age and a citizen by blood, of the Choctaw Nation; that I am the lawful wife of James W. Barnett, who is a citizen, by intermarriage of the Choctaw Nation; that a male child was born to me on 7th day of July, 1904; that said child has been named Clifford Barnett, and was living March 4, 1905.

Ella Barnett

Witnesses To Mark:

Subscribed and sworn to before me this 4th day of April, 1905

OL Johnson
Notary Public.

AFFIDAVIT OF ATTENDING PHYSICIAN OR MID-WIFE.

UNITED STATES OF AMERICA, Indian Territory,
Central   DISTRICT.

I, E. F. Hodges, a physician, on oath state that I attended on Mrs. Ella Barnett, wife of James W. Barnett on the 7th day of July, 1904; that there was born to her on said date a male child; that said child was living March 4, 1905, and is said to have been named Clifford Barnett

E.F. Hodges M.D.

Applications for Enrollment of Choctaw Newborn
Act of 1905   Volume X

Witnesses To Mark:
{
    Subscribed and sworn to before me this   4th day of   July   , 1905

                            OL Johnson
                                  Notary Public.

<u>Choc New Born 694</u>
    Vera C. James   b. 3-22[sic]-04

(The letter below typed as given.)

C.C.Smith   dealer in
General Merchandise.

                            Drake, I. T. April 3, 1905.

Commission to Five Civilized   Tribes   inclosed find affidavit of birth of Vera C. James Daughter of Black & Rebecca James who was enrolled as Rebecca Walker.

        C O P Y .

                                              Choctaw 2551.

                   Muskogee, Indian Territory, April 10, 1905.

Black James,
    Drake, Indian Territory.

Dear Sir:

    Receipt is hereby acknowledged of your letter of April 3, enclosing the affidavits of Rebecca James and T. A. Stevns[sic] to the birth of Vera C. James, daughter of Black and Rebecca James, March 21, 1904, and the same have been filed with our records as an application for the enrollment of said child.

                        Respectfully,
                                     Commissioner in Charge.

Applications for Enrollment of Choctaw Newborn
Act of 1905 Volume X

7-NB-694.

Muskogee, Indian Territory, May 27, 1905.

Black James,
    Nebo, Indian Territory.

Dear Sir:

There is enclosed you herewith for execution application for the enrollment of your infant child, Vera C. James.

In the affidavits of March 4, 1905, the physician gives the date of the applicant's birth as March 21, 1904, while the mother, in her affidavit of the 3rd ultimo, gives the date as March 22, 1904. In the enclosed application the date of the applicant's birth is left blank. Please insert the correct date and, when the affidavits are properly executed, return them to this office.

In having these affidavits executed care should be exercised to see that all names are written in full, as they appear in the body of the affidavit, and in the event that either of the persons signing the affidavit are unable to write, signatures by mark must be attested by two witnesses. Each affidavit must be executed before a Notary Public and the notarial seal and signature of the officer must be attached to each separate affidavit.

Respectfully,

VR 27-1.   Chairman.

7 NB 694

Muskogee, Indian Territory, June 17, 1905.

Black James,
    Nebo, Indian Territory.

Dear Sir:

Receipt is hereby acknowledged of the affidavits of Rebecca James and T. A. Stevens to the birth of Vera C. James, daughter of Black and Rebecca James, March 21, 1904, and the same have been filed with our records in the matter of the enrollment of said child.

Respectfully,

Chairman.

Applications for Enrollment of Choctaw Newborn
Act of 1905   Volume X

7-NB-694

Muskogee, Indian Territory, August 26, 1905.

Rebecca James,
    Crusher, Indian Territory.

Dear Madam:

Receipt is hereby acknowledged of your letter of August 18, 1905, asking if your child, Vera C. James has been approved.

In reply to your letter you are advised that the name of your child, Vera C. James, has been placed upon a schedule of citizens by blood of the Choctaw Nation, which has been forwarded to the Secretary of the Interior, and you will be notified when her enrollment is approved by the Department.

Respectfully,

Commissioner.

BIRTH AFFIDAVIT.

IN RE-APPLICATION FOR ENROLLMENT, as a citizen of the   Choctaw   Nation, of Vera C. James , born on the   21   day of   March , 190 4

Name of Father: Black James   a citizen of the   Choctaw   Nation.
Name of Mother: Rebecca James   a citizen of the   Choctaw   Nation.

Postoffice   Nebo I.T.

AFFIDAVIT OF MOTHER.

UNITED STATES OF AMERICA, INDIAN TERRITORY,
_____ District.

I,   Rebecca James   , on oath state that I am   22   years of age and a citizen by Blood   , of the   Choctaw   Nation; that I am the lawful wife of   Black James   , who is a citizen, by   Marriage   of the   Choctaw   Nation; that a   Girl   child was born to me on 22[sic]   day of   March , 1904, that said child has been named   Vera C James   , and is now living.

Rebecca James

Applications for Enrollment of Choctaw Newborn
Act of 1905   Volume X

Witnesses To Mark:
{ O H Smith
  R N Sheppfard[sic]

Subscribed and sworn to before me this 3 day of   April , 1905.

My commission expires Mar 2 1907   C.C. Smith
                                                        Notary Public.

AFFIDAVIT OF ATTENDING PHYSICIAN OR MID-WIFE.

UNITED STATES OF AMERICA, INDIAN TERRITORY,
  Northern   District.

I,   T A Stevens , a   physician , on oath state that I attended on Mrs. Rebecca James , wife of Black James on the 21" day of Mar , 1904; that there was born to her on said date a female child; that said child is now living and is said to have been named Vera

                                    T A Stevens

Witnesses To Mark:
{ Agnes Childers
  Emma Perry

Subscribed and sworn to before me this 4" day of March , 1905.

                        E. J. Buckley
                                Notary Public.
My commission expires March 15" 1908

BIRTH AFFIDAVIT.
DEPARTMENT OF THE INTERIOR.
COMMISSION TO THE FIVE CIVILIZED TRIBES.

IN RE APPLICATION FOR ENROLLMENT, as a citizen of the   Choctaw   Nation, of Vera C James , born on the 21 day of March , 1904

Name of Father: Black James   a citizen of the Choctaw Nation.
Name of Mother: Rebecca James   a citizen of the Choctaw Nation.

                    Postoffice   Nebo Ind Ter

Applications for Enrollment of Choctaw Newborn
Act of 1905 Volume X

AFFIDAVIT OF MOTHER.

UNITED STATES OF AMERICA, Indian Territory, }
    Southern 21   DISTRICT.

    I, Rebecca James, on oath state that I am 22 years of age and a citizen by blood, of the Choctaw Nation; that I am the lawful wife of Black James, who is a citizen, by ——— of the United States Nation; that a female child was born to me on 21 day of March, 1904; that said child has been named Vera C James, and was living March 4, 1905.

                                       Rebecca James

Witnesses To Mark:
  { A.P. Henry
    Effie Smith

    Subscribed and sworn to before me this 13 day of June, 1905

                                    C C Smith
My commission expires Mar 2 1907   Notary Public.

AFFIDAVIT OF ATTENDING PHYSICIAN OR MID-WIFE.

UNITED STATES OF AMERICA, Indian Territory, }
                              DISTRICT.

    I, T A Stevens, a physician, on oath state that I attended on Mrs. Rebecca James, wife of Black James on the 21" day of March, 1904; that there was born to her on said date a female child; that said child was living March 4, 1905, and is said to have been named Vera C James

                                         T A Stevens

Witnesses To Mark:
  { Wm Childers
    J. A. Roth

    Subscribed and sworn to before me this 3rd day of June, 1905

                                    E. J. Buckley
                                        Notary Public.
My commission expires March 15" 1908

Applications for Enrollment of Choctaw Newborn
Act of 1905 Volume X

Choc New Born 695
    James Leroy Key b. 12-11-03

Choctaw 343.

Muskogee, Indian Territory, April 10, 1905.

James H. Key,
    Madill, Indian Territory.

Dear Sir:

    Receipt is hereby acknowledged of the affidavits of Lula Key and Susan Arterbery to the birth of James LeRoy Key, son of James H. and Lula Key, December 11, 1903, and the same have been filed with our records as an application for the enrollment of said child.

                    Respectfully,

                                  Commissioner in Charge.

BIRTH AFFIDAVIT.

DEPARTMENT OF THE INTERIOR.
COMMISSION TO THE FIVE CIVILIZED TRIBES.

    IN RE APPLICATION FOR ENROLLMENT, as a citizen of the Choctaw Nation, of James Leroy Key , born on the 11th day of December , 190[sic]

Name of Father: James H. Key   a citizen of the United States xxxxx.
Name of Mother: Lula Key   a citizen of the Choctaw Nation.

                Postoffice   Madill, I.T.

AFFIDAVIT OF MOTHER.

UNITED STATES OF AMERICA, Indian Territory,
    Southern   DISTRICT.

    I, Lula Key , on oath state that I am 21 years of age and a citizen by blood , of the Choctaw Nation; that I am the lawful wife of James H. Key , who is a citizen, ~~by~~ ....of the United States xxxxxx; that a male child was born to me on 11th day of December , 1903; that said child has been named James LeRoy , and was living March 4, 1905.

                                        Lula Key

Applications for Enrollment of Choctaw Newborn
Act of 1905   Volume X

Witnesses To Mark:
{ *(Name Illegible)*
{ AJ Knight

    Subscribed and sworn to before me this 30th day of March , 1905

                        W.B. Hancock
                        Notary Public.

AFFIDAVIT OF ATTENDING PHYSICIAN OR MID-WIFE.

UNITED STATES OF AMERICA, Indian Territory,}
    Southern   DISTRICT. }

    I, Susan Arterbery , a Mid-wife , on oath state that I attended on Mrs. Lula Key , wife of James H Key on the 11th day of December , 1903; that there was born to her on said date a male child; that said child was living March 4, 1905, and is said to have been named ....

                        Susan Arterbery

Witnesses To Mark:
{
{

    Subscribed and sworn to before me this 30th day of March , 1905

                        W.B. Hancock
                        Notary Public.

<u>Choc New Born 696</u>
    Nellie Harrison   b. 2-25-05

                                           Choctaw 411.

                Muskogee, Indian Territory, April 10, 1905.

Lewis H. Harrison,
    Bailey, Indian Territory.

Dear Sir:

    Receipt is hereby acknowledged of your letter of April 3, transmitting the affidavits of Edga Lee Harrison and Emily Breazeale to the birth of Nellie Harrison,

Applications for Enrollment of Choctaw Newborn
Act of 1905   Volume X

daughter of Lewis H. and Edga Lee Harrison, February 25, 1905, and the same have been filed with our records as an application for the enrollment of said child.

Respectfully,

Commissioner in Charge.

BIRTH AFFIDAVIT.

DEPARTMENT OF THE INTERIOR.
COMMISSION TO THE FIVE CIVILIZED TRIBES.

IN RE APPLICATION FOR ENROLLMENT, as a citizen of the   Choctaw   Nation, of Nellie Harrison   , born on the 25th day of Feb   , 1905

Name of Father: Lewis H Harrison   a citizen of the   Choctaw   Nation.
Name of Mother: Edga Lee Harrison   a citizen of the   Choctaw   Nation.

Postoffice   Bailey, I.T.

AFFIDAVIT OF MOTHER.

UNITED STATES OF AMERICA, Indian Territory,
   Southern   DISTRICT.

I, Edga Lee Harrison   , on oath state that I am 34   years of age and a citizen by   Intermarriage   , of the   Choctaw   Nation; that I am the lawful wife of   Lewis H Harrison   , who is a citizen, by Blood   of the   Choctaw Nation; that a   female   child was born to me on 25th day of Feb   , 1905; that said child has been named   Nellie Harrison   , and was living March 4, 1905.

Edga Lee Harrison

Witnesses To Mark:

Subscribed and sworn to before me this 3 day of   April   , 1905

J.M. Gibbins
Notary Public.

4/27/1905

Applications for Enrollment of Choctaw Newborn
Act of 1905   Volume X

AFFIDAVIT OF ATTENDING PHYSICIAN OR MID-WIFE.

UNITED STATES OF AMERICA, Indian Territory,
Southern DISTRICT.

I, Emily Breazeale, a Midwife, on oath state that I attended on Mrs. Edga Lee Harrison, wife of Lewis H. Harrison on the 25th day of Feb, 1905; that there was born to her on said date a female child; that said child was living March 4, 1905, and is said to have been named Nellie Harrison

Emily Breazeale

Witnesses To Mark:

Subscribed and sworn to before me this 3 day of April, 1905

J.M. Gibbins
Notary Public.
My commission expires 4/27/1905

Choc New Born 697
    Thomas E. Campbell   b. 10-10-03

COPY   9 N.B. 697

Muskogee, Indian Territory, April 13, 1905.

William Campbell,
    Utica, Indian Territory.

Dear Sir:

You are hereby advised that before the application for the enrollment of your infant child, Thomas E. Campbell, can be finally disposed of, it will be necessary for you to furnish the Commission either the original or a certified copy of the license and certificate of your marriage to his mother, Idonia Campbell.

Please give this matter your immediate attention.

Respectfully,
SIGNED   *T. B. Needles.*
Commissioner in Charge.

Applications for Enrollment of Choctaw Newborn
Act of 1905 Volume X

COPY

Choctaw N.B. 697

Muskogee, Indian Territory, April 28, 1905.

W. G. Campbell,
　　Utica, Indian Territory.

Dear Sir:

　　Receipt is hereby acknowledged of your letter of April 25, transmitting a certified copy of marriage license and certificate which you offer in support of the application for the enrollment of your child, Thomas E. Campbell, and the same has been filed with the records in this case.

　　　　　　　　　　Respectfully,

　　　　　　　　　　SIGNED
　　　　　　　　　　Tams Bixby
　　　　　　　　　　　Chairman.

7-NB-697

Muskogee, Indian Territory September 30, 1905

William Campbell,
　　Durant, Indian Territory.

Dear Sir:

　　Receipt is hereby acknowledged of your letter of the 23rd instant in which you request this office to return to you the certified copy of the marriage license and certificate between you and Idonia Methvin, which evidence of marriage you filed with this office in the matter of the application for the enrollment of your minor son Thomas E. Campbell as a citizen by blood of the Choctaw Nation.

　　In reply to your letter you are advised that said evidence of marriage must be retained by this office and kept on file in the enrollment case of your said son.

　　You are further advised that should you desire to secure another certified copy of said marriage license and certificate the same may be obtained from Fred Wilson, Clerk of the Parish Red River, Louisiana.

　　　　　　　　　　Respectfully,

　　　　　　　　　　　Commissioner.

Applications for Enrollment of Choctaw Newborn
Act of 1905 Volume X

NEW-BORN AFFIDAVIT.

Number...............

...Choctaw Enrolling Commission...

IN THE MATTER OF THE APPLICATION FOR ENROLLMENT, as a citizen of the Choctaw Nation, of Thomas Campbell

born on the 10th day of ___Oct___ 190 3

Name of father William Campbell   a citizen of Choctaw
Nation final enrollment No. 10334
Name of mother Idonia Campbell   a citizen of white
Nation final enrollment No. ———

Postoffice   Utica I.T.

AFFIDAVIT OF MOTHER.

UNITED STATES OF AMERICA
INDIAN TERRITORY
Central   DISTRICT

I Idonia Campbell , on oath state that I am 21 years of age and a citizen by white of the ——— Nation, and as such have been placed upon the final roll of the ——— Nation, by the Honorable Secretary of the Interior my final enrollment number being ——— ; that I am the lawful wife of William Campbell , who is a citizen of the Choctaw Nation, and as such has been placed upon the final roll of said Nation by the Honorable Secretary of the Interior, his final enrollment number being 10337 and that a Male child was born to me on the 10th day of Oct 190 3; that said child has been named Thomas Campbell , and is now living.

Idonia Campbell

Witnesseth.

Must be two Witnesses who are Citizens. } Basil L. Gardner
Lula E Huggins

Subscribed and sworn to before me this 13 day of Feb 190 5

W.J. ODonby
Notary Public.

My commission expires: Dec 17th 1905

Applications for Enrollment of Choctaw Newborn
Act of 1905 Volume X

Affidavit of Attending Physician or Midwife

UNITED STATES OF AMERICA,
INDIAN TERRITORY,
Central DISTRICT

I, A. J. Pennington a Physician on oath state that I attended on Mrs. Idonia Campbell wife of William Campbell on the 10th day of Oct , 190 3, that there was born to her on said date a male child, that said child is now living, and is said to have been named Thomas Campbell

A.J. Pennington M. D.

Subscribed and sworn to before me this the 18th day of January 1905

W.H. Lazarus
Notary Public.

WITNESSETH:
Must be two witnesses who are citizens and know the child.
Basil L. Gardner
Lula E Huggins

We hereby certify that we are well acquainted with A J Pennington a Physician and know him to be reputable and of good standing in the community.

Must be two citizen witnesses.
(Name Illegible)
W. L. Hammer

State of Louisiana
Parish of Red River

I hereby certify that the within is a true and correct copy of the original on file, and of records in this office, given under my hand and seal this April 19 AD 1905.

Fred Wilson
Clerk County Court
& Ex officio
Notary Public

DEPARTMENT OF THE INTERIOR,
COMMISSION TO THE FIVE CIVILIZED TRIBES.
FILED

APR 27 1905
Tams Bixby CHAIRMAN.

Applications for Enrollment of Choctaw Newborn
Act of 1905 Volume X

State of Louisiana--Parish of Red River

To any Person authorized to Celebrate Marriage in the Parish of Red River--GREETING:

You are hereby licensed and permitted to unite in the bonds of matrimony, according to law and established rules, Mr. **William Campbell** and Miss Idonia Methvin

50#

Revenue stamps attached to original.

Given under my hand and seal of office as Clerk of the District Court in and for the Parish of Red River, the 24th day of November one thousand nine hundred ~~and~~ 1900

(Name Illegible) Clerk

CERTIFICATE OF MARRIAGE

State of Louisiana }
Parish of Red River }

Be it remembered. That in pursuance of a license issued by the Clerk of the District Court of the Parish of Red River, Louisiana, I have performed the solemn rites of Matrimony between Mr. **William Campbell** and Miss Idonia Methvin on the 25th day of November, 1900, in the presence of the undersigned subscribing witnesses.

Signed
JA Martin
L J McGraw
JW Chapman

Signed
W.C. Campbell
Idonia Methvin
T.G. McGraw J.P.

BIRTH AFFIDAVIT.

Department of the Interior,
COMMISSION TO THE FIVE CIVILIZED TRIBES.

IN RE APPLICATION FOR ENROLLMENT, as a citizen of the Choctaw Nation, of Thomas E Campbell, born on the 10th day of October, 1903

Name of Father: William Campbell   a citizen of the Choctaw Nation.
Name of Mother: Idonia Campbell   a citizen of the not a citizen Nation.

Post-Office: Utica, Indian Territory

Applications for Enrollment of Choctaw Newborn
Act of 1905 Volume X

AFFIDAVIT OF MOTHER.

UNITED STATES OF AMERICA,
   INDIAN TERRITORY,
  Central   District.

    I, Idonia Campbell , on oath state that I am 22 years of age and a citizen by ——— , of the ———Nation; that I am the lawful wife of William Campbell , who is a citizen, by blood of the Choctaw Nation; that a male child was born to me on 10th day of October , 190 3, that said child has been named Thomas E Campbell , and is now living.

                                    Idonia Campbell

WITNESSES TO MARK:

    Subscribed and sworn to before me this 4th day of April , 1905

                                      W.J. ODonby
                                      Notary Public.

AFFIDAVIT OF ATTENDING PHYSICIAN OR MID-WIFE.

UNITED STATES OF AMERICA,
   INDIAN TERRITORY,
  State of Louisiana District.

    I, A. J. Pennington , a Physician , on oath state that I attended on Mrs. Idonia Campbell , wife of William Campbell on the 10th day of October , 190 3; that there was born to her on said date a male child; that said child is now living and is said to have been named Thomas E Campbell

                                  A J Pennington M.D.

WITNESSES TO MARK:
    R.L. Rogers
    W T Holdman

    Subscribed and sworn to before me this 28 day of March , 1905

                                    W.H. Lazarus
                                      Notary Public.

Index

ADAMS
   Eliza 85
AINSWORTH
   Thomas D 158
AIRINGTON
   Elmina 101,102,103,104
   Henry Jackson 101,102,103,104
   Jackson 101,102,103,104
   M E 102
ALLEN
   L D 234,235
ANDERSON
   Robert 286,287
   Will 267
ANGELL
   W H 52,53,99,288
ARNOLD
   Mrs L L 288
ARNOTE
   A J 178,179
ARNOTE & DAVENPORT 178
ARTERBERY
   Susan 321,322
ASHLEY
   Jerry 229,231
ATKINSON
   Ed 259
   Fred Leonard 168,169,170
   John H 168,169,170
   Mary S 169,170
   Mary Susan 168,169

BACON
   Dave 21,22
   Mame 21,22
   Nonie Esner 21,22
BAKER
   Agustia 277,278
   Augustia 277,278,279,280
   Elisbeth 208,209
   Elizabeth 212,214
   Elum 75,77
   Harry L 60,61,62,65
   Jackson 277,278,279,280
   Mary Frances 279,280
   Mary Francis 277,278
BALL

   Dr J G 13
   J G 12,13,14
   J G, MD 13
BARNETT
   Clifford 313,314,315
   Ella 313,314,315
   Emmett Leroy 53,54,55,56
   James W 313,314,315
   Maud 205,206
   Sarah A 53,54,55,56
   W W 53
   William W 54,55
BARNWELL
   Clara 216,217
   Clare 215
BASCOM
   John 289,290
BEAMES
   Josiah 187,189
   Maudie Mutrie 189
   Maudie Myrtie 187
   Minnie 187,189
   Minnie E 189
   Wallace 181,182,184,185,186
BEAMS
   Joseph 186,187
   Josiah 187
   Maudie Myrtie 186,187
   Maudie Myrtle 187
   Minnie 186,187
BEANS
   Wallace 181
BECKETT
   J B 261
   J B, MD 261
   A L 72,73,132,133,149
BECKETTE
   J B 297,298
   J B, MD 298
BECKLE
   James H 238,239
BENGEMAN
   Josephine 51
BENJAMIN
   Betsy 52
   James 50,51,52
   Josephine 51

Index

Katie 50,51,52
Simeon 50,51,52
BENNETT
   Chas A 104
BENTON
   Julia 223,224
   Lola 223,224
   Rufus F 223,224
BILLE
   Dixie 72
   Lida 70,72
BILLIE
   Dixon 71
BIXBY
   Tams 9,10,17,32,33,38,75,101,
   102,120,163,196,198,199,216,243,244
   ,269,273,308,325,327
BOHANAN
   H J 279,280
BOND
   E H 34
   June H 277
   Ridgely 236,237,238
   Ridgely E, Jr 237,238
   Sina 236,237,238
BOWER
   James 47,88,96,115,131,159,
   255,256,267
   W L 169
BOWMAN
   Edward S 88
   Gertrude 88
   Lois Annie 88
BRADLEY
   W P 226
BRANAUGH
   V 22,23,24,25
BREAZEALE
   Emily 322,324
BREEDLOVE
   R T 151
BREWER
   John 278
BRIANS
   (Illegible) 55
   A E 300,302
   Mary M 300,301,302

Mrs A E 302
R E 53
R H 300,301,302
Wilbert M 300,301,302
BRIGHT
   Mrs L M 288
BRIMM
   Sam 22
BRUCE
   Kate 125,126
   Mrs J H 122,123,124
BUCKLEY
   E J 319,320
BURKES
   Lillie B 204
BURNES
   Mary 280
   Mary C 278
BURNS
   Mary 280
BURNSIDE
   D E 29,30,31
   Gladys 29,30,31
   Lizzie 26,29,30,31
BUTLER
   Delia 67,68,69
   Jane 211
   Jno M 67,68,69
   John M 69
   M D 102,103
   Pearl 66,67,68,69
BYINGTON
   Ben 43,44
   Henry 41
   Luvena 41
   Moody 285,286

CAIN
   P L 57,58,59
CALDWELL
   Willie 8
CALLAWAY
   A B 47,50
CAMPBELL
   C M 200,201
   Idonia 324,326,327,328,329
   Thomas 325,326,327

Index

Thomas E 324,325,328,329
W C 328
W G 325
William 324,325,326,327,328,329
CAPSHAW
   Mrs N L 57
   Nancy L 57,58
CARMICHAEL
   J D 222,223
CARR
   Dennis 57
   Jane 57
   Wm O 147,148
CART
   J L 55,56
CASS
   Maurice 96
CEPHAS
   Bessie 309,310
   Elliston 309,310
   Timothy J 309,310
CEPHUS
   Bessie 307,308,309,311,312
   Ellistan 307,308,310,311,312
   T J 307,308,310,311,312
   Timothy J 13
CHAPMAN
   J W 328
   Nancy 21,22
CHASTAIN
   J D 246,267
CHILDERS
   Agnes 319
   Wm 320
CHOATE
   Belle D 272,273,274,275,276
   David 272,273,274,275,276
   Ida 193,194
   James H 193,194
   James H, Jr 193
   James H, Junior 193,194
   James Luke 272,274,275,276
   Mary I 272,273,274
CHOATS
   W F 127,128
CINB
   D N 201

CLARK
   Edwin O 50
   J B 300
   J B, MD 300
CLEGG
   Lou 101,104
COBB
   Loren 252,253,254,257,267,268
   Loring 255,256
   Sarah E 253,254,255,256,257
   Sina 255,256
   Sinie 252,253,254,257
COELMAN
   D J 189
COFER
   J E 239,241
   J E, MD 239,241
COLBERT
   Charley 171,172
COLEMAN
   Arian 147
   N F 281
   N G 282
   R S 62,63,64,282
   S W 282
   Sarah Gaddy 148
COLEY
   Johnson 75,77
COLLIN
   (Illegible) 17
COLLINS
   Gracie A 89,90,91
   Henry Monroe 89,90,91
   Miles S 89,90,91
   Ollie Belle 89,90
COOPER
   Abel 131,132
   Ada 242,248,267
   Adah 246
   A B 227
   Corean 246
   Corine 242,245,246,248,267
   Corrine 243
   James 47
   Lucy Lucas 227,228
   Mrs S C 246
   S C 246

Index

Stephen 242,243,244,248,267
COUCH
  S E 224
COWAN
  George S 260,263,297,298
  Ira Lee Riley 297,298
  Sarah 297,298
CRABTREE
  C R 194,195
CRANFILL
  L J 202
  L J, MD 202
  Luther J 203
  Luther J, MD 199,204
CROSTHWAIT
  E 54
CROUTHAMEL
  A H 260,262,263,298,299
CROWDER
  Loran F 138,139,141,142
  Loring F 139,140
  Loui F 138
  Louis F 138
  Lydia 139,140
  Lydia A 138,139
  Lydia Ann 138,141,142
  Walter L 138,139,141,142
  Walter Lee 140
CROWELL
  Elizabeth 101,104
CULBERSON
  James 99
CUMMINGS
  A M 55,56
CURRIE
  W G 276
CURRY
  Guy A 175,235

DABNEY
  J A 138,139,140,141,142
  J A, MD 140,142
  J A. ,D 139
DAILY
  Mary 87
  Mary Ann 84
  Maryann 84

DALTON
  E M 306,307
DAVENPORT
  ? J 194,195
DAVIDSON
  W B 137
DAVIS
  Emma 160
  Jas H 209,210
  S P 143
DEAL
  Frank 196,197
  Ida I 195,196
  Ida Isabell 196,197
  John East 196
  Johnece 195,196,197
  Johnese 195
DIFENDAFER
  Chas T 208,221,227,228,229,251,
  255,266,295,297
DOLLAR
  Mary 223
DONNELLY
  W C 120,244,245
DORSET
  Carrie 37,38,39
  Ida 37
  John 37,38,39
DORSETT
  Carrie 37,38,39,42,43,44
  Ida 37,39,42,43
  John 37,38,39,42,43,44
DORSEY
  John 40
DOSHIER
  Etha M 163,164,165,166,167,168
  A G 163,164,165,166,167,168
  Mrs A G 166
  Pauline 163,164,165,166,167,168
DOWNING
  E A 231
DOWSET
  Carrey 40,41
  Ida 40,41
  John 40,41
DR L T JACKSON & CO 189
DUKES

Index

H C 3,4
DWIGHT
  E T 28
  Minerva 23
  Minervia 24,25

EATHERLY
  W B 175
EDMOND
  Emily 37,39,41,42,44
EDMONDS
  Emily 41
ELLIOTT
  Alice 125,126
  J H 122,123,124,125,126
  Joel H 121
ELLIS
  H A 1
  H A, MD 1
ERVIN
  Columbus C 239,240,241
  Lizzie H 239,240,241
  Rena Pauline 239,240,241
  William L 267
ESTES
  W N 267
EVANS
  C L 3,4,5,6,7
EVERIDGE
  J H 239,240
EVINS
  E L 283,284
  E L, MD 284
EWING
  C H 43,44,226

FANNIE
  E J 216,217,244
FANNIN
  E J 120,245,269,270
FENNELL
  Mrs T 13
  Thomas 13,107,108
  Thos 107,108
FERGUSON
  A H 116,117
FITZER
  James 145
FOLSOM
  Arnold 94,95,96
  A E 41
  Fletcher Daniel 80,82
  Frank 131,132,148
  Frank D 80,81,82
  Frank Davis 80,81
  Jincy 228,229
  Joseph 228,229
  Lizzie 94,95,96
  Mary G 80,81,82
  Nathan W 263
  Noel 93,94,167,168
  Oslin 94,95,96
  Walter 147
FOREST
  Minnie 44
FORREST
  Annie 44,48,49
  Minie 46
  Minnie 44,45,47,48,49,50
FORRET
  Minnie 47,48
FOSTER & DALTON 305
FOWLER
  H L 14,15,307,311,312,313
  J D 15,17,18,21
  J D, MD 17
  John 311
FRANKLIN
  James 213
  Wirt 69,89,90,91,92,93,110, 159,192,287
FRAZIER
  Andy 191
  Emma 157,158
  Gertie 26
  Julia 155,156
  Lona 155,156
  Ross 30
  Susan 190,191
  Thompson 155,156
  Wilson E 285,286
FULSOM
  Jancy 131,132
  Peter 213

Index

GARDNER
  Basil L 326,327
  J J 115
  Robert 267
GARLAND
  Arizona 133,134,135,136,137
  Clara Sterling 133
  Clara Stirling 134,136,137
  D N 222
  Davis 133,134,135,136,137
  Herman Newton 133,134,135,136
  Ida 97
  Inez C 222
  Josiah 97
  Louise 221,222
  Ward 134,136
GIBBINS
  J M 323,324
GIBSON
  Emma 176,177,179
  Jennie 97,98,99,100
  Melisis 178
  Melissie 176,177,178
  Wesley 97,98,99,100
  William 97,98,99,100
GIVENS
  J G 282
GLENN
  W T 28,279,280,309,310
GOFORTH
  J H 40
  A M 83,85
GOLD
  S M 127,128,129
GOLLIHARE
  Andrew J 86,87
  Andrew Jackson 83,84,85
  Harriet Cordelia 85
  Harriett Cordelia 83,84,85,86,87
  Harvey Andrew 83,84,86
  Harvie Andrew 86,87
  Hurbert 83,84,85,86
GOODNIGHT
  E G 83,84,85
  John H 84,85,87
GREEN
  J M 63,64

GRIST
  Maggie 150,151
HAKLOCHEE
  Elsie 213
HAMILTON
  N J 111,112,113
  N J, MD 112
  Vercy 271
  Versie 268,269,270
HAMMER
  W L 327
HAMPTON
  Annie Frances 225,226
  Annie Francis 226
  Frances 225,226
  Julius C 225,226
HANCOCK
  W B 322
HARBOUR
  I T 68,69
  I T, MD 68,69
HARDY
  J J 163,165,166,167
  J J, MD 166,167
HARKINS
  George Lafayett 231,232,233
  Giles W 232,233
  Mollie 232,233
HARLEY
  Montford 309,310
HARPER
  J H 224
  J L 231
  Tom 223
HARRISON
  Birdie Lee 180,183,184,185,186
  Edga Lee 322,323,324
  Lewis H 322,323,324
  Lorena 180,181,182,183,184,185
  Lyman 180,181,182,183,184,185
  Lymon 186
  Nellie 322,323,324
  Rhoda 180,181,182,183,185
HARTSHORNE
  W O 88,89,90
HENDERSON

Amanda 151,152,153,154
Lee O 151,152,153,154
W L 151,152,153
Wilson L 153,154

HENRY
A P 320

HESTER
P F 237

HICKMAN
J H 84,87
Minnie 87

HIGHTOWER
A M 202,203,204

HILL
Arthur T 137
A D 296,297
A T 134

HOBBS
Alice 128,129

HOBBY
Alic 126

HODGES
E F 314,315
E F, MD 314,315
Walter 231

HOLDMAN
W T 329

HOLLEY
G A 71,131,305

HOLMAN
Ellen 105,106

HOOVER
Andrew J, MD 197
D W 178,179
A J 197
J T 288

HORTON
L D 21,23,24,25,26

HUDLOW
W H 191

HUDSON
J F 209
Orvil 209
W H 156

HUGGINS
Lula E 326,327

HULSEY
Wm J 246,267,284

HULSEY & PATTERSON 243,283

HUNTER
Ada 243,244,245
T W 28

IMPSON
John 112
John A M 112,187,189
Mrs A 187

ISHAM
L N 14

IVIE
Charles W, MD 161
Charles William 161

JACK
Hanna 16,17
Loman 16,17,19,20

JACKS
Robin 77

JACKSON
D N 246
Joseph 16,17,20
L T 187,189
L T, MD 187,189

JAMES
Ben 92,93,94
Black 316,317,318,319,320
Dolly Elizabeth 192,193
Edward 173
Emily 92
Etha M 163,164,165,166
Gibson 91,92,93,94
Joseph 74,75,76,77,78
Katie 192
Nellie 74,75,76,77,78
Rebecca 316,317,318,319,320
Rhoda 92,93,94
Sarah E 253,254,256,257
Solomon 258
Vera 319
Vera C 316,317,318,319,320
Wesley 73,74,75,76,77,78
William Adolphus 192

JEFFERSON
Mary 76,77

Index

JEFLOW
  Joseph 282
JENNINGS
  B A 265
JOHNICE
  John 255,256,267,268
JOHNSON
  Abel H 283,284
  Alex 70,71,72,73,305
  Alexander 70,71,306
  Annie 207,208,209,210,211, 212,213,214,215
  Arbin 208,209,210,212,213, 214,215
  Auben 214
  Ben F 283,284
  E 236,237,238,239
  E, MD 237,238
  Elizabeth 70,71,72,73,305,306
  Emeline 283,284
  Lola 209
  Lula 207,208,210,212
  N J, MD 192,193
  Nelson 212
  O L .... 51,81,82,83,161,162, 208,211,218,219,221,227,228,229,251 ,252,254,255,261,264,266,295,296, 297,315,316
  Orbin 208,210,212,213
  Orlin 208
  Simon 70,71,72,73,306
  Sophia 211
  William 211
JOHNSTON
  P S 302,304
  P S, MD 304
JONES
  C C 95,134,135,136,137
  Dovie 78,79,80
  Dr C C 96,97
  Emma ... 289,290,291,292,293,294,295
  J N 29,78,79,80,95,136,288
  Jocie 80
  M W 291
  Meda 78,79,80
  Mike 289,290,291,292,293,294,295
  W S 134,136

  Willie 289,290,291,292,293,294,295
KENNEDY
  D S 139,140,141,142
KEY
  James H 321,322
  James Leroy 321
  Lula 321,322
KING
  C A 231
KNIGHT
  A J 322

LANCE
  Elizabeth 248
  Elizzie Beth 242,248
LAZARUS
  W H 327,329
LEFLORE
  Joseph 76
  Lorena 248,249,250,251,252
  Louis 157,158
  Mary 249,250,251,252
  Noel 248,249,250,251,252,292,293
  Noel E 249,250
LENZ
  John M 144,145
LEWIS
  Benjaman 234,235
  Calvin 234
  Cassie 233,234,235
  Eliza 175,176,177,178,179,180
  Frank 93,165,166,167,168
  George 190,191
  J L 259
  Johnson 176,177,178,179,180
  Mary 176,177,178,179,180
  Nancy 190,191
  Noa 190,191
  W J 258
LINDSAY
  J C 154
  J C, MD 154
LINDSEY
  Dr J C 153
  J C 151
  J C, MD 153

Index

LLOYD
J B 187
LOCKE
Victor M, Jr 92,180
LORING
W H 29,30
LUCAS
Lucy 227
LUNSFORD
F B 180,181,183,185
LYLE
Grady Edwin 224,225
Lula B 224,225
Robert Thomas 224,225

MCBRAYER
Dr W H 3
W H 3,5,7
W H, MD 3,5,7
MCCAIN
C E 301,302
Joe 71
Mrs C E 301
MCCANN
Betsey 290,291,293,294
J L 292
Joe 289,290,294
Joe L 249,250
MCCARLEY
W B 76
MCCLEARY
J E 22,23
MCCURTAIN
Green 237
Mollie 266,267,268
MCDANIEL
Thomas 180,183,186
MCGILBERRY
Osborne 293
MCGRAW
L J 328
T G 328
MCHENRY
J W 32,34,35,36
MCINTOSH
Alex 180,181,185
John 279,280

MCLAUGHLIN
Lula 5
MCMURTREY
Clyde 67,68
MCNEIL
Eastman 20

MANSFIELD, MCMURRAY &
CORNISH 10
MARTIN
Clarence 71,305,306,307
H H 99
J A 328
James 71,305,306,307
Kizzie 305,307
M ? 53
Maggie 71,305,306,307
William 307
Wm 47,53
MASSEY
Arizona C 108,109,110
Oliver 108,109,110
William B 108,109,110
MATHERS
I C 245
MAYNOR
M H 5
MAYSEY
Samuel A 248
MELTON
W J 226
W J, MD 226
METHVIN
Idonia 325,328
MILLER
Lucy 55
Mary A 53,54,55
MISHONTAMBE
Louisa 156
Lousa 155
MITCHELL
S E 146,148
S E, MD 148,149
MONTGOMERY
D M 225
MOORE
Clifford Welsey 160

Clifford Wesley 162
David A 160,161,162
Dora M 160,161,162
Elsie 234,235
J M 113,114
J R 198,200,201
Joseph R 198,199,202,203
Lena Cecile 110,111,112,113
Lizzie 198,199,202,203
Mary Kathleen 160,161
R F 111,113,190
Robbie A 197,198,199,202,203,204
Robert A 198
Robert F 111,112
Rosa 111,112,113

MORAN
Alton 1
Alton Olive 1
Fannie 1
James E 1

MORGAN
Thomas M 288
Thos M, MD 288

MORRIS
Nelson 207,212,214

MOSES
Marion 42,43

NEAL
John W 142,143,144,145
Julia 144,145
July 142,143,145
Susan 142,143,144,145

NEEDLES
T B 37,45,59,70,74,100,109,
118,164,198,204,215,243,308,324

NELSON
B A 239,240
Eastman 267
Joseph 131

NEVINS
Floyd 212,214

NEWMAN
E A 98
M W 71,72,249,250,289,290,293

NIVINS
Floyd 208,209

ODONBY
W J 326,329

OLIVER
John H 49

OLSAN
Maud 233

OTT
Bicy 170,172,173
Fannie 170,171,172,173
Green 170,171,172,173
John 170,171,172,173
Samuel A 171,172

OVERSTREET
Clara 218
John T 215,216,217,218
Mamie 215,218

PARKE
(Illegible) 209
Frank E 209
Frank R 209

PARKER
Chas G 270

PARROTT
F C 218,221

PARSONS
Mellie 272
Millie 274

PATE
B K 268,269,270,271
Nancy C 272,274,275
Vercy 268,271
Vernon 268,271

PATRICK
Lizzie 198,200,201

PAYTON
Allen 23,24
Josephine 23,24,25
Ned 23,24,25
Walter 23,25

PEARSON
Amelia E 126,127,128,129
Bernard Preston 126,127,128,129
Robert T 126,127,128,129

PENNINGTON
A J 327,329
A J, MD 327,329

PERKINS
- L H 127,128

PERRY
- Emma 319
- Frank 130,131,132,133
- Houston 130,131,132,133
- Lewis 227,228
- Lula 227,228
- Sallie 130,131,132,133

PHILIPS
- W H 258

PHILLIPS
- S F 209
- W H 152,153,154,257

PIERSOL
- Robert T 126

PILGREEN
- Hascot 67,68,69

PISACHUBBEE
- Edward 178,179

POWELL
- Edgar L 220,221
- Edgar Louis 219
- Mary Etta 220,221
- Vera 219,220,221

PRYOR
- S V 124

PUSLEY
- Abner 57,58
- Abner B 56
- Agnes 56,57,58
- Julian 59,61,62,63,64,65,66
- Lelan 60,61,62,63,64
- Sedalia 56,58
- Sedalie 57
- Sedlie 57
- Vivian Eloise 59,60,62,63,64,65,66
- William 60
- William W 59,60,61,62,63,64,65,66

PUTTY
- Geo T 225

QUINCY
- Jerome Ervin 123

RABON
- Devie 46,47
- Dovey 44,45,46,48,49,50
- J W 238,239
- Mary J 162
- Minnie 44
- Thomas 163
- Will 46
- William 44,48,49

RAPPOLEE
- H E 268,271
- J L 268,271,272

REYNOLDS
- J T 67,68

RICE
- T J 304,305

RIDER
- M A 233

RISENER
- Charles 28
- Charlie 26,27,28
- Lizzie 29,30
- Lucy 26,27,28
- William 26,27,28
- Wm 26,27

RITTER
- J H 193

ROBERTS
- Sam T, Jr 182,184

RODGERS
- M E 194
- Rice 157

ROGERS
- Jocie 78
- Josie 80
- M E 193
- R L 329

ROSE
- Annie 96
- Sam 160
- Vester W 92,286,287

ROSS
- M 156,191

ROTH
- J A 320

RUNTON
- Carnolie 15,16,17,18,19,20,21
- Dora M 15,17,18,19
- James C 15,16,17,20,21

Index

Tabitha A 15,16,17,18,20,21
RUTHERFORD
   B C 27,28,30,31
   B C, MD 27,28,30,31
SAUL
   Mary 189
SAULS
   Mary 187
SAVAGE
   C C 246,267
   C C, MD 246
SCANTLEN
   J M 136
SCOTT
   J C 140,141
SECOR
   Bessie May 280,281,282
   Lucy 281,282
   William H 281
   Wm H 282
SELF
   James 140,141
SENATE
   Harriette 63,64
   Mattie 63,64
SENNETT
   Harriet 60,61,62
SEXTON
   Cora 234,235
   Thos J 115
SHANAFELT
   Richard 98
SHEPPFARD
   R N 319
SHONEY
   W A 8,11,14,15,285,286
SLOAN
   Chas C 160
SMITH
   C C 316,319,320
   Effie 320
   Elmore 260,262,263,264
   Essie 262,263,264
   George L 260,261
   Georgia Lee 260
   Georgie Lee 260,261

   Hill T 263
   K R 263
   Mary E 260,261
   Milton 72
   O H 319
   Pauline 262,263,264
SMOOT
   John R 314
SNIDER
   C A 288
SOCKEY
   Lewis 154
SPAIN
   Jimmie B 32,34,35
   Minnie L 32,33,34
   Minnie Lee 32,34,35,36
   Minnie May 32,33,34,35,36
   Sidney B 32,34,35,36
   Sidney D 32,33,34
SPRADLIN
   Arrilla 114,115
   Emet 116
   Emmet J 114,115
   Jaunita 114
   Juanita 114,115
   Juanita Durant 116
   Orilla 114,116
SPRIGGS
   Claud P 12,13
   Claude P 107,108
STANFIELD
   J H 226
STATLER
   Price 1
STEPHENS
   Dr L K 133
   J J 115,116
   John J 169,170
   John J, MD 115
   L K 130,133
STEVENS
   T A 317,319,320
STEVNS
   T A 316
STIGLER
   J S 132,146,148,149
   Joseph S 147,148

Index

Mary J 146,147,148,149
Rupert Bernard 146,147,148,149
S J 149
STONE
   Wm B 269,270
SWISHER
   O P 110

TALBERT
   Jno E 106
TALIAFERRO
   John D 287,288
   Nannie Lucile 287,288
   Nora 287,288
TANTUBBEE
   Enos 309,310
TAYLOR
   Agnes 105,106,107,108
   Ellen 105,107,108
   James 314
   John 106,107
   Margaret 105
   Margred 106,107
   Margret 108
   Selin 105,106,107,108
TERRELL
   Emaline 254,255
   Emiline 255
   Emmaline 253,257
TERRILL
   Daniel 167,168
THOMAS
   D 182,184
   Isaac 258,259
   James 106,107
   Jno J 180,181,185
   Loman 209,215
   Marth 258
   Netty 81,82
   Sickey 259
   Silvia 285,286,287
   Siney 258
THOMPSON
   Jacob 112
   Jake 112
   Nelson 77
   A P 91

Thelma Lee 282
THREADGILL
   C M 232,233
TOHKUBBI
   Cephus 285,286,287
   Laura 284,285,286,287
   Seon 285,286,287
TOMAS
   Nettie 81,82
TOMPSON
   Joe 3
TRAHAN
   V P 154
TRAMMELL
   J F 205,206
   John Edgar 204,205
   Lillie B 205,206,207
   Margaret L 204,205,207
   Stella May 204,206,207
   Thomas J 205,206,207
TRASK
   F W 226
TUBBY
   Cora 296
   John William 296
   William 296,297
TUEY
   L C 238,239
TURNER
   Albert P 150,151
   Andrew J 273,274,275,277
   Artie M 150,151
   Eunice Melvina 150,151
   Harrol V 303
   Harrol Van 302,303,304
   Ida F 277
   J M 174
   James M 175
   James M, MD 175
   Lena 302,304
   Lila 118,120,121
   R S 303
   Robert S 302,304
TYE
   R P 222

UHLER

Jesse 217
UMBER
  Ida 38,39,42,43
UMBRA
  Ida 40,41
UNDERWOOD
  Mary 274
  W R 274

VANZANDT
  I N 282
VARNER
  T T 216,217

WADE
  Dennis 76
  Jennie 97,98,99,100
WADLEY
  George L 132
WALKER
  Chas T 97
  Rebecca 316
WALLACE
  Bessie 307,308,309,310,311,312
  Celia 307,308,310,311,312
WALLEN
  Isam 259
  Isom 258,259
  Sim 258,259
  Siney 258,259
WALLICE
  Bessie 310,311
  Cealis 311
WALLS
  J M 145
  Jennie 143
  Jess 144
  T J 144
WARD
  C B 314
WASHINGTON
  Marcus 43,44
WATKINS
  James 143
  Martha 143,145
WATSON
  Adam E 249

WEBB
  W G 124
WELLSHEAR
  C C 237
WES
  Geo W 264
  Geo W, MD 264
WESLEY
  Elias 122,123
WEST
  Geo W 263
  Geo W, MD 263
WHISTLER
  Lena 265,266,267
  Martin 255,256,265,266,267
  Nancy 265,266,267
WHITAKER
  E E 117,119,123,124,125
  E E, MD 123
WHITEMAN
  Henry A 2,3,4,5,6,7
  M C 4
  Mattie J 3,4,5,6,7
  W J 2,3,4,5,6,7
  William J 4
WHITENER
  Harland H 229,230,231
  A J 229,230,231
  Lizzie 229,230,231
WHITNER
  Harland H 229,230
WILKERSON
  P E 300
WILLCUTT
  F F 23
WILLIAM
  John 71
WILLIAMS
  Austin 99,100
  B W 26,27,28,29,30,31,79,80
  Frank 173
  H E 108,110
  J E 35,36,205,206,207
  J Ernest 204
  Jack 157,158,159,160
  Leola 156,157,158,159,160
  Leoler 157

Mary Jane 157,158,159,160
Vicey 99
Vicy 100

WILLIS
Edward 7,8,9,10,11
Gracie 8,9,11,12,13,14,15
Sam 7,12,13
Samuel 14
W 10,11,14
Willie 9,12,13

WILSON
Fred 325,327
Nelson 3,4
Rufus L 13

WILTSEY
Annie 299,300
James Ellis 299,300
John M 299,300

WOLLEY
Lela 117

WOOD
J R 171,172,173

WOOLERY
Annie 8,11,15
James 8,11

WOOLEY
Clara 124
Joseph 118
Joseph M 117,118,119,122,123, 124,125
Lela 117,119,122,123,124,125
S L 123,124
Samuel L 117,118,119,120,121, 122,123,124,125

YANDELL
J D 76,77,78

YOUNG
Catherine 174,175
J M 16,17,18,19,20,21
Jeff 174,175
Marion 174,175

www.ingramcontent.com/pod-product-compliance
Lightning Source LLC
Chambersburg PA
CBHW020240030426
42336CB00010B/562